WITTGENSTEIN'S
HOUSE

LANGUAGE, SPACE, & ARCHITECTURE

WITTGENSTEIN'S HOUSE

Nana Last

FORDHAM UNIVERSITY PRESS | NEW YORK | 2008

Copyright © 2008 Fordham University Press

All rights reserved. No part of this publication may be reproduced, stored in a retrieval system, or transmitted in any form or by any means—electronic, mechanical, photocopy, recording, or any other—except for brief quotations in printed reviews, without the prior permission of the publisher.

Library of Congress Cataloging-in-Publication Data
Last, Nana.
Wittgenstein's house : language, space, and architecture / Nana Last.—1st ed.
    p. cm.
  Includes bibliographical references and index.
  ISBN-13: 978-0-8232-2881-2 (pbk : alk. paper)
  1. Wittgenstein, Ludwig, 1889–1951—Criticism and interpretation. 2. Haus Wittgenstein.
3. Architecture—Philosophy. 4. Language and languages—Philosophy. I. Title.
NA1011.5.W5L37 2008
192—dc22

                            2008009121

Printed in the United States of America
10 09 08 5 4 3 2 1
First edition

List of Figures vii

Acknowledgments ix

INTRODUCTION Spatial Practices from Architecture to Philosophy 1

PART ONE TRANSGRESSIONS AND INHABITATIONS

1 Transgressions 33

2 From Without to Within: The Building of Inhabitation 61

3 The Stonborough-Wittgenstein House 78

4 The Practice of Architecture 95

PART TWO IMAGES OF ENTANGLEMENT

Images of Entanglement 123

Family Resemblance 125

The Landscape of Language 136

Nets and Webs 143

Crystalline Purity 146

Spatial Crises   149
Labyrinths and Mazes   155
Albums   161
Surface Practices   168
Boundaries   174
Shared Territory   182

Notes   191
Selected Bibliography   201
Index   205

LIST OF FIGURES

1. *Tractatus Logico-Philosophicus* — 6
2. *Philosophical Investigations* — 7
3. Stonborough-Wittgenstein House: view of the southwest facade, 1983–1984; new light fittings and stair railings are visible — 28
4. Stonborough-Wittgenstein House: view from the stairs of the hall toward the entrance, 1992 — 29
5. Stonborough-Wittgenstein House: ground-floor plan — 87
6. Stonborough-Wittgenstein House: northwest façade, original state, 1968 — 89
7. Stonborough-Wittgenstein House: south aspect, view of the southwest terrace, spring 1929 — 91
8. Stonborough-Wittgenstein House: the hall with a view of the sculpture "Discobolus" at the top of the stairs and the double-door leading to the salon, spring 1929 — 96
9. Stonborough-Wittgenstein House: the hall looking toward the southwest terrace, spring 1929 — 96
10. Stonborough-Wittgenstein House: the hall, looking toward the southwest terrace, original state, 1975 — 97
11. Stonborough-Wittgenstein House: the dining room, state in 1992 — 99
12. Stonborough-Wittgenstein House: the dining room, view of the southwest terrace through the open glass doors, state in 1989 — 100

13. Stonborough-Wittgenstein House: view from the library/living room into the salon to the right and the hall on the left, state in 1992; the opening between library and salon is not the original 101
14. Stonborough-Wittgenstein House: view of the stairs with the elevator shaft on the ground floor, 1983–1984, state after the renovation of 1976–1977 113
15. Stonborough-Wittgenstein House: plan of the ground floor showing the pattern of the joints on the floor 118
16. "The Jewish Type" 127

ACKNOWLEDGMENTS

The fundamental interdisciplinarity of this work has played a critical role in its coming into being. The range of people who influenced, supported, and entered into this project in various ways over the course of its development demonstrates the confluence of ideas involved; yet, looking back, it is clear to me that the disciplines and intellectual positions of these various persons are representative not of a set of discrete disciplines but of the broader, underlying connectivity of the issues at hand. As such, many of those acknowledged here, while drawn from specific disciplines—philosophy, Wittgenstein studies, architecture and art history, theory and criticism—did not contribute solely from the viewpoint of their respective fields but were fundamental in setting forth in comment, criticism, and by example the very broadness and interconnectivity of the central concerns.

As the ideas of this book originated as the topic of my doctoral dissertation completed at the Massachusetts Institute of Technology in Architecture and Art, History, Theory and Criticism, I want to begin by acknowledging my gratitude to my dissertation committee, Mark Jarzombek, Leila Kinney, Norman Bryson, Stanley Cavell, and K. Michael Hays, for their insights, support, and guidance over the course of that phase of this work and well beyond, insights with which I am still coming to grips. While each maintained his or her distinct viewpoint, approach, and disciplinary standing, their contributions to this project emerged not so much as distinct categories but as different approaches to the confluence of these ideas. Norman Bryson and Leila Kinney need thanks as well for their early recognition—

insistence, even—that my thoughts on Wittgenstein and spatiality constituted the basis of sustained work. And I want to thank Stanley Cavell for his example of scholarship on Wittgenstein and for his wider support of my work. Michael Hays needs to be singled out for first publishing my thoughts on Wittgenstein as well as for his long-standing support of my various endeavors over these years.

The ideas presented in this book made their first appearance long before I ever dreamed of the topic becoming a central focus of my work. That first inception began in response to a philosophy course on Wittgenstein taught by Paul Horwich at MIT, to whom I remain indebted for his comments and support despite the differences in our views. That undertaking, combined with my focus on architectural thought processes, incited me to address a series of concerns that over some years found their development in this book.

Other people who were in and around MIT and Harvard during that period contributed to and supported my work in various ways; these include Benjamin Buchloh, Sarah Goldhagen, Rosalyn Deutsche, Juli Carson, and Tim Hinton. I want to extend a particular note of thanks to Hilary Putnam, whose influence lies outside any particular category but whose overall and long-standing inspiration, involvement with, and support of my work from well before my dissertation have had a profound effect on my life.

Several people have lent their support and comments during the final phase of writing this book, including Elizabeth McQuitty and Theresa Papanikolas for their comments on sections of this book. I also want to acknowledge Cary Wolfe, whom I met later on in this project, for his immediate sense about my work that led him to direct me to Fordham Press. And I would like to extend my appreciation to Helen Tartar at Fordham for her understanding and support. Helena Michie deserves a particular expression of my gratitude for her intelligence and concern which have meant so much during the final phase of writing.

Sections of this book were published in *Assemblage* 35 (April 1998); *Architecture, Language, Critique: Around Paul Engelmann*, ed. J. Bakacsy, A. V. Munch, and A. L. Sommer, Studien zur Osterreichischen Philosophie 31 (Amsterdam and Atlanta: Rodopi Press, 2000); and the anthology *Penser, Dessiner, Construire: Wittgenstein et l'Architecture*, ed. Céline Poisson (Paris: Editions de l'éclat, 2007).

Finally, I want to acknowledge the people who made this project possible in the most fundamental of ways. I would first like to acknowledge my parents for their unending support of all I do and particularly my mother,

Miriam Last, who, with her belief in all things intellectual, more than anyone else taught me to write. I hope she would have found this book a worthy outcome. It is in her memory that this book makes its way into the world.

There are two people who mean the most to me and to whom I also dedicate this book. To my son, Milo, for all that he is and all that he will be. And to my husband, Lester Yuen, who has never let me forget the worth of this and all of my endeavors and without whose help in all phases and manners of this project—assistance given wholeheartedly and unfailingly—this book would not have come to be.

—NANA LAST
June 2007

WITTGENSTEIN'S
HOUSE

Spatial Practices from Architecture to Philosophy

We are talking about the spatial and temporal phenomenon of language, not about some non-spatial, non-temporal phantasm.—LUDWIG WITTGENSTEIN, *Philosophical Investigations*, sec. 108

To begin a project concerned with the relationship between Ludwig Wittgenstein's practices of architecture and philosophy is to enter a territory whose fundamental principles of operation are in question. Overflowing with possibilities latent in relations between linguistic practices and spatial ones, the territory in question is ripe. Its operations, however, have been mired in the entrenched presupposition that a gap exists between the linguistic and the spatial, between language and the world. But what if no gap exists? What if the field in which architecture and philosophy operate is inclusive of linguistic and spatial practices? What potentials stem from understanding the relations between language and not-language as constituting aspects of a shared territory of meaningful practice? This sense that language operates within a fluid territory of practice with the world it represents is the underlying premise of this book, a premise that culminates in the conclusion that Wittgenstein's practice of architecture contributed a central and active component to his philosophical development.

While Wittgenstein's practice of architecture lies outside the margins of most discussions of his philosophy, *Wittgenstein's House: Language, Space, &*

Architecture enacts a Copernican revolution of sorts to place that relationship at its core. Modeled on the image of language that Wittgenstein put forth in his late philosophy, *Wittgenstein's House* proposes not a smooth field of operation but an entangled one, a territory in which relations between language and space, philosophy and architecture are at times more distinct, at times inseparable, at times commingled, and at times at odds. Beginning with the premise that these disciplines, these constructs are already entangled, this book employs an interdisciplinary approach to the analysis of the case of Wittgenstein, house, philosophy, and all. To examine how Wittgenstein's practice of architecture insinuated itself into his philosophy, *Wittgenstein's House* restages the drama revolving around the philosopher's dramatic entry, departure, and return to philosophy by rereading his two main philosophical texts, the *Tractatus Logico-Philosophicus*[1] and the *Philosophical Investigations*,[2] in relation to his practice of architecture in his design of the Stonborough-Wittgenstein House.[3] The argument presented is that the practice of architecture occupies not just the historical position between Wittgenstein's early and late philosophy but the conceptual position as well.

Wittgenstein's involvement with architecture presents itself as a form of intermediary: the house's design as the intersection of philosophy and architecture, early and late Wittgenstein. But how is it to be read? The house was designed by a philosopher and bracketed between two distinct and oppositional phases of his work, so the history of its production cannot help but challenge the viewer to decipher within its walls some affinity between Wittgenstein's architecture and his philosophy. While the directness and repetitiveness of the house's exterior offers few clues in its austerity to unraveling this association, this inscrutable quality has only fueled speculation on the house's "meaning." The seeming blankness of its facade has often suggested a deep association with Viennese architectural modernism,[4] as has the sparse, "mysterious" prose of the *Tractatus*. But the Stonborough-Wittgenstein House itself is not blank. As the scene of Wittgenstein's practice of architecture, the house bears the signs of spatial conflict and questioning in many of the ways that become apparent in the late philosophy's examples of visual and spatial thinking.

Wittgenstein's two main texts, the *Tractatus Logico-Philosophicus*, completed in 1918, and the *Philosophical Investigations*, published in 1953, two years after his death, suggest very different relations between philosophy and architecture. In each text, Wittgenstein was concerned with the scope, limits, and operations of meaningful language, but what he believed language capable of communicating sensibly changed drastically from one work to the other. The *Tractatus* had attempted to define the limits of "what cannot be thought by working outwards through what can be thought."[5] Beyond the bounds of the thinkable or sayable was that which could only be shown. Effectively, this thinking subdivided philosophy's traditional territory, casting aesthetics and ethics out beyond language into the realm of showing and practice. Logic in the *Tractatus* held the privileged, if tenuous, position of connecting saying and showing and thereby allowing language to represent the world. The *Investigations* removed the limits that the *Tractatus* had imposed on language and philosophy by rejecting the *Tractatus*'s view that language represents the world in accordance with the rules of logic. Instead, Wittgenstein's late philosophy saw that the proper task of philosophy was to reconnect the philosophical study of language with language's everyday practices.

Wittgenstein completed the *Tractatus* in 1918 after just a seven-year association with philosophy. With its completion, Wittgenstein declared all philosophical problems solved and his involvement with philosophy over.[6] Following his abandonment of philosophy, Wittgenstein pursued what he referred to as a "completely unpretentious vocation," that of a grammar school teacher in an Austrian village primary school. In October 1926, at his sister's suggestion, Wittgenstein first collaborated with the architect Paul Engelmann and then quickly took over the design of his sister's house. In January 1929, immediately following the completion of the house, Wittgenstein returned to Cambridge and to philosophy. In light of Wittgenstein's previous renunciation of philosophy and accompanying declaration that all philosophical problems had been solved, the question becomes: What confronted the finality and closure of that position to pry open language and philosophy to reexamination? Wittgenstein himself hinted at an answer to this, an answer that points to the practice of architecture having provided a key component.

In a letter he wrote at the time to Moritz Schlick, the philosopher of the Vienna Circle, Wittgenstein expressed his desire to remain in Cambridge "for a few terms and work on visual space [*Gesichtsraum*] and other things."[7] While not explicitly addressing those concepts, Wittgenstein's late philosophy undertook that exploration as an implicit part of his reexamination of language and philosophy. Wittgenstein's continued concern with problems of vision and space is clearly evident in the philosophical problems with which he was involved; that is, the problems he focused on were already spatial ones, involving, for example, the mediation between the subject's interiority and the publicness of language or his continued concern with the scope and limits of language itself. Throughout these endeavors, Wittgenstein's postarchitecture *Investigations* is permeated with spatial and visual metaphors, references, and other signs of the incorporation of his spatiovisual practice of architecture. While the *Tractatus* had also involved itself deeply with spatial issues of the limits of language, the references emerging in the *Investigations* are of an entirely new type, different from that which had previously existed. It is the joint quality of expansion and invention permeating Wittgenstein's linguistic-spatial thought that makes it so striking.

Insinuating itself into his philosophical thinking, Wittgenstein's practice of architecture manifests itself in two main ways. The first, broader instance pertains to the distinction between Wittgenstein's early and late philosophy as occurring about the space from which language is viewed. I characterize this distinction as the shift or move from the view from *without* language, indicative of the early philosophy of the *Tractatus*, to the view from *within*, realized by the late philosophy of the *Investigations*. Underlying this instance is the practice of architecture that enters the philosophy to reframe how we position ourselves in relation to language. As a framing device, the practice of architecture acts on and transforms Wittgenstein's preexistent interest in and approach to philosophical problems—particularly those with spatial components. In the second related type of association between architecture and philosophy, Wittgenstein's practice of architecture enters the late philosophy as the lens through which his view of language is cast. Here the emphasis is on architecture as a practice. Architecture thereby becomes that through which philosophy looks, a look that transforms the specific understanding of the functioning and locating of language, shifting it from a basis in logic to being formed in everyday practice.

The importance of the initial spatial reframing process—the move from the view from without to the view from within—underlies the shift's ability to draw out the spatial practices between architecture and philosophy in Wittgenstein's work by pointing to the frameworks through which such discussion are themselves constituted. This is clearly apparent in the *Investigations*'s explicitly associating the restricted vision of the *Tractatus* with a particular apprehension of language. In referring to the *Tractatus*'s belief that the general form a proposition takes is: "This is how things are," Wittgenstein continues: "That is the kind of proposition that one repeats to oneself countless times. One thinks that one is tracing the outline of the thing's nature over and over again, and one is merely tracing the frame through which we look at it."⁸ And, referring to the *Tractatus*'s presupposition of an ideal form of language that at once frames and limits our view, Wittgenstein writes: "The ideal, as we think of it, is unshakeable. . . . Where does this idea come from? It is like a pair of glasses on our nose through which we see whatever we look at. It never occurs to us to take them off."⁹

The *Investigations*'s discussion of the glasses that limit the view of language by predefining it is in some ways analogous to the work undertaken by this book. The disenframing suggested by the removal of the glasses is, of course, never complete. Each frame is necessarily replaced by another one, no matter how wide the focus or unnoticed the profile. The importance of the removal of the glasses is thus not to produce a neutral, complete, or natural view *but to point to the existence of the view itself*. The resultant outlook is then in a position to redefine the relation between the understanding of language and our view of it, our—in Wittgenstein's terms—way of life. This repositioning is what allows for the second architecture-philosophy interaction, the concept of language as practice, to be a product of the view from within in the late philosophy. By the same token, this reframing of Wittgenstein's texts—alternately by his practice of architecture and as undertaken here—is as natural as it is estranged, an act that seeks repeatedly to reject the existence of any neutral or isolated views.

The *Tractatus* and the *Investigations* themselves contribute in yet another manner to indicate the devices by which they construct images and viewpoints of language and philosophy. The most overt of these is realized in the literal image of each text. Owing to its uniqueness and specificity, each image points to the visible form of the philosophical text—and of language itself—as a component of the philosophy. Here again the two images diverge. The *Tractatus* presents itself as a hierarchically and precisely structured series of propositions ordered by a numbering system calibrated to the fifth decimal place (fig. 1). In contrast, the *Investigations* offers an open-ended seriality in which the numbering system simply denotes its consecutive sections, 1 to 693 (fig. 2).¹⁰ Owing to the *Tractatus*'s complex numbering system that at once formally, conceptually, and visually structures its thoughts, the interdependence of form and content seems to suggest itself more urgently in the early philosophy than in the *Investigations*. Closer examination of the *Investigations*, however, reveals that its concepts are as dependent upon its formal structure as are those of the *Tractatus*. This suggests that Wittgenstein had not simply altered the numbering system

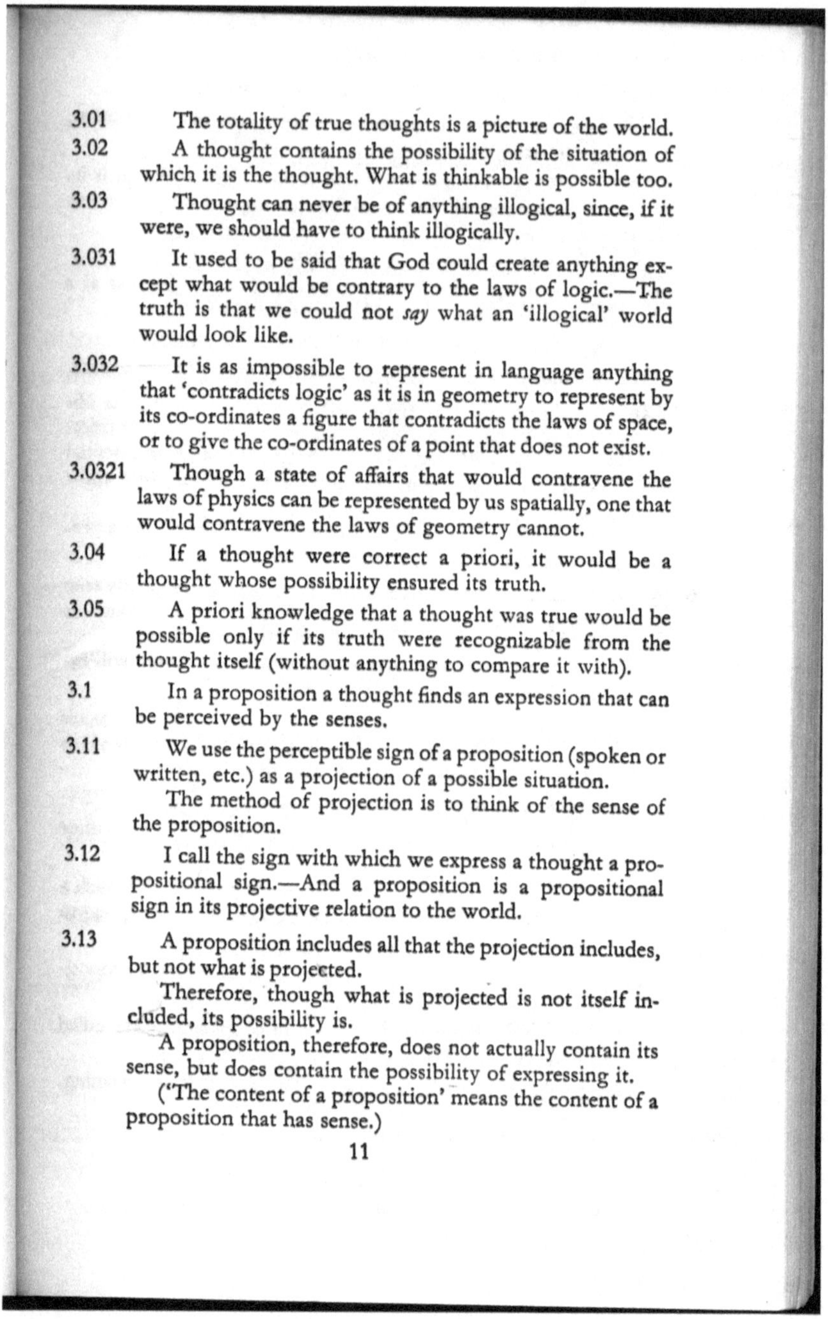

3.01   The totality of true thoughts is a picture of the world.

3.02   A thought contains the possibility of the situation of which it is the thought. What is thinkable is possible too.

3.03   Thought can never be of anything illogical, since, if it were, we should have to think illogically.

3.031 It used to be said that God could create anything except what would be contrary to the laws of logic.—The truth is that we could not *say* what an 'illogical' world would look like.

3.032 It is as impossible to represent in language anything that 'contradicts logic' as it is in geometry to represent by its co-ordinates a figure that contradicts the laws of space, or to give the co-ordinates of a point that does not exist.

3.0321 Though a state of affairs that would contravene the laws of physics can be represented by us spatially, one that would contravene the laws of geometry cannot.

3.04   If a thought were correct a priori, it would be a thought whose possibility ensured its truth.

3.05   A priori knowledge that a thought was true would be possible only if its truth were recognizable from the thought itself (without anything to compare it with).

3.1   In a proposition a thought finds an expression that can be perceived by the senses.

3.11   We use the perceptible sign of a proposition (spoken or written, etc.) as a projection of a possible situation.
The method of projection is to think of the sense of the proposition.

3.12   I call the sign with which we express a thought a propositional sign.—And a proposition is a propositional sign in its projective relation to the world.

3.13   A proposition includes all that the projection includes, but not what is projected.
Therefore, though what is projected is not itself included, its possibility is.
A proposition, therefore, does not actually contain its sense, but does contain the possibility of expressing it.
('The content of a proposition' means the content of a proposition that has sense.)

11

Figure 1. *Tractatus Logico-Philosophicus* (London: Routledge & Kegan Paul, 1961).

125. It is the business of philosophy, not to resolve a contradiction by means of a mathematical or logico-mathematical discovery, but to make it possible for us to get a clear view of the state of mathematics that troubles us: the state of affairs *before* the contradiction is resolved. (And this does not mean that one is sidestepping a difficulty.)

The fundamental fact here is that we lay down rules, a technique, for a game, and that then when we follow the rules, things do not turn out as we had assumed. That we are therefore as it were entangled in our own rules.

This entanglement in our rules is what we want to understand (i.e. get a clear view of).

It throws light on our concept of *meaning* something. For in those cases things turn out otherwise than we had meant, foreseen. That is just what we say when, for example, a contradiction appears: "I didn't mean it like that."

The civil status of a contradiction, or its status in civil life: there is the philosophical problem.

126. Philosophy simply puts everything before us, and neither explains nor deduces anything.—Since everything lies open to view there is nothing to explain. For what is hidden, for example, is of no interest to us.

One might also give the name "philosophy" to what is possible *before* all new discoveries and inventions.

127. The work of the philosopher consists in assembling reminders for a particular purpose.

128. If one tried to advance *theses* in philosophy, it would never be possible to debate them, because everyone would agree to them.

129. The aspects of things that are most important for us are hidden because of their simplicity and familiarity. (One is unable to notice something—because it is always before one's eyes.) The real foundations of his enquiry do not strike a man at all. Unless *that* fact has at some time struck him.—And this means: we fail to be struck by what, once seen, is most striking and most powerful.

130. Our clear and simple language-games are not preparatory studies for a future regularization of language—as it were first approximations, ignoring friction and air-resistance. The language-games are rather set up as *objects of comparison* which are meant to throw light on the facts of our language by way not only of similarities, but also of dissimilarities.

Figure 2. *Philosophical Investigations* (New York: Macmillan, 1953).

from one text to the other but had also altered the relations between the numbered sections and the conception of language.

While the *Tractatus*'s hierarchical structuring attempts to produce an absolute correspondence of language, meaning, and place, the *Investigations*, in replacing the strictly structured ordering of the *Tractatus* and instituting an otherwise undifferentiated seriality, reveals the *Tractatus*'s structure to be not the incarnation of meaning itself but an idealized and limited image of meaning. Analyzing these images reveals them to be an integral part of both Wittgenstein's theories of language and his production of those theories, intimating that form and content in Wittgenstein's work are mutually productive to a greater degree than in most works of philosophy. Once the texts are begun to be read in this manner, the productivity of the approach becomes immediately apparent, as it reveals a correlation of form and content not just within each text but also between the texts, thereby underscoring the view that the inseparability of form and content is not just in evidence in Wittgenstein's work but lies at the heart of the philosophy.

Revealing this interrelation of form and content in Wittgenstein's philosophy does more than inform a reading of Wittgenstein's texts: it opens the door to a wider examination of the implications of such an approach both for the study of architecture and for philosophy. The most central of these implications argues that spatial and visual practices and constructs are *involved in the very processes of concept formation in language, subjectivity, aesthetics, ethics, and throughout philosophy*. Furthermore, this finding points to the essential need to develop forms of analysis capable of combining contributions from aesthetic associations, epistemology, and the philosophy of language (as well as myriad other potential practices). Such tools, in exposing spatiovisual and linguistic practices, including architecture and philosophy, underscore that interdisciplinary *meaning is always already in operation. As such, interdisciplinarity is not so much produced at specific moments between disciplinary practices—say, architecture and philosophy—as it is revealed and made explicit in all of the discourses involved*. Broadening interdisciplinary knowledge thus equally broadens our knowledge of the various disciplines and practices involved. Understanding such associations to preexist their acknowledged entry into discourse by, for example, unmasking the spatial and visual aspects *within a given philosophical text* no longer undertakes the impossible task of bridging some insurmountable language-space gap. Rather, it lays the foundation for a fluid territory through which to discuss the relationships between philosophy and architecture, language and space.

What immediately emerges from the methodological possibility of approaching language, spatiality, philosophy, and architecture from within a shared and fluid territory is a double promise. Beginning with Wittgenstein's discussion of the builders in the opening sections of the late philosophy of the *Investigations*[11] and continuing throughout with such central metaphors as that of the glasses framing philosophy, visual and spatial thinking provides a considerable model of thought to the *Investigations*. Accordingly, *Wittgenstein's House* pursues three interrelated forms of analysis: the spatial and visual metaphors of the *Tractatus* and the *Investigations*, the specific references made by the texts to architecture, space, visuality, construction, and so on, and the philosophical and spatial concepts employed by Wittgenstein in the practice of architecture.

In many ways, the concept of metaphor itself operates as a preeminent tool of analysis in this process as it maintains persistent (rather than transparent) relations between the architecture and the philosophy.[12] Such constructs as boundary, limit, transparency, hidden, enframing, and so on operate on both metaphorical and literal or physical levels and therefore populate equally the texts and the architecture to create inroads to and potential models of the workings of a shared practice (although not one without conflict). As such, analyzing the visual and spatial metaphors in the texts reveals another level of functioning of the philosophy. Unlike the operations of logical form described in the *Tractatus*, this newly revealed level is neither hidden nor disguised. Instead, it is found in the *Investigations*'s surface maneuvers which encompass philosophical as well as spatial constructs. These remain readily apparent in both text and building, even when unacknowledged.

The central acting supposition of this book—that there are not just different sets of spatial and visual images in the *Tractatus* and the *Investigations* but *different spatialities at work*—at once accords with the widely held view that Wittgenstein's late philosophy of language marks a decisive break from his early work while also providing a new understanding or reformulation of that break. Signaling something fundamental at stake, the conjunction of these sets of distinctions *is* more than mere coincidence or discrete markers of otherwise unrelated attributes. Rather, this compound break points to alignments between spatial and visual constructs, epistemology, and the philosophy of language. Adding to the understanding that the early work and the late work produce divergent theories of language, logic, and epistemology, I argue that they also produce alternate spatialities or spatial epistemologies. This finding holds the potential to speak—and loudly—not just about Wittgenstein's philosophy but toward the question of the association, the entanglement, of language, space, and knowledge. In literally introducing a new framework for its emergence, the practice of architecture achieves more than a new model of space and spatial thinking to replace that of the *Tractatus*; instead, it acts as a catalyst for Wittgenstein's reconsideration of the philosophy of language.

The implication of this line of study is that the inseparability of form and content in Wittgenstein's philosophy and its imbrication in spatial and visual thought are as much epistemological constructs as aesthetic or linguistic ones. The potential of this finding is undeniable; its revelation directly supports the connection between Wittgenstein's practice of architecture, as his engagement with a specifically spatial practice, and the emergence of not just a new philosophy of language but a new spatiality in the later work. Beyond the concern with Wittgenstein's philosophy, the wide-reaching implication of this is that *spatial constructs subtend many aspects of philosophy and thought, that the spatial cannot simply be peeled away to leave philosophical thought intact, and that, therefore, in challenging the spatial constructs of the philosophy of language of the* Tractatus, *the philosophy itself was challenged and a new philosophy of language emerged.*

Architecture, it becomes apparent, is not the originating source of spatiality in Wittgenstein's philosophy. Rather than providing an introduction to spatial thinking and issues, Wittgenstein's practice of architecture provides a means for the dismantling of the philosophy of the *Tractatus*, not because it introduces spatiality into philosophy but because it challenges the attenuated and restrictive spatiality definitive of the *Tractatus*. This bears repeating. The power of the practice of architecture to challenge the tenets of the early philosophy lies in the fact that the early philosophy was already deeply involved with visual and spatial thought. Interdisciplinarity is effective, then, not in bringing disciplines together, but in making apparent and harnessing their preexistent and underlying associations. In this manner, Wittgenstein's involvement with and incorporation into his philosophy of the spatial practice of architecture provided a deep yet unseen and unacknowledged lure. As such, the *Tractatus* provides as much a field or site upon which the practice of architecture can operate as the practice of architecture provides for the late philosophy—even if these associations are at times more conflictual than confirmative.

This approach, this redefining of the relationship between architecture and philosophy, form and content, in Wittgenstein's work comprises a departure from the manner in which relations between Wittgenstein's architecture and philosophy have previously been explored.[13] As the vast majority of the study of Wittgenstein's work comes from within the discourse of philosophy, it almost without exception does not deal seriously with Wittgenstein's practice of architecture, even when given an ideal opportunity to enter into this discussion. For example, when a philosophical journal of aesthetics and art criticism reviewed the book *Ludwig Wittgenstein: Architect*,[14] disciplinary separation was enforced; philosophy and aesthetics were placed to one side, the house and architecture to the other. After summarizing the book's discussion of the relationship between Wittgenstein's philosophy and architecture, the reviewer concluded: "For the philosopher there are two questions. Does [the author] correctly understand Wittgenstein's thinking about aesthetics, and does that thinking help us resolve philosophical problems about aesthetics? These, however, are questions for another day."[15]

Posed in this manner, the reviewer's concerns succeed only in divorcing the formulation of a Wittgensteinian aesthetics from its architectural associations. This leaves the reviewer's questions disconnected from their origin in the book on the philosopher's architecture and summarily displaced to within the "secure" bounds of "philosophy." Consequently, the practice of architecture remains unrecognized as an active participant in the construction of Wittgenstein's "aesthetics" and no less in his philosophy of language. The end result of this maneuver is to remove aesthetic concerns from an aesthetic practice—architecture—and place them in the discipline of philosophy, where Wittgenstein's practice has no acknowledged role, despite its being the generator of the interpretation of the aesthetics in question.

The book reviewer, however, is not singularly at fault in this enforced disciplinary segregation, as the book itself does not find a way to bridge the philosophy-architecture gap, declaring at a critical juncture: "[I]t still remains difficult to compare the connections between architectural precision, consisting in visual-spatial-tactile relationships and in a certain use of building elements, with philosophical or linguistic precision, consisting in semantic relationships and in a certain use of words and concepts."[16] This statement is crucial to understanding the problem at hand—not just in its inability to bridge a gap but in its dual defining of the gap as that, on the one hand, between visiospatial relations and linguistic precision and, on the other hand, between the mute elements of architecture and the written words of philosophy.[17] Wittgenstein's work on the house, in its forcing of the architecture/philosophy discussion, ultimately defines a unique and oddly both contentious and desolate place, an image reminiscent of that of the house itself.

The very uniqueness of the case of Wittgenstein, with its dual architecture-philosophy involvement, is what opens up the much broader issue at hand, that of linguistic-spatial philosophy-architecture involvements. In its directness, the case of Wittgenstein is able to provide keys inaccessible elsewhere. Equally, the rigid disciplinary separation that limited the discussion of architecture and philosophy around Wittgenstein's practice—just as it was most warranted—is not unique but extends broadly to encompass other philosophy-architecture and linguistic-spatiovisual associations. It is that directness of association that is most at issue and counters approaches that invoke various additional modes of mediation.

A number of theorists writing on relations between architecture and philosophy, the visual and the verbal, have made attempts to bridge a presumed gap between the disciplines or modes of thought by, for example, positing a third, mediating term or space in between, in which the initial two terms may interact. Such a mediating term is designed to bridge some presumably nonnavigable gap between the initial two disciplines. This is the case whether that gap be defined as a formal, spatial, social, or political one. The heralded position of in-between, however, rather than summarily solving the situation, potentially confronts exactly those issues of connectivity and privilege faced by the original disciplines. This is not because some mediation between the existing realms does not or cannot profitably exist but because the search for the site in between functions largely by shifting the concerns at issue to an alternate interval of space, form, or functioning. The suggestion implicit in turning to a third term is that it is positioned with no—or a more limited—gap or space between it and the original terms. But is that the case? Or, more precisely, what unique properties does that middle term or position possess that are *unavailable* to the first two terms? Consider this: if, for example, the space in between is in some way contiguous or of like association with the original terms, then does that not imply that the original terms were in some manner *already* related or capable of interacting? In this case, what allows that third term to perform this mediating function and prevents the first two terms from doing the same? This is to suggest that the in-between term—if it performs as desired—may do so less because it is in between and more because it occupies a shared territory or aspects of a shared practice.

Consider, for example, Elizabeth Grosz's construct of the outside, a concept she institutes with the goal of defining a space of nonprivileged interaction between philosophy and architecture. In her *Architecture from the Outside*, Grosz posits the need for an outside space of interaction between architecture and philosophy as a necessary space for the two disciplines—

which are "fundamentally outside of each other"—to interact equally without subjecting one to the other, as would otherwise be necessary. "Outside" for Grosz reflects both her own position as:

> an interested outsider, not trained in architecture . . . and the position of . . . discourses or frameworks . . . which are all in some sense outside the mainstreams of both architecture and philosophy. . . . [18]
>
> [Architecture and philosophy] require a third space in which to interact without hierarchy, a space or position outside both, a space that doesn't yet exist. To explore architecture philosophically would entail submitting architectural design, construction, and theory to the requirements and exigencies of philosophical discourse, the rigor of philosophical argument, and the abstraction of philosophical speculation. And to examine philosophy architecturally would require using philosophical concepts and propositions, wrenched from their own theoretical context and transformed, perhaps mutilated, for architectural purposes. In either case, one discipline would submit the other to its own internal needs and constraints, reducing it to its subordinated other. It is only by subsuming *both* to a third term, to a position or place outside of both, that they can be explored *beside* each other as equivalent and interconnected discourse and practices. That third space, which I call the outside has rarely been theorized.[19]

While Grosz presents the problem of relating architecture and philosophy in terms that do not privilege one discourse or position over the other, her argument employs much of the same terminology of disciplinary separation found in Paul Wijdeveld's book.[20] For instance, Grosz contrasts the "requirements and exigencies of philosophical discourse, the rigor of philosophical argument, and the abstraction of philosophical speculation" to a philosophy "transformed, perhaps mutilated, for architectural purposes."

Although Grosz's stated position reinforces the autonomy and separation of the disciplines involved, her discussion suggests another possibility. In her presentation of the outside, Grosz alludes to underlying spatialities or spatial epistemologies that function to distinguish various philosophical approaches from one another. The example she offers compares the philosophies of Jacques Derrida and Gilles Deleuze spatially in their interdisciplinary negotiations. Grosz describes both philosophers as not attempting to reject binarized thought or replace it with an alternative but instead playing the binarized categories off each other to allow for the possibility of their reconnection or realignment in different systems.

Grosz, however, discerns a fundamental difference between the two philosophers in their interactions between the disciplines, specifically as to the degree by which each upholds the relative autonomy of the practices involved. As to that separation, Grosz notes that Derrida has been involved directly in both architectural contributions and appropriations, while Deleuze remains a philosopher who analyzes, from the outside, artworks, architecture, cinema, and literature. Grosz finds that this distinction allows Deleuze to be interested while maintaining the "the autonomy, the specificity of these different practices and their modes of manner of interchange with their outside."[21] More interestingly, however, Grosz continues on to define this Derrida-Deleuze distinction in spatial terms.

> Where Derrida could be described as the philosopher who insists on bringing the outside, the expelled, repressed, or excluded, into the inside by showing the constitutive trace it must leave on that which must expel it (that is, the impossibility of keeping borders and delimitations clear-cut), Deleuze could be understood as the philosopher who evacuates the inside (whether of a subject, an organism, or a text), forcing it to confront its outside and thereby unloosing its systematicity or organization, its usual or habitual functioning, allowing a part, function, or feature to spin off or mutate into a new organization or system, to endlessly deflect, become, make.[22]

The question of autonomy is of particular issue here as it is tied both to disciplinarity and to the question of authority, terms Grosz is attempting to navigate and mediate with her theorization of the outside. Discussing these same issues with an equal emphasis on sociopolitical standing, Michel de Certeau, in his *Practice of Everyday Life*, defines a fundamental association between specialization, expertise, and authority.[23] Despite describing disciplinarity as tied to the strict definitions of its own limits and rather than underscoring the need to mediate between disciplines, de Certeau *points to the relevance and importance of the general as that which itself mediates*. De Certeau describes the philosopher and expert as performing similar tasks of mediating between the wider society and a body of knowledge. The roles they perform, however, are fundamentally different. While the expert introduces specialization and an accompanying competence associated with authority, the philosopher bears the crucial responsibility of reestablishing the relevance of the general.

Experts, for de Certeau, come into being through the conversion of competence in a particular discipline into authority about or over that discipline, an authority that upholds a discipline's sense of autonomy and separation from other disciplines. As depicted by de Certeau, however, a curious thing happens to an expert's knowledge as authority is produced: the status of authority ultimately leads to a reduction in the expert's competence. This occurs as the expert is increasingly drawn out of his or her orbit or field by the social demands and political responsibilities associated with the role of mediator, thereby causing the expert to produce a discourse which is no longer a function of knowledge but rather of the socioeconomic order. The effect of this, as de Certeau describes, is to confuse social place with technical discourse to the point where the expert can no longer know what he or she is saying, a process that blurs a discipline's limits even as it tries to establish them. In other words, the production of expertise cannot but produce an unsustainable autonomy, one that ironically confuses what knowledge comes from "within" a discipline and what comes from that which is defined as outside.

To provide a countermodel that allows for the production of knowledge without producing expertise and the concomitant loss of knowledge, de Certeau introduces the Wittgensteinian model of ordinary language. De Certeau finds in Wittgenstein a radical critique of the expert, including the notion of the philosopher as expert. As described by de Certeau, Wittgenstein's ordinary language philosophy allows for rigorous examination of a philosophical topic, language, in a manner that does not convert competence into authority but instead reintroduces the relevance of the general. Emblematic of this is the avowed goal of Wittgenstein's late philosophy, of retrieving words from estranging philosophical uses that render them nonfunctioning and restoring them to their rightful and meaningful place in ordinary language. As Wittgenstein writes in the *Investigations:* "What *we* do is to bring words back from their metaphysical to their everyday use."[24]

The Wittgensteinian model of ordinary language is a product of the late philosophy, as it is only then that Wittgenstein occasions to bring language back from philosophical uses to ordinary ones. This is of particular importance as it is a critique directed as much toward Wittgenstein's own early philosophy as toward that of others. Wittgenstein's early philosophy of the *Tractatus*, while deeply involved with locating the limits of the meaningful use of language, did so by modeling the functioning of all of language on logic rather than on ordinary or everyday language. This meant that the limits of language were effectively greatly reduced so as to be coincident with the limits of logical thought and representation, a view Wittgenstein reveals in the *Investigations* to result from the removal of the previously unnoticed glasses. The *Tractatus* was thus able to delineate the limits of language not by locating them but by imposing those limits a priori and then—necessarily—transgressing them in order to render them visible. Wittgenstein's late philosophy of the *Investigations* removed those limits in order not to investigate a limited and specialized philosophical use of language that produces expertise but to examine how language as it is ordinarily used is already meaningful. In that way, the late philosophy was involved in the returning of language to its everyday home, a home that forms the foundation of de Certeau's practices of everyday life.

The reimaging through which ordinary language becomes a model for philosophy also entails a repositioning in the relationship between philosophy and language. The limits of language envisioned in the *Tractatus* were a product of its extraordinary view from without—the position of transgression. From the *Investigations*'s vantage point within language, the limits of language are no longer clearly visible and the late philosophy no longer toils to locate precisely the boundaries of (meaningful) language. Instead, it reconsiders the persistent philosophical desire (as enacted in the *Tractatus*) to require language fit a particular mold of operation in order to be meaningful. That is, it examines (among other things) the philosophical temptation to try to surpass ordinary language not by moving beyond it but by *requiring that it function in extraordinary ways*—as akin to the model of logic. This process reveals a complex spatial model where what seems from the viewpoint of the early philosophy to exceed language (such as ethics, aesthetics, or the realm of practice) is revealed only to exceed the imposed limitations and expectations that language function in a particular way. As a result, much of what had seemed to be beyond language (practice for example) becomes understood to be internal to it.

Writing in the *Investigations*, Wittgenstein records the results of this process: "The results of philosophy are the uncovering of one or another piece of plain nonsense and of bumps that the understanding has got by running its head up against the limits of language. These bumps make us see the value of the discovery."[25] The section immediately following reiterates this understanding that even in philosophy one can act only within ordinary language, although the temptation to try to surpass language—by placing impossible demands on it—remains. "When I talk about language (words, sentences, etc.) I must speak the language of every day.... Your questions refer to words; so I have to talk about words."[26]

It is the late philosophy's insistent focus on the model of the ordinary that repeatedly rejects as its very method or practice any purifying process (such as that undertaken by the *Tractatus*) that attempts to eliminate the ordinary and replace it with an artificial language akin to those completely clarified forms of expression sought by the logical positivists during the first decades of the twentieth century.[27] Describing this, de Certeau writes:

> Rarely has the reality of language—that is, the *fact* that it defines our historicity, that it dominates and envelops us in the mode of the ordinary, that no discourse can therefore "escape from it," put itself at the distance from it in order to observe it and tell us its meaning—been taken seriously with so much rigor."[28]

Most pertinent to the discussion here is de Certeau's comment that no discourse can escape from ordinary language, that ordinary language is integral to all discourse. De Certeau sees Wittgenstein's unwavering involvement with ordinary language as combating philosophy's professionalization and with it the concomitant reduction of philosophy to a technological positivist discourse. It is that characteristic, via its basis in ordinary language, which allows Wittgenstein's philosophy to fulfill its role in reestablishing the relevance of the general.

In rejecting the privileged view of a technical discourse—one based in logic or metaphysics—Wittgenstein's late philosophy institutes an understanding of ordinary language as practice capable of incorporating a potentially unlimited number of other seemingly outside practices, including architecture. De Certeau alludes to this:

> Wittgenstein sees the metaphors of *foreign* analytical procedures *inside* the very language that circumscribes them. . . . And since one does not "leave" this language, since one cannot find another place from which to interpret it, . . . since in short there is no *way out*, the fact remains that we are *foreigners* on the inside—*but there is no outside*.[29]

> By being "caught" within ordinary language, the philosopher no longer has his own (*propre*) appropriable place. Any position of mastery is denied him. The analyzing discourse and the analyzed "object" are in the same situation: both are organized by the practical activity with which they are concerned, both are determined by rules they neither establish nor see clearly, equally scattered in differentiated ways of working (Wittgenstein wanted his work itself to be composed only of fragments), inscribed in a texture in which each can by turns "appeal" to the other, cite it and refer to it. There is a continual exchange of distinct places.[30]

Wittgenstein's shift to the model of ordinary language is itself a spatial model that repositions philosophy, philosopher, and language user alike.

De Certeau's description of Wittgenstein, with its undeniable spatial implications, emerges from Wittgenstein's philosophy itself to make its way (as spatial epistemologies do) into de Certeau's thinking in both acknowledged and unrecognized ways. De Certeau notes that Wittgenstein's attack on the "presumption that leads philosophy to proceed 'as if' it gave meaning to ordinary use, and to suppose that it has its own place from which it can reflect on the everyday"[31] denies philosophy a superior (literally above) position. That is, it denies the view from above. De Certeau acknowledges this in his description of what it is like to be awash in ordinary language.[32] "We are subject to, but not identified with, ordinary language. As in the ship of fools, we are embarked, without the possibility of an aerial view or any sort of totalization. That is the 'prose of the world' Merleau-Ponty spoke of."[33]

It is clear, then, that de Certeau recognizes in Wittgenstein's rejection of the authoritarian an equal rejection of the totalizing or aerial view of a discipline or language. He further understands this positioning within ordinary language in spatial terms as a continual movement or oscillation rather than the reinforcing of a prescribed or sharply defined territory. That is, de Certeau detects (even if he does not characterize its use as such) the rejection by Wittgenstein of a particular spatialization of philosophy. He does not, however, tie that approach explicitly back to Wittgenstein's spatial order in the practice of philosophy, although the implications of this spatiality are developed in de Certeau's emphasis on practice and the view from the street.

Wittgenstein's model of ordinary language proposes that language is entered into as an everyday practice, one entangled with but not overseeing an enormous range of other practices. As such, it cannot be presided over nor is it outside other discourses—even if it can be host to "foreign analytical procedures." This view of language stems from the late philosophy's construct of family resemblance. Family resemblance depicts language as a complex accumulation of interdependent practices, games, rules, words, drawings, forms of life. Wittgenstein introduces the construct of family resemblance to describe how language comes to be meaningful without being reliant on one-to-one correlations of word and meaning. In this view, no particular meaning or use of a word is more essential than any others; instead, meaning is dispersed throughout all usages and appearances of a term in practice. To describe family resemblance Wittgenstein employs an image of entanglement itself: the image of the fibers that come together, one upon the next, to form a thread, a process in which no one fiber runs throughout the entirety of the thread, allowing the fibers to remain at once discrete and yet entangled. By extension, family resemblance defines an infusive understanding of language as a productive entanglement of various practices and uses of language, including architecture.

Given this model, language is both product and producer of everyday practices and hence is neither over them nor beneath them but is integrally interwoven. Owing to this, Wittgenstein's "radical critique of the expert" fostered by the model of family resemblance counters, in emphasizing the inescapability of ordinary language, the necessity for a third, mediating term or space in which architecture and philosophy may interact. Ordinary language thus is shown to provide a site of interaction—not because it is outside other disciplines, including philosophy, but rather because it is already entangled with them. Grosz's focus on a place outside autonomous disciplines as the site that allows there to be an equal or unprivileged discourse is confronted by the Wittgensteinian model of ordinary language that produces such an unprivileged position from within—a position that simultaneously rejects the production of expertise and autonomy.

The practice of ordinary language provides a model in which philosophy and architecture are entwined and entangled, thereby producing numerous possibilities by which to make this association visible. Rejecting the a priori existence of such a language-space gap opens up new framing possibilities, including the examining of both the late philosophy and the relation between it and the early work in visual and spatial terms, a process that itself can be understood in spatiovisual terms.

In the opening paragraph of *Looking Awry: An Introduction to Jacques Lacan through Popular Culture*, Slavov Žižek introduces the spatiovisual practice of "looking awry" at theoretical motifs as a procedure already to be found in Wittgenstein's late philosophy. Curiously, Žižek posits this view without further reference or explanation, leaving it unclear why he believes the late philosophy constitutes such a practice. Wittgenstein's philosophy, however, presents its own clues. The practice of looking awry, as Žižek describes it, entails the endeavor to look at theoretical motifs or high theory as they emerge in popular culture not simply with the goal of making high theory accessible but with the more far-reaching aim of "rendering visible" aspects of theory that would have "otherwise remained unnoticed" were the theory approached "straight on" as traditionally undertaken.[34] Given this, the question is: Why (whatever Žižek's view) might this practice be attributed to the later Wittgenstein? In what way can late Wittgensteinian philosophy be said to look awry—and at or through what is that look cast?

An answer to this question is implied in Žižek's attributing the practice of looking awry to the late philosophy rather than to the early work, an act akin to declaring them to possess different spatial practices or different spatial epistemologies, such as in the distinction between the view from outside language and that from within. Following Žižek's approach, the distinction between Wittgenstein's early and late philosophy can be characterized as the product of alternative practices of viewing language and philosophy: the straight-on view of the *Tractatus* and the awry look of the *Investigations*. This distinction reinforces the premise of *Wittgenstein's House* that there is something fundamental and *yet unseen* in the straight-on view of language and philosophy—that something becomes visible through other spatiovisual approaches, including the awry look through the practice of architecture undertaken here.

Looking awry also needs to be understood as itself a spatial practice, the product of a shift in spatial location by the viewer.[35] It should be made clear, however, that despite involving or being comprehensible as a shift enacted by the viewer, looking awry is no more an "outside" practice than the straight-on view. Instead, this act of repositioning not only reveals the inherent spatiality and nonneutrality of the (typically unacknowledged) straight-on view, it questions which frameworks, concepts, constructs, subjects, and so on are "rightly" included in a given practice or discipline. That is part of what is at stake in looking awry—made clear in Žižek's merging of high theory and popular culture: the question of what disciplines or practices are understood to be entitled to or capable of engaging in the production of specific concepts, practices, or knowledge. Traditionally, from within the practice of philosophy, the practice of architecture is considered to be an outside practice, discipline, or site, but through the awry look that I am instituting, the practice of architecture, through the sharing of spatial practices and philosophical concepts between the architecture and the texts, emerges substantively as a component of Wittgenstein's philosophy. With the awry look, components or aspects previously thought to be outside the practice of architecture or philosophy become incorporated at a fundamental level.

This reframing of Wittgenstein's philosophy is central to the argument I am proposing: that understanding the late philosophy requires admitting into its core components, concepts, and disciplines previously thought to be external or tangential to the philosophy. These inclusions recast our vision in much the way Wittgenstein claims occurs in the *Investigations* with the removal of the glasses' restrictive frame that had previously defined the view of philosophy in the *Tractatus*.

Rendering this approach operative, architecture needs to be understood not as an autonomous discipline but more broadly as a spatial or spatiovisual practice. Approaching architecture as a spatial practice allows for the more ready examination of how it relates to other disciplines that may also have spatial components. Such a theory of architecture as entanglement is discussed here not in the abstract but as it resides in the pages of Wittgenstein's philosophy and in the specifics of the Stonborough-Wittgenstein House. As is implicit in the act of looking awry, such a view allows conceptual theory, philosophy, and the visible and material realms to be continuous with one another, blurring or reimagining boundaries to the point where they no longer function solely as limits but come forth as markers or concepts within this newly defined domain.

Ultimately, I have come to see all of these components coming together to produce as much the foundation for a theory of architecture as a reading of Wittgenstein's philosophy. As a product of this approach, such an architecture theory is not a traditional object-based theory but an entangled one that strives to apprehend how architecture—its practices, operations, objects, and constructs—interrelate with other forms of knowledge. Although entangled within the pages of the text and spaces of the house, the association between architecture, spatiality, and visuality benefits from delineation. While each of these constructs covers an extensive and related area, they are neither mutually exclusive nor mutually inclusive.

For the purposes of this discussion, this argument is premised on the understanding that architecture is a fundamentally spatial practice that itself constructs complex relations between the spatial and the visual. While these terms cannot be wholly separated, it needs to be emphasized that they are not equivalent, although all are at play in Wittgenstein's texts and in the Stonborough-Wittgenstein House as well. This framework can best be described as a spatial analysis of Wittgenstein's philosophy initiated by the influence of his practice of architecture, a practice that binds or compiles these issues but does not align their boundaries. The visual is thus most ardently present as it emerges through the spatial locating of viewpoints and viewing subjects. Architecture, apparent in typical practices of building, also surfaces to present itself within associated broader visual and spatial concepts. To that end, Wittgenstein's specific architecture references—to building, construction, houses, measured drawings, and so on—are the most distinct, while the spatial references to such constructs as indistinct areas and the intermingling of attributes that define family resemblance are the most far-reaching.

The twentieth century's linguistic turn, in which Wittgenstein and the philosophy of language play a considerable role, has constructed the historical and theoretical ground for the full development of an interdisciplinary discourse capable of redefining each component within it. Employing that foundation set by the linguistic turn and made widely viable by Wittgenstein's philosophy of ordinary language is one of the things that this book hopes to achieve. The premise lies in understanding that the linguistic basis, in encroaching upon the assumed borders between philosophical discourse and aesthetic objects, holds a key to reuniting aesthetic practice and thought, to allow—even demand—practice to "speak" and language to be made visible. The correlated gesture found in Wittgenstein's focus on language as practice does just that by declaring practice and speech to be inseparable.

Wittgenstein's House is divided into two main sections: "Transgressions and Inhabitations" and "Images of Entanglement." The first part of the book, "Transgressions and Inhabitations," defines the views and frameworks of space constructed by the three main actors in this enterprise: the *Tractatus*, the *Investigations*, and the Stonborough-Wittgenstein House. The compound construct of transgressions and inhabitations details the shift that develops between the texts from the *Tractatus*'s view from without, which is indicative of transgression, to the *Investigations*'s view from within, the product of inhabitation. The part includes chapters on the practices of transgression produced by and in the *Tractatus*, the construction of inhabitation in both the practice of architecture and in the *Investigations*, and an analysis of the formal, conceptual, and practical makeup of the Stonborough-Wittgenstein House. This last chapter reveals the practice of architecture's contribution to Wittgenstein's subsequent rejection of the *Tractatus*'s prescriptive approach to philosophy realized in his development of the *Investigations*'s practice-based philosophy of language.

In this part, the *Tractatus*'s spatial logic, its view from without, is the working datum for evaluating the impact of the practice of architecture on Wittgenstein's subsequent philosophy of language. The *Tractatus* develops its view from without as part and parcel of its philosophical objectives through its attempt to define the limits of sensible or meaningful uses of language. What becomes clear in examining the *Tractatus*'s spatial framework is that its very comprehension of language and philosophy is dependent upon the positioning of the viewer as if above and outside language, looking downward so as to discern clearly a particular relation between language, logic, and philosophy. From that viewpoint, all three seem to share a coincident series of boundaries. The *Tractatus* describes these as a series of spatial limits appearing throughout the text, including: "*The limits of my language* mean the limits of my world" and "Logic pervades the world: the limits of the world are also its limits."[36]

The view from without has certain attributes or characteristics that presents the workings of meaningful language as determinate and unambiguous, the product of a necessary and a priori structure of language akin to logic. The *Tractatus* unearths this logical determinacy of language from its hiding place beneath the surface of an everyday language, a surface that masks its own analytic structure and thereby obfuscates its meaning. Problematically, this confusion of meaning produces pseudo-problems that are mistaken for valid philosophical ones about the world and the relation of language to the world it represents. These illusory problems are understood by the *Tractatus* to form the contents and focus of philosophy (particularly of metaphysics and epistemology). In response to this situation, the *Tractatus* contends that once the propositions of philosophy are properly analyzed for their logical structure, the philosophical problems they describe will not simply be solved but will, in effect, dissolve. In this light, the only remaining purpose for philosophy is to rid the discipline of such "pseudo" problems, its only method a repetitive procedure of self-correction directed toward ending philosophy as we know it. The *Tractatus* thus undertakes the transformation of philosophy into a discipline whose reason for being is to empty continually its own contents and qualities.

The *Tractatus* develops these central ideas not solely by isolating language, logic, and truth but by examining their emergence through issues of visuality, subjectivity, ethics, and aesthetics. Wittgenstein's involvement with the visual and spatial is most apparent in the *Tractatus* in the importance of the constructs of showing and saying for his argument. It is the relation between showing and saying that Wittgenstein employs to define the limits of the sensible use of language. Although both showing and saying are manifestly subjective practices and the subject in the *Tractatus* shares (nominally) these limits, the philosophy of the *Tractatus* makes no room for the subject, finding instead that "The subject does not belong to the world: rather, it is a limit of the world,"[37] and the subject "must," according to the text, "transcend these propositions, and then he will see the world aright. . . . (He must, so to speak, throw away the ladder after he has climbed up it.)."[38]

Beyond this explicit content, the visual and spatial thinking that proves crucial to the *Tractatus*'s production of the view from without yields three main images of transgression that are discussed in the first chapter: the numbering system, the picture theory of meaning, and the paradigmatic image of the ladder. This dispelling of the subject is a product of the *Tractatus*'s paradoxical construction of the view from without, which in order to depict the limits of language must transcend those same limits. As such, the view from without each image of transgression operates by replicating this process of positing a construct or rule which in order to be followed must be transgressed.

The first image of transgression, the *Tractatus*'s numbering system, is equally responsible for the text's unique image. The numbering system is both the primary image of the *Tractatus* and an image of transgression. It divides the text into hierarchically and precisely numbered propositions that aim to produce absolute clarity of expression by constructing clearly defined and utterly unambiguous relations between the propositions that form the text. Although at times referred to as idiosyncratic, insignificant, or simply a temporary working method,[39] the numbering system that produces the *Tractatus*'s unique image—and it *is* its image—is indicative of far more. The numbering system that orders the text is the single most fundamental and significant site of the *Tractatus*'s spatial thinking. It is the place from which the *Tractatus*'s spatiality has lodged—wholly apparent and wholly undetected—to emerge most ardently. Its meaning at once hidden and open to inspection, the numbering system frames and organizes the *Tractatus* by forming the locus of both the *Tractatus*'s spatiality and its logic-based attempt to produce a fully clarified form of expression. Despite these intentions, the numbering system itself paradoxically yields spatial contradictions. In its attempt to fix meaning through the impositions of a strict but ultimately untenable correspondence of word, meaning, and place, the numbering system, I argue, problematically sacrifices spatial associations to logical reference, thereby also sacrificing meaning.

In a similar attempt to that of the numbering system to fix correspondence of meaning to word, the *Tractatus*'s picture theory, its second image of transgression, provides a model of how language operates. That model allows for the grammatical structure of propositions to operate as models of reality. This allows elements in the sentences to stand for objects in the world, all the while demanding a form of correspondence denied by everyday practice. Transgressions of these self-created rules result, once again, from the inability to produce the act of meaning propounded by the theory: to connect language unambiguously with the world that it describes.

Offered in the closing lines as that which must be climbed in order to move beyond the text itself, the *Tractatus*'s image of the ladder provides transgression's third and most explicit manifestation. Via this image, the propositions of the text are equated with rungs on a ladder that must be climbed in order to gain a proper view of those same propositions. The result is the construction of an external view, the view from without, a view in direct violation of the *Tractatus*'s self-declared limits of language and the subject.

Following the discussions of the *Tractatus*'s images of transgression are three chapters that detail the production of inhabitation in the late philosophy and in the Stonborough-Wittgenstein House. While transgression defines the spatial practices of the *Tractatus*, inhabitation plays a comparable role in the *Investigations*. This series of inhabitations follows the *Tractatus*'s acts of transgression and its associated view from without. Inhabitation is initiated by Wittgenstein's practice of architecture with the Stonborough-Wittgenstein House and is developed further in the late philosophy's creation of the builders as the imaginary figures who set the *Investigations* and the construction of the view from within language in motion.

The *Investigations*, written over the course of sixteen years beginning in 1929, forms the core of Wittgenstein's late philosophy. With it Wittgenstein embarked on the fundamental project of reconsidering language and philosophy as he characterized them in the *Tractatus*. That assessment denies two fundamental views critical to the *Tractatus*: that language requires an essential nature or an a priori structure to be meaningful, and that language's surface illusion masks the meaning it harbors in its deeper structure. In this pursuit, the *Investigations* reexamines many of the themes found in both the *Tractatus* and in the Stonborough-Wittgenstein House: boundaries, limits, rules, meaning, practice, and so on. Most important, however, is that the *Investigations* rejects the sharp distinction between showing and saying that propelled the *Tractatus*'s production of the view from without. This shift alters the focus of the *Investigations* from a basis in the logical structure hidden beneath ordinary language's surface and accessible only through logical analysis to the visually accessible surface itself. The hallmark of this realignment is found in Wittgenstein's exhortation to the reader, "don't think, but look!"[40] when searching for the associations between various uses of a word. That is, rather than presume an ideal meaning, the *Investigations* impels the reader to look at how the word—now viewed as part of a practice—is manifest in everyday practice. The thrust of this shift supports a continued search, pressed on by the activity of the search itself, that requires the subject's entanglement with language as a necessary component of investigation.

Focusing on the construction of the view from within initiated in the opening pages of the *Investigations* by "the builders," the first discussion of inhabitation describes the shift from the view from without to that from within. The builders and their language lie at the forefront of the *Investigations*'s construction of the space of language as an ongoing practice of construction and inhabitation. Presented as the first example of a language-game that forms the basis for the rejection of a *Tractatus*-like conception of language, their language consists of four words: "block," "pillar," "slab," and "beam," with an associated series of actions. Language-games model constructs that Wittgenstein employs in the *Investigations* as his primary method for the study of language, provide specific models of the functioning of everyday language. With the builders' model Wittgenstein at once introduces a counterexample to a *Tractatus*-like conception of language, presents the idea of the language-game as a way to study language, and posits the idea of practice, particularly that of building, at its impetus.

The scene of the builders imagines language as the continual processes of self-learning and construction, deeply related in the conjoined practice of architecture and the philosophy of language. Both practices are shown as being capable of fostering the creation of habitable space and the subsequent construction of the *Investigations*'s view from within the space of language. This view differs dramatically from the view from without in how it positions the subject in relation to language and the study of language. While the view from above, as the *Tractatus*'s specific form of the view from without, implies that everything is available to vision, the view from within is incapable of offering such seemingly ideal clarity. Instead it points to a series of possible and potentially unlimited practices of vision and movement through space. This transposition alters the role of vision itself. From within, vision is no longer privileged as it can no longer oversee. It becomes instead one of the many possible ways of interacting with the world. Another way of understanding this distinction between the view from without and within is to see the aerial view of the *Tractatus* as having been replaced by the view from the streets, a view that later forms the everyday of Michel de Certeau.[41]

The introduction of the view from within implements a radical development from the *Tractatus*'s goal of formal and logical clarity. By advancing a philosophy of the everyday use of language in which language does not function by either describing reality or masking it, the *Investigations* approaches language as an engaged practice inseparable from the "form of life" it at once produces and represents. In this process, the *Investigations* rejects the restrictions the *Tractatus* placed on language, accepting instead that ambiguity and confusion may be inherent in meaningful uses of language. In explicitly allowing that any use of words—even drawings at times[42]—may be a language, the *Investigations* suggests that there are no definitive limits to the use of language, no definitive rules of language, and that as such, language itself is indeterminate, but that this indeterminacy does not preclude understanding. Integral to this view of language is an ongoing entanglement with the world of practice, an entanglement that includes Wittgenstein's practice of architecture as a constitutive component.

This book's second and third discussions of inhabitation focus on the Stonborough-Wittgenstein House and Wittgenstein's practice of architecture, respectively. The discussion begins by detailing the history of the production of the house and continues on to examine Wittgenstein's engagement with the practice of architecture in his work on the design of the house and his overseeing of its construction. The Stonborough-Wittgenstein House, designed between 1926 and 1929 for Wittgenstein's sister, Margarethe, presents two well-known images: its austere exterior of asymmetrically grouped cubic white blocks marked by regular vertical windows, and its central interior space which inverts that image to forefront the multilayered paired glass-and-steel doors that breathe life into its walls (figs. 3, 4). Within and between those walls, the house resonates with many of the themes and preoccupations of Wittgenstein's philosophy, including a concern with boundaries, limits, rules, and the relationships between inner and outer, public and private, hidden and manifest. These constructs are all brought to bear in the house, frequently in the form of spatial and visual conflicts over what it means to follow a rule or how to define a boundary.

The central hall of the house presents the paramount case for study as it is a meeting point both spatially and practically for the complex relations between interior and exterior and the various programmatic concerns of the main floor. The central hall also acts to mediate Wittgenstein's work on the house with that of the architect, Paul Engelmann, who initiated the house's design. As with Wittgenstein's fascinating construction of double-layered doors that present different images and degrees of transparency to each room, these relations have been precisely visually and spatially modulated by Wittgenstein, both in their physical locations and in their access and associations. The complex U-shaped composition of the central hall, along with the compound construction of its iconic doors themselves,

Figure 3. Stonborough-Wittgenstein House: view of the southwest facade, 1983–1984; new light fittings and stair railings are visible. Photographer: Margherita Spiluttini. Copyright: Wittgenstein Archive, Cambridge.

becomes Wittgenstein's preeminent tool for the construction and discussion of the concept of boundary and the relation between inner and outer, private and public.

Focusing on the practice of architecture as inhabitation sets up the spatial reading of the *Investigations* by depicting how the practice of architecture challenges the incipient or restricted spatiality of the *Tractatus*, as found, for example, in the numbering system. This focus provides a crucial connection between the early philosophy and the more developed and complex spatiality produced in the *Investigations*. How the practice of architecture performed this function is an important part of this rereading. Specifically, *Wittgenstein's House* proposes that the practice of architecture provides a model of how space operates akin to the manner by which Wittgenstein himself offers specific language-games in the *Investigations* as models of language's everyday functioning. In much the same manner that Wittgenstein introduces language-games to force the reader to reconsider entrenched assumptions about specific aspects of language, the spatial models introduced by the practice of architecture similarly challenge

Figure 4. Stonborough-Wittgenstein House: view from the stairs of the hall toward the entrance, 1992. Photographer: Margherita Spiluttini. Copyright: Wittgenstein Archive, Cambridge.

the isolated view of language produced by the *Tractatus*. In so doing, architecture defines a "site" for Wittgenstein's development of the view of language as a practice, an approach that permeates the late philosophy.

While the first part of the book, "Transgressions and Inhabitations" discusses the construction of frameworks or views by which Wittgenstein sees and discusses language and philosophy, the second part, "Images of Entanglement," analyzes the images constructed by the late philosophy's view from within. These images emerge from their architectural inception in the Stonborough-Wittgenstein House to appear explicitly in Wittgenstein's philosophy in his 1929 lecture on ethics. Such images of entanglement develop further in the *Investigations*, where the influence of Wittgenstein's immersion in spatial practices become fully apparent. It is there that Wittgenstein's reconceived understanding of space produces a new criterion of clarity, one born from entanglement. Images of entanglement define how the *Investigations*'s view from within produces a new spatiovisual basis for philosophical clarity. While the *Tractatus* demanded the absolute clarity promised by the view from without as a prerequisite for meaning, the *Investigations*'s view from within challenges the possibility of an absolute separation of view from language or subject from object, constructing in its place a meaningful practice emerging from the spatial entanglement between the subject and language.

Strategically employed in the late philosophy, these snapshot-like images of entanglement arise at crucial moments throughout the *Investigations* to define the philosophical approach and imprint its processes of concept formation. Images of entanglement thereby function to define sites in Wittgenstein's work—both textual and architectural—where the enmeshment of spatial practices between architecture and philosophy coalesce into a series of specific images. Examples of images of entanglement include the central hall of the Stonborough-Wittgenstein House, Wittgenstein's definition of language as a labyrinth of paths, his discussion of the philosopher's involvement with philosophical problems as the attempt to repair a torn spiderweb with one's fingers, his description of meaning as akin to the intertwining of characteristics that produce family resemblance, and the ordering of the *Investigations* itself, with its interwoven concepts and interrupting interlocutor.

I recognize at this point that what began as an analysis first of the relationship between the form and the content and then of the spatial metaphors in Wittgenstein's philosophy has become less a traditional analysis and more of an occupation. The approach, then, is in ways as wide as it is limited. While it offers a very specified and focused reading of Wittgenstein's philosophy, this approach is meant not to replace but to complement and interrelate with the extensive material that already exists on Wittgenstein's texts. The realignment of Wittgenstein's practices of architecture and philosophy is not proposed solely to rectify the lack of inclusion of his architecture in discussions of the texts; rather, it is initiated in an attempt to reexamine the very bases of interdisciplinarity and of the possibilities for relating linguistic and spatial practices. Inclusivity, it needs to be emphasized, does not deny difference but understands that these disciplines already operate in a field or shared territory of meaningful practice. The hope of this endeavor is that it will shed light on Wittgenstein's architectural and philosophical thought while fostering the reconsideration of the presumed limitations of those existing domains.[43] It is into this encroached-upon but untapped territory that *Wittgenstein's House* enters.

PART ONE

TRANSGRESSIONS AND INHABITATIONS

Transgressions

The current of this book lies in discerning the influence of Wittgenstein's practice of architecture on his subsequent philosophy of language. Toward this end, the approach is in many ways from the point of view of the practice of architecture and the late philosophy of the *Investigations*. In this scenario, Wittgenstein's early philosophy of the *Tractatus*, as the site of his pre-practice of architecture, serves as a form of datum or measure of comparison by which to gauge the impact of architecture's influence. That measure comes in large part from an examination of the spatial epistemologies or problematics underlying each phase of Wittgenstein's philosophical output. Attending to these fundamental spatial constructs in the philosophy opens up new aspects of similar concepts instituted in both the early and late work and becomes useful in establishing grounds that transpire between the architecture and philosophy. The fundamental conception of space that this examination identifies within the *Tractatus* is what I characterize as the view from above or without and whose operative construct I propose to be that of transgression.

THE VIEW FROM ABOVE

Central to the *Tractatus*'s development of its thought, philosophy, and textual production is an interrelated set of spatial and visual concerns. These range from its construction of the view from above, by which it depicts language, to its reliance on the spatial acts of positioning to define the limits of sensible thought, its division between showing and saying, and ultimately its diagnosis of linguistic and surface confusion as the underlying basis of philosophical problems—problems the *Tractatus* hopes to rectify by instituting the view from above.

Underlying these complex spatial constructs are the interrelated and explicitly spatial concepts of limit, boundary, and transgression that the *Tractatus* relies upon to accomplish its philosophical work. The concepts involved not only refer to some understanding of spatiality, however, *but are themselves inconceivable without committing to certain conceptions of space* that embed spatiality into the very core of the *Tractatus*, making it necessary to approach the text itself as a spatial construct integral to grasping its own philosophy. This is to say that the *Tractatus, in attempting to define the limits of the thinkable, is itself unthinkable outside the severely restricted understanding of space it produces, a space determined by the view from above.*

The philosophy that results from this view differentiates itself by striving to produce a completely clarified view of language from which a completely clarified form of expression may become apparent. Outlined in the preface to the *Tractatus* is the philosophy's fundamental goal of defining the limits of sensible language:

> the aim of this book is to draw a limit to thought, or rather—not to thought, but to the expression of thoughts: for in order to be able to draw a limit to thought, we should have to find both sides of the limit thinkable (i.e., we should have to be able to think what cannot be thought). It will therefore only be in language that the limit can be drawn, and what lies on the other side of the limit will simply be nonsense.

Envisioning that limit becomes the work of the *Tractatus*, work that of necessity violates its stated tenets by transgressing the limits of language in order to envision them as the view from above language. It is in this paradoxical and circular process that the view from above and the operation of transgression become entangled as inseparable partners of an impossible dialectic.

As its operative principle, transgression sets the construction of the view from above into motion through an acknowledged transgression of the limits of sensible thought, moving the *Tractatus* beyond what it admits of language. Transgression in the *Tractatus* is thus both product and productive: while it serves as the central operation that the *Tractatus* executes to institute the view from above, it is a direct product of the extremely limited and limiting activity of philosophy in the *Tractatus*, limitations that extend into the view itself.

The *Tractatus*'s understanding of language and philosophy depends upon positioning the viewer of language above language, looking downward. The formation of the view from above is evinced with the *Tractatus*'s derivation of a series of spatial limits dispersed throughout the text. The *Tractatus* repeatedly details language, logic, the subject, and the world in terms of these limits. The series begins with the text's opening lines and its suggestion of the world as a limiting factor of knowledge and continues on to reinforce that limit by making it coextensive with the limits of logic, of the self, of the sayable, and ultimately of silence. The view from above comes about in the attempt to locate the point at which the viewing subject becomes capable of seeing these limits.

1   The world is all that is the case.
1.1   The world is the totality of facts, not of things.
5.6   The limits of my language mean the limits of my world.
5.61   Logic pervades the world: the limits of the world are also its limits. So we cannot say in logic, "The world has this in it, and this, but not that."

      For that would appear to presuppose that we were excluding certain possibilities, and this cannot be the case, since it would require that logic should go beyond the limits of the world; for only in that way could it view those limits from the other side as well.

      We cannot think what we cannot think; so what we cannot think we cannot *say* either.

5.632 The subject does not belong to the world: rather it is a limit of the world. . . .
7   What we cannot speak about we must pass over in silence.

While the *Tractatus* presents these limits as absolute statements about the world, they are definitive less of the world or language in total than of a specific, idealized, and limited viewpoint from which the limits of language are presented. The equating or aligning of the limits of language, logic, and the subject (while not differentiating their functionings) is reiterative of the structure of logic—not solely because it is privileged but because its privilege resides in its definitively demarcating language itself. Yet the continued reassociations between logic, the world, and the subject in their interworkings cannot help but expand that limit—against the *Tractatus*'s protestations. In connecting the limits of language to the limits of the subject, the *Tractatus* necessarily introduces the viewing subject to the view it constructs. What the limits describe, then, are the particulars of the view from above and outside that which is defined. Such a series of depictions details a seeming command through the (over)seeing of language, philosophy, subjectivity, and so on, setting a correlated theory of representation into motion.

With the avowed goal of setting limits to what cannot be thought, the *Tractatus* acknowledges this process of representation as working "outwards through what can be thought."[1] Yet this particular process necessarily entails not only the acknowledged locating of the constellation of constructs or arenas of language, logic, sense, boundary, and limit involved, but transgression as that which enables the view from above. The *Tractatus* thus lays out a spatiovisual problem: to detail the limits of or access to meaningful language, only to solve it through transgression. As such, it is transgression in constructing the view from above rather than logic that supplies the sought-after linguistic clarity—by turning it into visual clarity. As logic provides the *Tractatus* with the structure through which language represents the world, that view is constructed in the image of logic. Logic in the *Tractatus* thus does not come to define the internal, a priori order of language that it claims, but places extraordinary demands on the functioning of language, demands necessitating that language accord with logical clarity in order to be meaningful. It is those demands that generate the transgressive structure of the view from above that privileges the image of logic.

The view from above combines two transgressive spatial structures that mirror the *Tractatus*'s two main components: its logical mandate to produce a fully clarified form of expression, and its so-called mystical one to delineate the realm of value. The first spatial structure is associated with the philosophy's logical mandate. It initiates the spatial search for a completely clarified form of expression, which it ferrets out from beneath the surface of everyday language in which philosophical propositions are formed. The logical section of the book encompasses its theory of the general form of a proposition, its picture theory of representation, and its discussion of logic, including truth tables, tautologies, contradictions, and mathematics.

The text's second spatial structure is associated with the mystical. It is located not beneath the surface of language but beyond language's proper operations. The "mystical" component subsumes the discussions of solipsism, subjectivity, ethics, and aesthetics. Permeating this divided landscape is the *Tractatus*'s primary pursuit of distinguishing between what meaningful propositions in language can say and what they can only show, a pursuit necessitating the search for the limits of sensible language. It is that required mediation that institutes the *Tractatus*'s spatiality. As much as this endeavor is engrossed in a search for the designating of meaning, its operations generate spatial acts and produce spatial constructs integral to the production of meaning and the concomitant division between sense and nonsense. The two spatial structures/components of the text are related by the act of transgression. As the mystical realm of showing ultimately needs to be entered in order to see through language to the logical structure embedded beneath language's surface, the two spatial structures/components become inseparable. To enter the mystical is to move beyond the sayable into that which can only be shown, experienced, or practiced.

The *Tractatus*'s structure, similarly to its mandates, divides language into two parts: logically founded sensible propositions that define the realm of the sayable, and nonsensible pseudo-propositions that try to state what can only be shown. The *Tractatus* levies this latter status on many of the concerns of philosophy, beginning with the realm of value and practice and extending to its own propositions. Invalidated in the attempt to say what can only be shown, these uses of language are contrasted to propositions from the natural sciences that depict factual states of affairs in the world and accord with logical grammar.

This fundamental and divisive distinction between showing and saying goes to the heart of the *Tractatus*'s very formation. The division pits its delimiting of meaningful propositions against the status of the *Tractatus*'s own propositions, thereby generating the central spatial paradox that structures the *Tractatus:* its acknowledgment that its failure to state definitively the limits of language succeeds negatively by culminating in the act of showing. In other words, the *Tractatus* succeeds in revealing the limits of language only when it transgresses those limits as its only means of envisioning them. Consequently, the bounding of language culminates in showing. Out of that paradoxical need to exceed the limits and propositions of the text in order to construct a point from which they can be seen, a space and structure of transgression emerges as the view from beyond. The transgression of the bounds of sensible thought, thus, while producing nonsense also produces enlightenment in the formal clarity of the view from above.

THE LOGICAL SPATIAL STRUCTURE

Wittgenstein's goal in constructing the view from above was to define a completely clarified form of expression, one in which the laws of logic and of language coincide, a goal shared by the philosophers Bertrand Russell and G. E. Moore. The view from above is central to this endeavor as it provides an overview by constructing a linguistic picture of the relations between logic and language. Accordingly, Wittgenstein's discussion of logic in the *Tractatus* develops as an integral component of an investigation of the space and spatial constructs governing language, logic, philosophy, and the text of the *Tractatus*. In the *Tractatus*, logic bears unique relation to the more general *concept* of limit or boundary as much as it does to the *specific* boundaries of language set forth in the text. "Logic pervades the world: the limits of the world are also its limits. So we cannot say in logic, 'The world has this in it, and this, but not that.'"[2] Assuming this role, logic subtends the spatial construct of limit in the *Tractatus*.

The *Tractatus*'s view from above clearly bound together logic and language along a shared boundary. This needs to be addressed operatively, in that logic's requirement that sense be determinate becomes impressed on ordinary language to require that sensible, determinate thought become not just logic's criterion but language's as well. By demarcating the boundary of sense to coincide with that of logic, the two become operatively and spatially inseparable, yet are not the same. This magnifies the importance of logic in the *Tractatus*, allowing it to play two crucial roles. First, it furnishes the necessary a priori structure of thought that allows language to hook onto the world and thereby perform its primary function of representing reality as described in the *Tractatus*'s picture theory. This is accomplished by virtue of logic's unique and privileged position of belonging equally to the realm of the factual and to the transcendental, a position that allows logic to serve as the connection between language and the world but in so doing, demands that we see the world through its lens.

Logic's role as connector sets up its second essential role in the *Tractatus*, that of constructing the boundary between showing and saying that Wittgenstein claims delimits the meaningful use of language. In this role, the model of logic is positioned to define the limits to sensible language.

> 4.121 Propositions cannot represent logical form: it is mirrored in them.
> What finds its reflection in language, language cannot represent.
> What expresses *itself* in language, I cannot express by means of language.
> Propositions *show* the logical form of reality.
> They display it.

For all of its defining of how we see language and despite its privileged mediating position, logical form can only be shown. This sharply contrasts it with statements of fact, such as those from the natural sciences, while aligning it with such philosophical topics as aesthetics and epistemology. But once more, logic's disposition is more complex: while ethics and aesthetics are viewed by the *Tractatus* as complementary to the world, logic is inextricably bound to it. The reason that the logical form and the rules of logical syntax that configure the core of logic cannot be put into words is because they themselves produce a precondition to linguistic representation. They therefore concern essential features shared between language and reality necessary for language to represent the world, logic's primary role. As such, according to the *Tractatus*, they can only be shown.

The reasons the realm of value can only be shown are different. They are deemed unsayable as such propositions defy determinate (factual) form, thereby violating another of the *Tractatus*'s dictums regarding the meaningful usage of language. This leaves the realm of value (including ethics and aesthetics) as delimited from *within* the text yet profoundly absent from it.[3] As Wittgenstein writes in prop. 6.421 of the *Tractatus*, "It is clear that ethics cannot be put into words. Ethics is transcendental. (Ethics and aesthetics are one and the same.)" The only philosophically relevant propositions that the *Tractatus* does condone are those involved in the process of logical clarification whose aim it is to present clearly what can be said. While this aspect has been acknowledged, its crucial spatial functioning that oversees these processes has been left untheorized.

In determining the position of the boundary between showing and saying, logic correlates two sets of distinctions: that between sense and nonsense, and that between showing and saying. These of distinctions are related, as nonsense is that which results when the bounds of sense are surpassed or transgressed so as to correlate content with spatial positioning. Each distinction must necessarily be understood according to both its determining content and its demarcating spatial location. In terms of content, sensible propositions are propositions about the world that make definitive—that is, factual—statements. These are underscored by Wittgenstein in the *Tractatus*'s opening lines: "*The world is the totality of facts, not of things.*"[4] Such factual propositions conform equally to the prescribed boundaries between showing and saying that demarcate sense in relation to logic and to line in space—a boundary that cannot be crossed without sense being diminished.

While defining the limits of sense, such a boundary also serves to distinguish between showing and saying. Enabling this, the *Tractatus* offers a series of rules of sense that define what language can sensibly or meaningfully say compared to what it can only show,[5] including the following (incomplete) list of rules that the *Tractatus* presents:

> 4.022 A proposition *shows* its sense.
>
> A proposition *shows* how things stand if it is true. And it *says that* they do so stand. . . .
>
> 4.114 [Philosophy] must set limits to what can be thought; and, in doing so, to what cannot be thought.
>
> It must set limits to what cannot be thought by working outwards through what can be thought. . . .
>
> 4.1212 What *can* be shown, *cannot* be said.

A curious thing about overstepping the show/say boundary and producing nonsense is that crossing this threshold does not make itself immediately apparent. It has no unique visual appearance, no appearance *as nonsense per se*, but instead defines a visual construct: the state of appearing to make sense while not doing so. Nonsense, as it turns out, typically takes form as grammatically correct ordinary language. Its determining factor is thus not its surface appearance but the disconnect between its surface appearance and its underlying logic.

This paradox forms another place where the visual component of language in the *Tractatus* emerges—in this instance as a contradiction between the proper grammatical appearance of nonsense and its literal lack of logical sense. As the sense/nonsense distinction is a prime place from which Wittgenstein saw philosophical problems emerge, this confusion of appearance is not a side effect of the *Tractatus's* functioning order *but constitutive of it*. The confusion between what only *appears* to be meaningful and what actually *is* sayable ultimately forms the impetus for the work of the *Tractatus*, as it is in response to the philosophical ambiguity of ordinary language that the *Tractatus* invokes the view from without as a place of removal—as a place from which the viewer may clearly discern distinctions between sensible language and nonsense. The view from without thus allows the viewer not to be drawn into—tricked by—language's confusing appearance of grammatical order. That sense or fear of being drawn into confusion later makes its appearance in the *Investigations's* repeated images of webs, mazes, and labyrinths.

Logical analysis in the *Tractatus* ultimately concludes that what appear to be philosophical problems in epistemology or metaphysics, problems somehow in, of, and about the world, are produced instead by our inability to understand completely our own language or, more specifically, to see the logical structure contained within that of ordinary language. In response, Wittgenstein proposes that the proper task of philosophy need be the logical clarification of its own propositions, a process that reveals those propositions to be pseudo-problems masquerading as important problems about the world. Toward that end, the *Tractatus* offers one "strictly correct" method, summarized in the closing paragraphs of the text:

> 6.53 The correct method in philosophy would really be the following: to say nothing except what can be said, i.e. propositions of natural science—i.e. something that has nothing to do with philosophy—and then, whenever someone else wanted to say something metaphysical, to demonstrate to him that he had failed to give a meaning to certain signs in his propositions. Although it would not be satisfying to the other person—he would not have the feeling that we were teaching him philosophy—*this* method would be the only strictly correct one.[6]

Following the approach of logical clarification, the misunderstandings that produce philosophical problems are seen to arise from within the gap or misalignment between a proposition and the logical form underlying it. Pseudo-problems are therefore problems of vision; specifically, they are problems of illusion and the obstruction of vision that the view from above, in its directness and seeming completeness, is established to eliminate. Wittgenstein's understanding that philosophical problems arise from an inability to see the correct logical form *beneath* ordinary language makes clear that the *Tractatus* defines a specified relation between language, logic, and vision. Such a view correlates visual qualities to linguistic forms—with ordinary language seen as opaque and logical form understood as transparent. The end result of the clarification process is thus intended to be the transformation of the ordinarily ambiguous and opaque surface of everyday language into the completely clear and transparent form of the logic that subtends it.

Once the expression of the philosophical problem is clarified, that is, once the propositions in "ordinary" language forming philosophical problems are brought completely in line with logic—those problems are shown to be illusory, the result of the inability, when *looking* at the *surface* of language, to apprehend the properly analyzed form of the proposition embedded within it. The philosophy of the *Tractatus* thus institutes a fundamentally self-correcting mechanism. The *Tractatus*'s method, however, is guided not so much toward solving the problems it uncovers as it is toward dissolving them, and with them, vision and the viewing subject. In so doing, the process or practice threatens not just philosophy's pseudo-problems but philosophy's continued (recognizable) existence. The *Tractatus*'s proposed painstaking analysis of language threatens to yield, then, a philosophy that is transparent, but only by virtue of being empty, one rid of philosophical problems, but equally rid of philosophical *discourse*.

THE MYSTICAL STRUCTURE OF TRANSGRESSION

In enlisting the view from above to depict language, the *Tractatus* depicts only the part of language that lies within the bounds of logic. The view from outside and above is one of presiding over. Both arising from and as a necessary component of the *Tractatus*'s attempt to describe the limits of meaningful language and the relation between language and the world, the view from above presents itself as a clear and concise picture of how language functions as well as how to avoid misusing it. Its apparent visual command of the world it oversees is the result of remaining at a distance from it, as it is only from outside of language, *disentangled from potential obstacles to clear vision,* that the limits of language are ostensibly visible and describable.

The clarity that the view from above lends to language, however, is the product of its emphasizing specific qualities of language—those in accord with logic—rather than in its depicting all of language. The late philosophy shows just this in challenging that such a view from without is possible and, more important, challenging that the *Tractatus*'s position does in fact characterize all of language. In the *Investigations*, Wittgenstein explicitly discusses the limitations of the view of language presented in the *Tractatus,* suggesting early on that while the *Tractatus* implied that it described the whole of language, it was in fact detailing only a limited area of language. In referring to Augustine's *Tractatus*-like description of language quoted in the opening paragraph of the *Investigations*, Wittgenstein writes: "And one has to say this in many cases where the question arises 'Is this an appropriate description or not?' The answer is: 'Yes, it is appropriate, but only for this narrowly circumscribed region, not for the whole of what you were claiming to describe.'"[7]

That narrowly circumscribed region is the realm of logic and the limits of a theory of representation following from it. Those limits are used to produce a frame around the limits of sensible thought. The *Investigations* enacts the unmasking of that frame and the release of its associated spatiality and subjectivity also arising from the idealized viewpoint from without:

> (*Tractatus Logico-Philosophicus*, 4.5): "The general form of a proposition is: This is how things are."—That is the kind of proposition that one repeats to oneself countless times. One thinks that one is tracing the outline of the thing's nature over and over again, and one is merely tracing round the frame through which we look at it.[8]

Part of the move from the *Tractatus* to the *Investigations* thus involves the realization of the limitations of the view from above constructed by the *Tractatus*, particularly the flatness and immobility of its implied space. The *Investigations* details those restrictions from its newly defined position within language but outside the narrow limits of logic, a place where space, vision, and subjectivity are neither wholly interchangeable nor entirely separable.

Even from its removed position, the view from above necessarily associates viewing subject with constructed view, despite attempts to exile the subject from the *Tractatus* or at least to its limits. While the *Tractatus* strains to keep the interactions between subject and language in check, it is that involvement that fuels the *Investigations*'s understanding of language as a form of life. The realization that the *Tractatus*'s depiction of language—a depiction in which language, logic, and the subject all share the same boundaries—is the result of a particular view disrupts, in a number of ways, the self-contained, objectified character of the logic-permeated view presented in the *Tractatus*. No longer understood as a given objective fact, the realization of a view works backward to the realization of a viewer and from there to the understanding that a viewer needs to be located both in space and in history. But how can the *Tractatus* locate a viewer or characterize the subjectivity, language, and logic that viewer introduces? Part of what makes the view from above and without language ideal is exactly the impossible situation or position it posits of a viewer outside language. Yet understanding the position of the viewer remains vital to this issue, as it is the viewer's ideal position that allows for—or at least is tied by the text to—detailing the limits of language.

The impossibility of the view from above is paired in the *Tractatus* with an equally impossible solipsistic view of the subject to produce a shared and essential solipsism between subjectivity and view of language. Wittgenstein writes in prop. 5.62 of the *Tractatus* that:

This remark provides the key to the problem, how much truth there is in solipsism. For what the solipsist *means* is quite correct; only it cannot be *said,* but makes itself manifest. The world is my world: this is manifest in the fact that the limits of *language* (of that language which I alone understand) mean the limits of *my* world.

Following the *Tractatus* to its word, the text constructs the view from without that defines the solipsistic position of the subject presiding over language, a position that renders the subject speechless and hence outside language.

Considering the viewer and not just the view of language makes it clear that despite its seeming clarity, the view from above is more paradoxical than it first appears. On the one hand it attempts to offer the widest, most commanding position possible—a position capable of apprehending the limits to thought and language. Yet on the other hand, it produces a severely constrained activity, one that fixes the viewer to one position, or at least one plane in space. Although the subject (the metaphysical subject, according to Wittgenstein) shares (nominally) the limits of the world, "The subject does not belong to the world: rather it is a limit of the world."[9] The text of the *Tractatus* effectively makes no room for the subject, finding instead that the subject "must transcend these propositions, and then he will see the world aright. . . . (He must, so to speak, throw away the ladder after he has climbed up it.)"[10] That is, the subject has to move beyond the text of the *Tractatus*, beyond its limits of thought and language in order to discern and apprehend them. That movement forms a transgression of language. But this transgression, as an initial and incomplete act, literally leaves the reader suspended in midair. Having climbed up the ladder, the subject is stranded, incapable of movement, left solely with vision as the way of perceiving or interacting with the world.

Wittgenstein's discussion of the visual field in the *Tractatus* makes this clear:

5.633   Where *in* the world is a metaphysical subject to be found?
     You will say that this is exactly like the case of the eye and the visual field. But really you do not *see* the eye.
     And nothing *in the visual field* allows you to infer that it is seen by an eye.
5.6331 For the form of the visual field is surely not like this [diagram of the eye and the visual field].

Wittgenstein's comment that: "And nothing in the visual field allows you to infer that it is seen by an eye" points to the complete exclusion of society and person alike from the *Tractatus*'s conception of language and subjectivity. Wittgenstein's focus is only on the solipsistic subject. Taken another way, there is clearly evidence in our everyday visual fields through which we can infer an eye—the existence of other seeing subjects. But in making no room for the subject, the *Tractatus* finds none.[11]

That transgression of the limits of language opens up a space or gap in which the viewer is paradoxically separated from self and society alike, while language is separated from the world it nevertheless continues to depict. This leaves unanswered—in effect constructs—the crucial question of how language as the product of the view from above connects or hooks onto the world. While the act of viewing reassociates the viewer with the world below, it makes no room for the viewer to be actively involved. Wittgenstein's position of the subject at the limits of language creates this paradoxical stance, leaving the viewer more involved than the "objectivity" of the view suggests, yet strained and limited in the association constructed between viewer and view.

Arising out of the method of logical clarification defined in the *Tractatus*, and mentioned on the heels of it in the closing propositions of the text, is the *Tractatus*'s explicit acknowledgment that its own propositions violate or transgress the very rules and boundaries that they posit. Those propositions are therefore nonsensical in attempting to say what can only be shown. Owing to this history of production, transgression proves central to the *Tractatus*'s operations, as the nonsense it produces is constitutive of its philosophy, and its actions, however repressed, produce images of transgression as the fallout of its coming into being. The *Tractatus* is thus not seemingly able to stop itself from violating its fundamental dictum by trying to say what it acknowledges can only be made manifest. And while the *Tractatus* suggests those violations define the limits of language and the world, it is that series of violations that is manifest throughout the text as a series of images of transgression.

IMAGES OF TRANSGRESSION

The *Tractatus*'s moves beyond both language and text form a double transgression. As moving beyond the limits of language is required (if impossible) in order to see the whole of language, the graphic and conceptual constructions of the view from above become necessary participants in the claims of the *Tractatus*, producing images of transgression in the process. These images include the literal, graphic image of the book's numbering system that organizes its propositions and represents logical order; the metaphorical, allusive image of the ladder as the component or mechanism that facilitates the view from above and ultimately leads to the late philosophy, and the picture theory of meaning and representation based in correspondence whose formation encompasses and echoes the metaphorical and literal images of the *Tractatus* alike.

The Numbering System

With its hierarchically ordered and numbered propositions calibrated to the fifth decimal place, the highly recognizable format of the *Tractatus*'s text presents a unique image in the history of philosophical texts (fig. 1). The numbering system, which has been called a working method and an idiosyncratic gesture,[12] was implemented to imbue the philosophical propositions that it harbored with, as Brian McGuinness noted, "the lack of ambiguity and the quite definite logical relations . . . of a logical system."[13] The system has, however, a number of anomalies that have also been noted. For example, Marjorie Perloff in *Wittgenstein's Ladder* has pointed to the occasionally illogical ordering of propositions and numbers. Alluding to the interaction between the *Tractatus*'s logical and mystical vocations, she proposes that "Perhaps the best way to regard the number anomaly is as a kind of *clinamen*, a bend or swerve where logic gives way to mystery."[14]

Another understanding presents itself once the spatial thinking of the *Tractatus* is taken into account: the anomalies of the numbering system are *signs of a repressed spatial battleground located within the text*. The latent conflict ensues from the implementation of a rigid, logical system instituted to contain and control the otherwise ambiguous functioning of the ordinary language in which the text is necessarily formulated. The image of the numbering system's forefronting of logic in effect reverses the *Tractatus*'s analysis of logic as that which underlies the meaningful use of language *to situate logic as the image of language*. But the system's attempt to perform spatially the philosophy of language that it details comes up against its own desire for absolute precision, setting the linearity of the text against the spatiality of the subject matter it specifies.

The system organizes the propositions of the *Tractatus* around seven main propositions that occupy the positions of the whole numbers 1 to 7. Between any two whole numbers, or main propositions, lie anywhere from 6 (between props. 1.0 and 2.0) to 149 (between props. 5.0 and 6.0) additional propositions. There are no propositions following number 7, the final proposition, which threatens—and delivers—silence. The propositions are organized so that any one proposition either continues on to another proposition at the same decimal place—and thus degree of logical importance—or locates any number of increasingly subservient propositions between that one and the next of equal or greater importance. This complex system attempts both to organize and to construct meaning by stressing which propositions are of greater or lesser "logical importance" and by indicating which propositions any set of other propositions refers to or follows from.

Appearing on the first page of the text to explain this system is the *Tractatus*'s sole footnote:

> The decimal numbers assigned to the individual propositions indicate the logical importance of the propositions, the stress laid on them in my exposition. The propositions n.1, n.2, n.3, etc. are comments on proposition no. n; the propositions n.m1, n.m2, etc. are comments on proposition no. n.m; and so on.

As a spatial organizer, the *Tractatus*'s numbering/structuring system acts to fix a series of associations and meanings that it puts forth as logically determined relations. The explicit structuring of these relations is not, however, a given but instead forms an attempt to be the final arbiter of meaning. The *Tractatus*'s numbering system parallels the fundamental relationship the text defines between word and meaning in its picture theory. As such, the numbering system, with its hierarchical construction and exacting association of elements, attempts to enact what the picture theory imagines—a one-to-one correlation between word and meaning. Importantly, however, in the association between proposition and meaning the system imbeds the additional spatial correlate of *place*.

As with the *Tractatus*'s focus on the inherent logical structure of language, the numbering system initiates a logical structuring of meaning based on the spatial situating of propositions, in effect assembling a now-intricate *trio* of correspondences between language, meaning, and place. In introducing this spatial component into the discussion of the correspondence between words and meaning, the *Tractatus* explicitly manifests the spatial implications of the concept of correspondence. *Situating each proposition in a specific position in relation to the others and to the whole of the Tractatus, the numbering system implicitly enlists spatial location as a component of the text and as an indicator of meaning.* This introduction of position highlights the fact that "correlation" and "correspondence" are spatial concepts and not purely "philosophical" or "linguistic" ones, a result that underscores the inseparability of spatial constructs from the philosophical ones defining the *Tractatus*. Even when unrecognized as such, these constructs—limits, boundary, correspondence, and so on—function spatially, defining spatiality as an implicit component of the philosophy that implements them.

Despite its attempt otherwise, the numbering system of the *Tractatus* ultimately fails to fix meaning. Instead, it inaugurates the unraveling of the *Tractatus*'s conception of language that the hierarchical structure was instituted simultaneously to produce and safeguard. In other words, rather than being an icon of a final and absolute structure, the numbering system is an act and image of transgression. The reason for this is that although meant to insure or secure specified logical relations, the system's incorporation of spatial relations impresses on the philosophical text an additional set of requirements that must be fulfilled in order for the *Tractatus*'s structure of meaning to be maintained. In setting out an additional requirement, these spatial relations also provide a point of incursion into the system, one particularly susceptible to the spatial practices associated with architecture. Any challenge to those spatial associations defining the *Tractatus*, then, equally becomes a challenge to the series of correspondences between word, meaning, and place upon which the *Tractatus* relies. As such, the unraveling of the *Tractatus*'s strict spatial order necessarily constitutes a challenge to the concept of correspondence between word and meaning, language and the world.

Challenges to the *Tractatus*'s numbering system are predominantly manifest through contradictions that arise in the system and the spatial implications of place they introduce. The first challenge occurs through the contradictory spatial locations of the system itself. To function in the desired manner, the system requires a unique order, one that associates a (specified) meaning to a (specified) place so as to yield the one "correct" way in which the propositions of the *Tractatus* should be taken. But the system is a more complex spatial arrangement than the proposal of direct correspondence or sequential linearity suggests. Despite the assignment of specific numbers to the propositions, their locations within the system are not fixed. Instead, the possibility of other orders capable of equally fulfilling the dual structural purpose laid out in the footnote lie latent within the system. Their existence initiates a conflict between the spatial implications of the numbering system, as a series of associations, stresses, and references, and other ordering systems, particularly the linearity of incremental counting. The conflict does not stop there, though; the multiple orderings inherent to the structure disrupt the presentation of the *Tractatus* as possessing a single unique meaning in accordance with the rules of logic. What this points to is that the complexities of the numbering system suggests less a linear/hierarchical ordering than one that incorporates a more dispersed network that can include nodal relations and the possibility of repeated entries.

Consider these sequences that occur in the *Tractatus:* 1, 1.1, 1.11, 1.12, 1.13, 1.2, 1.21; 5.6, 5.61, 5.62, 5.621, 5.63, 5.631; 3, 3.001, 3.01, 3.02, 3.03, 3.031, 3.032, 3.04, 3.05, 3.1, 3.11. Wittgenstein tells us in the footnote that the decimal numbers indicate the logical importance or stress laid on the propositions. Accordingly, the whole numbers are most important, followed decreasingly by those with one decimal place and so on down to the fifth and final decimal place. Equally, the note tells us that the propositions n.1, n.2, and so on are comments on propositions no. n and that the propositions n.m1, n.m2, and so on are comments on n.m, and so on, again down to the final decimal place. Given this, the first two sequences—1 to 1.21 and 5.6 to 5.631—seem in order. The third example throws all that into question by suggesting alternate possibilities. How is it that proposition 3.001 can precede proposition 3.01? In other words, how does n.m1 precede n.m? Importantly, this is not an isolated situation but occurs throughout the text, as in the sequence 4, 4.001, 4.002, 4.003, 4.0031, 4.01, where 4.001 and so on precede 4.01. But how can a comment be made on an as-yet-unstated proposition?

Organized spatially in accordance with the rule of reference the *Tractatus* outlines, the order from 3 to 3.1 would seem to have additional possibilities to the one instituted. For example, an alternate spatial organization of the *Tractatus*'s development of 3, 3.001, 3.01, 3.02, 3.03, 3.031, 3.032, 3.04, 3.05, 3.1, 3.11 could be 3, 3.1, 3.01, 3.001, 3.02, 3.03, 3.031, 3.032, 3.04, 3.05, 3.11 or perhaps 3, 3.01, 3.001, and so on, continuing on as in the *Tractatus*. It is not that any one of these is necessarily more correct than the others—including the *Tractatus*'s version—but rather that each is possible, given the dictates of the footnote. What the versions or permutations reveal is a conflict or gap between Wittgenstein's complex desire that each proposition have a specified degree of stress or importance and that each one also occupy a specified location or place of reference in relation to the other propositions. That is to say, the image that the *Tractatus* constructs—its numbering system—is at odds with what it proposes as a model of meaning.

What transpires in the *Tractatus* is that its attempt to balance the aim of numbering as an assignment of logical importance with the strict a priori ordering of counting (where each successive number is higher than the previous one) sacrifices spatial association to logical reference. The result of this is that the numbering system cannot produce a single determinate possibility. Instead, when the image/structure is spatially analyzed, multiple possibilities are revealed in the form of multiple potential orders, and with that, alternate structural forms or even logics, such as those associated with distributed networks. This happens in part because the *Tractatus*'s image is a flattened or collapsed version of a more complex spatial construct. The seemingly exacting numbering of the propositions thus belies inherent and repressed spatial-linguistic conflicts.

All this points to the fact that the *Tractatus*'s numbering system is not—despite the intention and the image constructed—completely fixed, even or especially when taken on its own terms. Instead, the numbering system/structure is *logically* open to rearrangement or reordering practices central to Wittgenstein's late philosophy. This leaves the *image* of a highly hierarchically structured order attempting to control the system in a way that the numbering system cannot. Which is also to say that the image of a unique logical order or structure that the *Tractatus* constructs conceals a more complex and ambiguous numbering system and association of concepts, a system that necessarily transgresses the *Tractatus*'s dictates of determinate order. This is, of course, the opposite of the *Tractatus*'s diagnosis of philosophical problems arising from the manner in which language's ambiguous surface occludes its underlying logical form.

At the same time, by making meaning, logical place, and spatial location inseparable, the numbering system, with its footnoted explanation, implements—however unintendedly—literal and metaphorical understandings of spatial relations in order to enforce a given reading of the *Tractatus*. Even if the *Tractatus*'s numbering system were to perform ideally, it would not be able to ensure the reading that Wittgenstein seemingly intended. That is, despite Wittgenstein's extreme efforts to impart a given meaning based on the logical ordering of propositions, the propositions remain in ordinary language, with all its ambiguities. As a result, the propositions may still elude the logical form Wittgenstein sees embedded within their ordering and the logical scaffolding of the numbering system by which he envelops them.[15] Given this, the numbering system's institution of a spatial order ultimately becomes more than a way of organizing the propositions on a page: it defines how we approach the text or language. It exhibits its manifest form to be not that of a solely logical order. Rather, it discloses the conflict between constrained order and transgression that reappears at multiple levels throughout the text.

Beyond explaining the numbering system itself, the *Tractatus*'s single footnote offers an image of the possibility of transgression of its own rules found in the system. The implementation of the footnote, by which Wittgenstein explains the numbering system *outside* of the propositions themselves, is an attempt to say what it shows, thereby paralleling, even initiating, the transgressive structure of the *Tractatus* with its need to move beyond the limits of language to see those limits and thereby produce the text. Both acts, the external structuring imposed by the numbering system and the view from above, constitute transgressions of the body of the text of the *Tractatus*. The footnote, by exaggerating the method of control rather than removing all doubt or ambiguity, points paradoxically to the fragility and ambiguity of meaning and to the contingency rather than the necessity of the specific logical structuring of the propositions of the *Tractatus*.

The image of the text imparted by the numbering system is thus paradoxical in its presentation of a strict order despite an underlying and ongoing spatial-epistemological conflict brought to the fore by Wittgenstein's subsequent practice of architecture. Emerging through the rethinking of spatial associations that resulted from that practice is the suggestion that in many ways architecture's spatiality is exactly what was absent from Wittgenstein's early work. At first glance, the *Tractatus*, with its strictly ordered and structured sections, seems more "architectural" than the *Investigations*. But that structure *represents* a purely two-dimensional, visual order based in a one-to-one-to-one correlation of language, meaning, and place. The practice of architecture challenged those strict associations by introducing a new spatiality that dismantled the singular view of the *Tractatus*, leaving in its place the realization that the absolute correlation of meaning and place was not a given reality but a particular way of seeing, one dependent upon a fixed viewer and a frozen image.

The late philosophy presents a new textual image. It rejects the strictly structured ordering of the *Tractatus*'s propositions and institutes an otherwise undifferentiated and open-ended seriality. Accordingly, the *Investigations* replaces the hierarchical ordering of the *Tractatus* with 693 sequentially numbered paragraphs[16] ranging in length from one line to more than one page and from a single paragraph to a complex of several paragraphs, lists, and diagrams. The *Investigations*, in lieu of a linear and hierarchical order, constructs multiple views of language that disrupt the fixity of the view from above by revealing it to be an imposed constraint rather than an absolute limit to language. One of the ways that Wittgenstein describes this constraint in the *Investigations* is as literally formed by the frame of a previously unnoticed pair of glasses.[17] What was believed given is shown to have been constructed. The element of place, as evidenced by the *Tractatus*'s numbering system, once dislodged replaces the one-to-one-to-one series of correspondences with the more unwieldy spatial association of "family resemblance."[18] Via this new construct, word and meaning are inextricably interwoven through spatial and other practices rather than directly correlated. These complex sections are a development from the relatively isolated propositions of the *Tractatus* that were akin to the rungs of the ladder.

The Ladder

Beyond the image of the text itself, the single image most associated with the *Tractatus* is that of the ladder. The ladder makes its appearance in the second-to-last proposition of the *Tractatus*, where its position heralds both the end of the text and the shift to Wittgenstein's late philosophy:

> 6.54 My propositions serve as elucidations in the following way: anyone who understands me eventually recognizes them as nonsensical, when he has used them—as steps—to climb up beyond them. (He must so to speak, throw away the ladder after he has climbed up it.)
>
> He must transcend these propositions, and then he will see the world aright.

Following this entry, Wittgenstein concludes the *Tractatus* with its famous final proposition: "What we cannot speak about we must pass over in silence" (T prop. 7.0). As described, the ladder is composed of the propositions of the *Tractatus*, with each proposition contributing a rung to the ladder and collectively their comprising the whole. The ladder furthers the literal image of the numbering system with its suggestion of discrete and ordered steps.

The *Tractatus* suggests the purpose of the ladder to be twofold. First the ladder is meant to provide a way—steps—toward the understanding of the text as a whole. This the ladder achieves by joining together in a particular order the discrete propositions of the *Tractatus*. Second, the ladder is meant to provide a position from which the *Tractatus* can be surveyed and understood. Toward this end, the ladder, literally in its climbing up, allows for an *over*view of varyingly the text, language, and philosophy, and most specifically, the limits of language. From that vantage point it offers the understanding that the propositions of the *Tractatus* are themselves nonsense. As such, the two aspects of the ladder, its joining together of the propositions and its providing an overview, work together to allow the propositions of the text or the rungs of the ladder to produce the understanding that the entirety of the endeavor of the *Tractatus*, the climb up the rungs of the ladder, is nonsensical *but enlightening in moving the reader beyond its propositions.*

There is the further statement that this act of knowing, of making one's way up the ladder, is transcendent, but it is a transcendence associated with the more literal act of transgression. Transgression here, as the rungs of the ladder themselves, is cumulative. It gathers together the *Tractatus*'s various acts of transgression, its movements beyond the bounds of sense, beyond the surface of the text and language, and potentially, or ultimately, beyond the ladder itself, to obtain the view from above and without. Transgression of these bounds and hence of the ladder itself is necessary as it is what allows one to reach a position from which the ladder may be removed, thrown away, as Wittgenstein suggests, something impossible in the midst of climbing.

From the attained correct point of view of clarity that climbing the ladder facilitates, the ladder itself appears problematic. The understanding achieved through the ladder is thus paradoxical in its ability to produce enlightenment of the nonsensical status of its own steps. In other words, it is the vantage point provided by the ladder—rather than the rungs themselves—that Wittgenstein finds important. While violating the bounds of sense in the process of attaining the correct logical point of view via the ladder, the *Tractatus* simultaneously constructs a place from which logical clarity and analysis is possible. Yet the steps themselves never fully enact this process but only offer access to the point of view of clarity: the view of the world aright. The ladder thus at once opens up the space of paradox with all of its indeterminacy and transgresses it in order to trade that indeterminacy for the clarity of determinate relations.

The ladder brings about this paradoxical achievement by functioning as a filter that separates important nonsense (such as the propositions of the *Tractatus* that produce the ladder) from nonsense that merely confuses logical syntax and is dissolved through logical clarification. This filtering, akin to but not the process of logical clarification, serves to distinguish the philosophy of the *Tractatus* from much of the rest of philosophical problems that Wittgenstein claimed were not really problems at all:

4.003 Most of the propositions and questions to be found in philosophical works are not false but nonsensical. Consequently we cannot give any answers to questions of this kind, but can only point out that they are nonsensical. Most of the propositions and questions of philosophers arise from our failure to understand the logic of our language.

(They belong to the same class as the question whether the good is more or less identical than the beautiful.)

And it is not surprising that the deepest problems are in fact *not* problems at all.

The problematic status of the ladder arises from its role as an explicit act of attainment and learning, yet one that in many ways presents an ambiguous situation, one that is in flux. In that manner it is similar to those situations that became one of the operative tropes in Wittgenstein's late work and that Stanley Cavell has referred to as "scenes of instruction."[19] Such scenes describe instances where it is unclear whether a child (or adult engaged in the act of learning) has, for example, acquired language, knows how to read, or is able to follow a mathematical rule.

These scenes reemerge repeatedly in the *Investigations* to raise a series of questions such as: What does it mean to follow a rule or to possess some particular knowledge or ability? What does it mean for language to be complete? What tolerance of error or degree of precision is allowable in determining the success of particular practices? The repeated concerns of how to assess the results of these practices follow from the situations where the event may be the same (the issuing of identical responses) but different possibilities emerge as to what those responses represent; for example, differences between knowing how to add but erring in the act, compared to an incorrect answer indicating that the person in question (possibly a child) does not understand the mathematical principle involved. In the late work, such issues of tolerance and precision are repeatedly raised for the range of possibilities they offer, while in the *Tractatus* such indeterminacy is something to be gotten past or through in order to achieve a clear view via the ladder. In other words, although the ladder is immersed in this indeterminacy, it is intended as *a way out of the indeterminacy* of such inherently ambiguous practices as the ordinary use of language, the learning of a practice, or the paradoxical status of the *Tractatus*'s own propositions.

Perhaps not surprisingly, language's surface ambiguity, from which the ladder simultaneously emanates and is offered as a means of escape, proves inescapable. The ladder, with its suggestion of rigid, if transcendent, logical form, is not as clear as it suggests. This is the case even given its metaphorical functioning within the text. One reason for this is the material basis of the rungs of the ladder, their being composed of the ordinary language that forms the propositions of the text. In *Wittgenstein's Ladder*, Perloff refers to this aspect when she finds that the movement up the ladder is a practice that is never finished. Instead, she says, it is necessarily embarked upon again and again without ever being repeated exactly. Despite the fact that each rung or philosophical proposition depends on the propositions that preceded it, difference emerges through the act of repetition itself, an act that always "entails a shift in context as well as use."[20] This view builds on the idea of ladders as portable objects readily available for use in new and varied situations, much like language itself.

In another way, ambiguity translates from the surface of ordinary language *up* the structure of the ladder itself. A ladder is composed of a series of consecutive and typically evenly spaced horizontal steps or rungs connected along their sides by two upright posts. In other words, it is a complex structure composed of interdependent rungs and posts meant for climbing up to allow access or reach beyond one's initial floor-bound condition. Equally, that situation can be reversed and those same steps can be employed to climb down to another level. In either situation, ladders are designed to navigate in a linear manner, one step at a time, to attain some level above or below the climber's current position.

While the *Tractatus*'s comments clearly relate the steps or rungs of the ladder to the propositions that form the book, what supplies the ladder's upright posts? They cannot simply be implied from the steps as they are what both connects them and gives them order. They are guides yet remain unmentioned, as it is the steps which are assumed to supply (here in the *Tractatus* as well as elsewhere) the quintessential elements comprising the ladder. Given that, the vertical elements that connect the steps to make ascending the ladder possible are a form of ordering that may include logical syntax as well as other types of understanding employed to provide the connections between propositions. Yet the ladder is also tied to transgression. Understanding the propositions means that one has understood them to try to say what they proclaim can only be shown. And following their trajectory, the rungs of the ladder leads beyond both propositions and text alike.

In equating the steps/propositions to the traditional straight-up-and-down image of the ladder, Wittgenstein is suggesting something about the arrangement of the propositions. If we follow the ordering of the propositions as they appear in the text from first to last, it is possible to produce a regular if rather long (and hence structurally prone to instability) ladder extending through all of the propositions. But are the propositions/rungs equal? And is their order strictly linear? The footnote and numbering system tell us no. What does that do to the act of climbing? Echoes of the numbering system remain. Although the ladder lacks the complexity of the text's hierarchical numbering system, nevertheless, in being built from those same propositions it cannot avoid some of its problems—nor does Wittgenstein do much to allay those issues. Two central questions lurk: Do the propositions—*in terms of understanding*—relate directly to the order in which they are presented in the text? And how does that order of understanding relate to the numbering system which is also correlated to the propositions and provides their ready reference?

If the numbering system is instituted to provide the foundational structure that guarantees the meaning of the text, the order in which the propositions occur to produce understanding are tied to the steps of the ladder and their elucidatory service. This associates the numbering system with the structure by which the propositions become understandable—by which they literally, through the dual acts of construction and climbing—*make* sense. And it is *that* structure that is symbolized by the image of the ladder.

Wittgenstein's description of the transgressive structure of the text—with the climb up the ladder—constitutes the final substantiation that the *Tractatus*'s view of language is that from both outside and above. The importance of this cannot be overstated. It is the fundamental organizing construct of the *Tractatus*. The view from the ladder, what Wittgenstein claims allows us to "see the world aright," is just that, *a view*. As such, the traits attributed to language and philosophy are the result of the particular visual framework, which exhibits a series of specific characteristics: it lies below, it is framed, it is presented as a horizontal surface, and it is dependent upon a fixed viewer. When the reader climbs up the ladder to "see the world aright," the view is from above and outside, looking down, where language and the world are reduced to a flat, horizontal, and seemingly bounded image. By positioning the reader-viewer in the ideal position outside language from which all of language is visible, Wittgenstein has effectively worked him and us outside of the sayable and into the realm of supposed silence, the realm of showing. As such, in some ways the one statement spoken fully from that view is the text's final proposition. This the *Tractatus* acknowledges. But what it cannot acknowledge is the depth to which this suggests that *saying (in the* Tractatus *and elsewhere) is integrally dependent upon the practice of showing.*

The Picture Theory

- 2.1   We picture facts to ourselves.
- 2.11   A picture presents a situation in logical space, the existence and non-existence of states of affairs.
- 2.12   A picture is a model of reality.
- 2.13   In a picture objects have the elements of the picture corresponding to them.
- 2.131 In a picture the elements of the picture are the representatives of objects.
- 2.14   What constitutes a picture is that its elements are related to one another in a determinate way.
- 2.141 A picture is a fact.
- 2.2   A picture has logico-pictorial form in common with what it depicts.

The *Tractatus*'s picture theory of meaning lays out the structural groundwork by which language corresponds with the world. Similarly to the workings of the numbering system and the ladder, the picture theory defines a complex system produced through the combination of discrete entities fixed in place through a series of correspondences. The main premise of the picture theory is that propositions are logical pictures or facts that correlate propositional elements with their counterparts in reality. This correspondence is what allows propositions to describe, either truly or falsely, possible states of affairs in the world. The picture theory thereby details representation by language as a logical isomorphic correspondence between the elements that form the proposition and the possible combination of things they describe, between what represents and what is represented. This makes meaningful language dependent upon a one-to-one correlation of elements that depict and what they depict.

The *Tractatus*'s understanding that logic underlies the functioning of meaningful language and therefore lays the groundwork for symbolic/linguistic representation leaves its picture theory of representation inseparable from its logical thinking. Hence it maintains an idea of propositions as logical pictures possessing all the necessity associated with the logical: "A proposition communicates a situation to us, and so it must be *essentially* connected to the situation. And the connexion is precisely that it is its logical picture."[21] In proposing that a given proposition's components are related to each other in a certain, *essentially* connected way, the picture theory describes a necessary structural correspondence in which linguistic components are combined in propositions to mirror their counterparts (those things they stand for) in the world. Proposition 4.04 of the *Tractatus* states: "In a proposition there must be exactly as many distinguishable parts as in the situation that it represents." It is this mirroring correspondence that makes the symbolic act of representation of the world possible.

The components at the base of this system of linguistic representation are elementary propositions composed of names that cannot be analyzed into simpler units and therefore can be directly correlated, as the picture theory proposes, to the simple objects for which they stand. As logic throughout the *Tractatus* is depicted as underlying meaningful language, elementary propositions are not formed in ordinary language but are the product of the process of logical analysis of more complex ordinary-language propositions. As such, elementary propositions are composed not of subject and predicate but of the logical terms of function and argument. The rules of logical syntax combine these elementary propositions into logical pictures:

4.411   It immediately strikes one as probable that the introduction of elementary propositions provides the basis for understanding all other kinds of proposition. Indeed the understanding of general propositions palpably depends on the understanding of elementary propositions.

The existence of these elementary propositions serves the important function of providing a limit or end point to the process of logical analysis. That is, they are devised to allow the process of logical clarification to be definitively terminated. That point of termination is the moment of correspondence with the world. Direct correspondence is thus enacted to close down any additional or residual play of meaning. The picture theory positions elementary propositions to act similarly to the imposition of the numbering system, so that the numbering system on one end and the picture theory on the other end act as if to bracket the extent of meaning between logic's image and its connection to the world.

This action recalls how the *Tractatus*, as I am detailing, is all about the constructing of a view, a representation of a particular kind enacted by transgression and made meaningful (according to the picture theory) through the specific mechanism of correspondence. Discussions of the picture theory, echoing the *Tractatus*'s own depiction of language, largely limit the understanding of the theory to occupying a defined portion of the text rather than understanding its constructs to be definitive of the text in its entirety. When considered spatially and structurally, the picture theory's attempt to fix correspondence by directly relating language and the world is quite indirect, as it first reassociates language through analysis to its underlying logical structure. Rather than securing meaning, the picture of direct correspondence is instead an attempt *to locate—and therefore fix—the act of meaning.*

In this imaging, the picture theory operates as the primary description of the *Tractatus*'s aims and functioning. But it is also an image of transgression in its presupposition of a gap between language and the world that must be somehow filled for meaning to be possible. And the *Tractatus* fills that gap with logical entities such as elementary propositions whose operations are restrained by the picture theory's frame, which reiterates the limitations of the *Tractatus*'s view from above. In other words, it begins with the view of language as separated from the world rather than embedded in it.

The inability of the *Tractatus* to maintain the very categories and distinctions it proposes sets up Wittgenstein's late work either to accept these paradoxes and remake the *Tractatus* so as to maintain those distinctions and realize those determinate categories or to try to grasp and describe language's shared territory of showing and saying, logic and practice. It chooses the latter. In response to the *Tractatus*'s acts of transgression, the *Investigations* reconceptualizes philosophy as inhabitation by displacing the *Tractatus*'s exiled viewpoint back within language and by reconceiving philosophy and language as constructive practices as exemplified by Wittgenstein's invention of "the builders." As the manifestation of subjectivity and inhabitation, it is the builders who set the *Investigations* in motion at the onset of the text. The effects of these two approaches force a series of shifts in the makeup of philosophy that allow the late work to incorporate the realm of ethics and aesthetics, practice and the subject within the limits of language, thereby in many ways questioning the existence of definitive limits of sensible language.

From the vantage point of the *Investigations*, then, the transgressions of language and philosophy enacted by the *Tractatus* are a necessary stage of development. The transgression beyond the restrictions of the *Tractatus* allows for a more inclusive practice of philosophy and understanding of language, a shift that allows for the subject to inhabit both language and philosophy. What initially seems to be Wittgenstein's movement outside philosophy, both beyond the bounds of the *Tractatus* and into other practices such as architecture, ultimately serves to form the basis for both his reengagement with and reconceptualization of the discipline.

CHAPTER 2

From Without to Within: The Building of Inhabitation

2. Let us imagine a language for which the description given by Augustine is right. The language is meant to serve for communication between a builder A and his assistant B. A is building with building stones: there are blocks, pillars, slabs and beams. B has to pass the stone, and that in the order in which A needs them. For this purpose they use a language consisting of the words "block," "pillar," "slab," "beam." A calls them out: B brings the stone which he has learnt to bring at such-and-such a call. Conceive this as a complete primitive language.—*Philosophical Investigations*

One of Wittgenstein's later criticisms of philosophy is that it is closed from the outside or larger culture from which it presumably arose. While Wittgenstein's early philosophy is clearly subject to (and the subject of) this criticism, the late philosophy is quite different in its approach. The *Tractatus* propounds a critique of traditional philosophical discourse in order to rework and redefine the basis of philosophical problems as problems of language and logic. The late philosophy of the *Investigations*, in its critique of the *Tractatus*, instead moves beyond those self-imposed limits to relocate language back into the realm of everyday practices. To accomplish this, the *text* generates a space of inhabitation inclusive of the subject and practice alike. Wittgenstein lays the groundwork for this in the *Investigations* by bisecting the starting point of the text to postulate two complex spheres of interaction as the bases for the study of language: one in philosophy and the other in the practice of architecture.

In its opening paragraph, the *Investigations*'s dual starting point begins, literally, with the words and memory of another, that of Augustine. In the succeeding paragraph, Wittgenstein complements those words with the act of construction in the builders' language-game. The first passage of the *Investigations* quotes from a passage in the *Confessions* wherein Augustine describes his memory of the acquisition of language as learning to apply names to objects:

> When they (my elders) named some object, and accordingly moved towards something, I saw this and I grasped that the thing was called by the sound they uttered when they meant to point it out. Their intention was shewn by their bodily movements, as it were the natural language of all peoples: the expression of the face, the play of the eyes, the movement of other parts of the body, and the tone of voice which expresses our state of mind in seeking, having, rejecting, or avoiding something. Thus, as I heard words repeatedly used in their proper places in various sentences, I gradually learnt to understand what objects they signified; and after I had trained my mouth to form these signs, I used them to express my own desires.[1]

Following this opening section, Wittgenstein submits the builders' language as a seeming enactment of Augustine's description of language. The figures and actions of "the builders" lie at the core of the *Investigations*'s construction of the space of inhabitation, and accordingly, the work of the *Investigations* begins with the scene of the builders. Their simple language, presented as the first model for the use of language in the *Investigations*, initially contains a series of four words: "block," "pillar," "slab," and "beam," with an associated series of actions. The scene of the builders does more than present an alternative usage of language to Augustine's; it simultaneously illustrates both Augustine's description of language and the failure of that description to characterize all of language. In so doing, by implicitly intertwining the realm of practice with linguistic expression, the builders subtend the simultaneous construction and inhabitation of the space and operations of language, an occupation that instills the means for the rejection of a *Tractatus*-like conception of language.

The builders' language conforms to Augustine's picture of language in two ways. First, it manifests the notion that words in language name objects, as each of the builders' four words is correlated to a particular type of building stone. In this paradigm, "block," "pillar," "slab," and "beam" refer respectively to blocks, pillars, slabs, and beams. The builders' use of words seemingly upholds the idea that the meaning of a word is the object to which it refers, and as all of the words are used in this way, it upholds Augustine's description that all of language acts accordingly. Second, this manner of using words exhibits a particular exercise or training for learning language or, more precisely, for learning a use of words. "A calls them out: B brings the stone which he has learnt to bring at such-and-such a call." Accordingly, Stanley Cavell understands both the builders' language and Augustine's description of language to be not so much the description or example *of* a language but *of the learning* of a language.[2] By extension, Wittgenstein is thereby revealing that our idea of what a language is is bound up with our ideas about acquiring that language.

Wittgenstein describes "the builders" varyingly as the first language-game, as a primitive language, as a language more primitive than ours, and as an origin or example of the learning of language. In recalling the history of the development of language both socially and individually, these descriptions emphasize the inseparability of language from the learning of language, an integral association that explicitly marks language as a practice from the onset of the *Investigations*. The example of the builders yields the concept of acquiring language through the act of building, a practice deeply associated with architecture.

Emerging through the practice of building with building stones, the association of language with the acquisition of language instigates the redefining of language from a collection of an objectlike set of words to a practice. This transformation begins to undermine Augustine's description of language by first requiring and then allowing words to perform functions beyond the labeling of preexistent objects. The builders' use of "slab," which in referring to a particular kind of building stone had ostensibly conformed to Augustine's description conceived as a practice, needs also to function akin to what Wittgenstein calls the command "Slab!" to permit the builders to communicate with one another. This transforms "slab" from its role as a label to something comparable to the phrase "Bring me a slab." It also highlights the language's need to be intelligible beyond the labeling of an object in order to explain why it is that B's bringing the stone is a fulfillment of A's call.

The example of the builders confronts Augustine's memory with Wittgenstein's own memory of learning (about) language in the practice of architecture, a recalling of the design and construction of the Stonborough-Wittgenstein House. Depicting learning language through learning to build, Wittgenstein's engagement with construction practices thus simultaneously constitutes Wittgenstein's earliest words in the *Investigations* as well as his response to Augustine's characterization of language. The language of the builders, with its mechanical, repetitive, and determinate nature, initially appears akin less to the functioning of language Wittgenstein develops in the *Investigations* than to the *Tractatus*'s conception. It is exactly this dual quality of language that Wittgenstein puts to the test of practice in the *Investigations* and which he ultimately employs to provide the criteria for rejecting the *Tractatus*'s view of language.

While seemingly supporting the Augustinian approach to language, the builders' language, via the practice of building, provides a vehicle by which to apprehend language beyond the *Tractatus*'s limits. As such, the builders' language is at once a simulation of what Augustine's words describe and a move away from them: "That philosophical concept of meaning has its place in a primitive idea of the way language functions. But one can also say that it is the idea of a language more primitive than ours."[3] In opposition to Augustine, the practice of building, with its implication of progress, permits development impossible in memory. Equally, in its ability to associate a public and external practice with the acquisition of language, the practice of building, once incorporated, shifts the *Investigations*'s focus from the individual learning of language to the social construction of language.

Whereas the quote from Augustine acts as proxy for preexisting philosophical problems that Wittgenstein is engaged with in the *Tractatus*, it also recalls an individual memory of the acquisition of language. Similarly, the builders recall Wittgenstein's own way back to "philosophy" from his ten-year hiatus. However, as Augustine's individual memory represents a commonly held view of language, it is also a shared memory that Wittgenstein understands must be addressed, although he separates himself from that memory by offering it in another's words and contrasting it to his own. As a corrective to that conception of language, Wittgenstein does not submit his own childhood memories but rather restages his learning process through architecture as a primitive learning of language in the example of the builders. Importantly, though, the example involves not a child but (presumably) two adults.

The building process and the builders, while metaphors of Wittgenstein's view of language and its acquisition, are equally real, a shorthand notation for Wittgenstein's experience as an architect. Through the introduction of the builders and in adding his memory to Augustine's, Wittgenstein constitutes his practice of architecture as the (unacknowledged) site from which to reexamine his early philosophy of language. That same site also presents a readily visible practice capable of supporting and supplying a view of language's complex functioning beyond the limitations of a determinate logical syntax.

In combining Augustine's memory with that of the builders' actions, the duality of the *Investigations*'s opening also brings forth the relation between the *Investigations* and the *Tractatus*. As Augustine's characterization of language shares with the *Tractatus* a narrow conception of language, in conjoining the two, the practice of building is able to challenge both at once. As a constructed act of memory, the builders reenact not Wittgenstein's acquisition of language but his acquisition of a new understanding of language. The "memory" or example of the builders that Wittgenstein uses to counter Augustine's description of the acquisition and functioning of language differs by entailing the development of a useful language, one whose construction is envisioned as practice (through acts of building). Consequently it relays how the memory of acquiring language is a memory of the acquiring of a practice.

The opposing images of language that unfold in the opening sections of the *Investigations* itself derive from an initial commonality or compatibility of the builders and their (primitive) language with Augustine's description of language as the naming of objects. Contrast develops when each word of the builders' language also corresponds to a given practice. Portrayed by Wittgenstein in the scene of the builders, words indicate actions as much as they name objects. In that way, the example of the builders' language introduces a fundamental ambiguity or complexity as an integral component of language. This culminates with Wittgenstein's detailing the scope of language in section 23 of the *Investigations* as including words, objects, practices, commands, and so on. The slippage that occurs in the opening of the *Investigations* between that which is at once the same (language as the naming of objects) and different (language as performing a function) is a method that reappears throughout the *Investigations*. That method draws the reader into the practices laid out in the text.

By spatially insinuating themselves into the discussion to provide an alternate and literal image of the acquisition and use of language for consideration, the builders—and by extension, the practice of architecture—make the narrowness of the Augustinian/*Tractatian* picture of language apparent. Following the presentation of the builders, Wittgenstein finds that Augustine's model of language describes "a system of communication; only not everything that we call language is that system." The limitations of Augustine's depiction instead make it "appropriate but only for this narrowly circumscribed region, not for the whole of what it is claiming to describe."[4]

The builders' acts of construction (of whatever it may be) serve to suggest metaphorically the ongoing development or construction of language by introducing a language *inseparable* from a given set of actions, what Wittgenstein later designates "forms of life." This suggests that embedded in the beginning of the *Investigations* is both the confrontation between the *Tractatus*'s and the *Investigations*'s views of language and the development through the practice of architecture of a new understanding of language and philosophy. That relation lies poised between commonality and opposition; beginning with the shared concerns of the *Tractatus*, it also reenacts a challenge to the *Tractatus* as posed by Wittgenstein's practice of architecture. The practice of architecture thereby enters the scene effectually to broaden the limits of language and philosophy for Wittgenstein beyond those *thinkable* (no less sayable) within the *Tractatus*'s framework.

The practice of architecture that the builders interject into the philosophy of language is what allows the *Investigations* to create habitable space and subsequently to construct the view from within the space of language. In the way that it positions the subject in relation to language and the study of language, this view differs dramatically from the view from without constructed by the *Tractatus*. Although the view from within is able to accommodate the subject fully, it loses the clarity that the view from without rendered. The view from within is incapable of offering the clarity of the view from above and without, in that it can no longer imply that the entirety of language is available to vision.

The inauguration of inhabitation alters the role of vision itself. From within, vision is no longer privileged—it does not *over*see the world but becomes one of the many possible ways of interacting with the world as developed in the everyday view from the streets of Michel de Certeau or even Henri Lefebvre.[5] De Certeau is of particular interest here in his implementation of Wittgenstein's view of language as a practice in his *Practice of Everyday Life*. That incorporation implicitly acknowledges the spatiality of the *Investigations*'s view of language as underscoring the spatial and urban practices that de Certeau theorizes and for which Wittgenstein's philosophy of language serves as a foundation for the book's subsequent development of urban strategies.

Toward the later part of the *Investigations,* Wittgenstein explicitly establishes the association between language, communication, and building. In section 491 he writes: "Not: 'without language we could not communicate with one another'—but for sure: without language we cannot influence other people in such-and-such ways; cannot build roads and machines, etc." Building on this in the following section, Wittgenstein further associates language with "inventing":

> 492. To invent a language could mean to invent an instrument for a particular purpose on the basis of the laws of nature (or consistently with them); but it also has the other sense, analogous to that in which we speak of the invention of a game.
>
> Here I am stating something about the grammar of the word "language," by connecting it with the grammar of the word "invent."

The relation between language and invent is informative in its coupling of a noun and a verb, both in the suggestion of inventing a language, as the builders must, and in the direct comparison of the terms "language" and "invent." In section 6 of the *Investigations,* Wittgenstein raises the issue of what it is to understand the call "Slab!" The question arises from Wittgenstein's discussion of the establishment of an "association between the word and the thing" and the "ostensive teaching" of words. Rather than basing the meaningful association between words and referents in private mental images, Wittgenstein claims, "[I]n the language of §2 it is *not* the purpose of the words to evoke images." Instead Wittgenstein looks to the calls, actions, and responses between the builders, that is, to their outward, visible practices, to gauge comprehension. "Don't you understand the call 'Slab!' if you act upon it in such and such a way?" These literal expressions of language shift linguistic meaning from being the product of the association of word and thing to being the act of associating a word with an action or practice. The object of the word, its referent, becomes poised between the thing—a slab—and the command or action of bringing a slab for a particular purpose.[6]

The relation between the call "Slab!" and its associated actions is central to surmising the builders' language and its role in the *Investigations.* Stanley Cavell finds the builders' language's unmediated directness between word and action too mechanical to be truly perceived as language because their use of words affords the builders no alternatives to the actions they perform. Cavell sees this lack of possibilities in the builders' lives extending to their language, a lack that threatens to leave the builders short both of using language and of being human.

The need for language to permit alternative possibilities also proves central to Rush Rhees's discussion of the builders' language. Based on the inflexibility of those calls and the life he envisions accompanying such a restricted use of words, Rhees, in his *Wittgenstein's Builders*, also finds the builders' calls and actions falling short of speech. As he indicates, the inflexibility of language becomes an impediment even to the task of building as it does not allow for communication when construction does not proceed precisely as planned. If words cannot be used for any other purposes than A calling for and B bringing the appropriate stone, then the builders are incapable of discussing either any problem that arises or how to alleviate it. Rhees also finds that their calls are unusable outside their particular routine. This is important, as it is the use of language elsewhere that typically defines the way we come to know whether and how language makes sense with reference to a particular instance. In other words, it challenges the construction of criteria for the meaningful use of language. And with that loss of criteria, the builders' language precludes any wider basis for communication or the establishment of alternative practices.

It is not just the builders' limited vocabulary, in the sense of the actual number of words, that calls the builders' language into question but, as has been pointed out, the sense that either their actions and communications would have to be so restricted or they would need to invent a new word for every new occasion that arises in order to continue communication. That constitutes the fundamental distinction between the builders' language and our sense of language. It is, rather, this reciprocal need for development of both their language and their lives that obtains the greatest hope for the builders' language. It is possible then, to imagine the builders' language as a language that is developing not simply by adding to itself through the accumulation of words but by beginning to take on some of the connectedness to and use in other situations. This also explains Wittgenstein's presentation of the builder's language as a complete primitive—that is, undeveloped—language.

That process of development might be seen to begin the first time something goes wrong in the building process. At that point, construction is no longer able to continue in the same manner and their repetitive commands become useless. The builders' language can become comprehendible as a "complete primitive language" if we understand the language not to be *frozen* forever in time but to be in an ongoing process of construction entailing occasions that require the addition of not just new words but new kinds of words to the lexicon. This fashions a practice in which building (in this case) is directed and develops according to its own needs. Although the builders' language is not ours, it remains possible to imagine it transforming—rapidly, even—into something we readily recognize as language.

Considering the builder's language directly in relation to the practice of architecture, yet another possibility and emerging criteria suggests itself. The response to the command "Slab!" associates the object "slab" with the structure that it is being used to erect. This process bestows on the slab a role defined by its place in the structure being built and suggests an additional functioning of the word "slab," along with an associated criterion for its use. Even if this seems initially to be beyond assistant builder's (B's) actions, it plays an equally strong role in B's learning to understand "Slab!" by providing a function for or effect of the addition of the slab into the structure. The builders' language loses some of its mechanical nature when seen not to conclude with B's correct retrieval and A's implied approval. Rather, the criteria by which B understands the correctness of her or his actions are primarily in the structure that B is assisting to construct. This extended communication involves recognizing that a slab is the correct building stone to bring according to its role in that phase of the construction.

This process of learning and building may proceed in any number of ways, allowing, for example, for a stage whereby following the call "Slab!" B brings a pillar instead and is shown by A that a pillar is inappropriate for the work at hand, that it does not, for example, fit the space allotted or allow for a level area or for continued building and so on. A could point to the lack of fit and suggest the dimension and form of the stone required at that time and in that place to allow B to learn the difference between slabs and pillars or between the call "Slab!" and the call "Pillar!" It is easy to see that as the building process changes or becomes more complicated or as unexpected events transpire, the builders can expand both building processes and words as required in order for construction to proceed.

It still remains unclear what the structure being built is (if it is a structure) or how, where, or if it is to be found in the *Investigations* at all. A possible answer does lie in what preceded the *Investigations*, however: in the house Wittgenstein built in Vienna for his sister immediately prior to his return to philosophy. The starting point of Wittgenstein's return to philosophy is important given the conclusions Wittgenstein propounded in the *Tractatus*. Those conclusions make Wittgenstein's return to philosophy contingent upon his finding a new understanding, a practice, really, not just of language but of philosophical problems that would suggest, against the end-of-philosophy declaration of the *Tractatus*, that all philosophical problems had not been solved or at least that the dissolution or emptying of philosophy indicative of the *Tractatus* could itself not proceed as planned—that the *Tractatus*'s repetitive philosophical practice of emptying philosophy, similar to the builders' repetitive calls and actions, must evolve. Although it cannot fully account for it, Wittgenstein's reentry into philosophy undeniably occurs through the practice of architecture: first, historically, in the house he designed for his sister, and then as introduced in the opening paragraphs of the *Investigations*, where the builders intervene to transform the discussion of language.

Wittgenstein's exhortation to the reader regarding the builder's language to "Conceive this as a complete primitive language" raises the question of what it means for a language to be complete. This question becomes all the more interesting in that it arises from a scene of ongoing construction. This juxtaposition hints at what Wittgenstein will later state very explicitly: that the idea of a continually developing language does not imply that prior to a given development, the language was incomplete. What appears incomplete in the scene of the builders and their language of orders is not necessarily the language but Wittgenstein's focus itself. And it is that incompleteness that accounts for the stultified language (or not-quite-language) indicated by Cavell and Rhees. That incompleteness, once conceived as a restricted view, parallels the narrowness of Augustine's and the *Tractatus*'s descriptions of language.

Further on in the *Investigations*, Wittgenstein examines how the *Tractatus*'s view of language explicitly results from such a restricted focus. Although the builders' language is the result of a limited view devised, at least in part, to comply with Augustine's description, it maintains an inherent break from that thinking, arising around the act of construction and the implication of a wider scene of which A and B are a small part. In that sense, the extent of the limitation of the focus on the scene of the builders varies throughout the *Investigations* in relation to how far along the act of construction has proceeded. Accordingly, the focus or view of the scene of the builders changes the language itself, leaving language to expand in the *Investigations* in contrast to the *Tractatus*'s reliance upon a fixed image.

The initial scene of the builders can thus be understood simultaneously as a fixed image from the *Tractatus* and as an evolving image in its description of an ongoing process entailing the continued piling up and rearranging of building stones. The compound nature of this image confronts the initial narrowly framed view to shift the focus back to the viewer and to the site and practice of viewing. Because of this inherent possibility, the builders are capable of constructing an extended world and producing new views—in the forms of additional language-games—of that emerging reality. In that way, the language introduced in section 2 offers as much an example of a language-game,[7] the core of Wittgenstein's study of language in the *Investigations*, as it does an example of the limited view Wittgenstein explicitly associates with the *Tractatus*.

What begins, then, to expand the builders' primitive language in the *Investigations* is the existence of the building site itself. In specifically referring to the building site, the *Investigations*'s evolving builders' language—as the first language-game—reinforces the existence of some form of structure under construction. This spatiolinguistic advancement occurs in section 8 in the form of the order "this-there" given by A and accompanied by the act of pointing to the desired stones and to a specified location on the building site. The builder's language thus develops from the objects of building—slabs and so on—more readily coincident with the understanding of language as naming, to the more complex notion of site and spatiality with the introduction of the shifter terms "there" and "this."

Emanating from the builders' example, the addition of these words, along with numerals and colors, forms the beginning of the differentiation of types of words and language games in the *Investigations*. Unlike the discussion of whether "Slab!" is a simple reference to a particular object or a sort of shorthand for the order "Bring me a slab!" the differentiation of types of words into nouns, colors, numbers, and indexical terms including "this" and "there" further implicates the concept of use:

> It will be possible to say: In language (8) [the expanded language] we have different *kinds of word*. For the functions of the word "slab" and the word "block" are more alike than those of "slab" and "d" [used to designate different colors] But how we group words into kinds will depend on the aim of the classification,—and on our own inclination.[8]

In rejecting attempts to assimilate the descriptions of uses of words, Wittgenstein supports this view by declaring that it "cannot make the uses themselves any more like one another. For, as we see, they are absolutely unlike."[9] Distinguishing between different types of words questions the idea of language as the applying of labels to preexistent objects, as the applying of labels largely holds true only for nouns rather than number terms or indexical ones. Wittgenstein likens these distinctions to the varying types of tools in a toolbox. The differentiation of language via the metaphor of the tools accordingly acts to breathe life into the building stones by offering potential ways of manipulating them. Literally, Wittgenstein is importing the tools by which the building stones, and our ability to act with and on them, are greatly enhanced, advancing the learning of how to build by expanding the types of tools available for use:

> 11. Think of the tools in a tool-box: there is hammer, pliers, a saw, a screwdriver, a rule, a glue-pot, glue, nails and screws.—The functions of words are as diverse as the functions of these objects. (And in both cases there are similarities.)
>
> Of course, what confuses us is the uniform appearance of words when we hear them spoken or meet them in script and print. For their *application* is not presented to us clearly. Especially when we are doing philosophy!

The association between the "tools" and the builders, although not explicit, is undeniable. These associations are borne out in Wittgenstein's concern with precision and fabrication in the design and construction of the Stonborough-Wittgenstein House. The ability of the builders to continue and further their work is based on their ability to differentiate materials, types of construction, particulars of the situation, and so on. The multiplicity of linguistic components and language-games is central to the development of language, not just for the builders but in the evolution from the *Tractatus*'s conception of language to the *Investigations*'s. Wittgenstein elucidates this a few sections later: "It is interesting to compare the multiplicity of the tools in language and of the ways they are used, the multiplicity of kinds of word and sentence, with what logicians have said about the structure of language. (Including the author of the *Tractatus Logico-Philosophicus*.)"[10]

Similarly, further on in his discussion of disparate types of words, numbers, lengths, and colors, Wittgenstein raises the issue of how such dissimilar types of words are defined. The question is: How do we understand a number to be a number type of word when we use it, without already having a definition of what "number" means? That is, how do we learn to use numbers in the language-games Wittgenstein is discussing, such as the call for "five slabs"? The issue extends readily to include all of language, as all our definitions of words are by means of other words. The search for continued definitions of the definitions quickly produces a reiterative chain threatening to become endless. Asking: "And what about the last definition in this chain?" as if in acknowledgment that construction's move forward works as if to balance the backing up of one definition by another, Wittgenstein turns to architecture, building, and the city to tackle the question of intelligible language: "(Do not say: 'There isn't a "last" definition.' That is just as if you chose to say: 'There isn't a last house in this road; one can always build an additional one.')"[11]

Despite Wittgenstein's introduction of the multiplicity of types of words, he does not want us to dismiss the prospect of there being a language consisting solely of orders, as in the initial language of the builders. Wittgenstein's admonition that we should "not be troubled by the fact that languages (2) and (8) consist only of orders"[12] presents another basis for differentiation, that between the many kinds of sentences. The seeming limitation of language with the builders is itself the product of an idea of what a fuller or more complete language would be. Wittgenstein questions this concept of a "complete" language in two ways. The first approach is based on the restricted or enframed language of the builders, while the second relies on the knowledge that those limitations can be understood as one of endless possible types of sentences or language-games, some of which Wittgenstein lists in section 23:

> 23. But how many kinds of sentences are there? Say assertion, question, and command?—There are *countless* kinds: countless different kinds of use of what we call "symbols," "words," "sentences." And this multiplicity is not something fixed, given once for all; but new types of language, new language-games, as we may say, come into existence, and others become obsolete and get forgotten. (We can get a *rough picture* of this from the changes in mathematics.)
>
> Here the term "language-*game*" is meant to bring into prominence the fact that the *speaking* of language is part of an activity, or of a form of life.
>
> Review the multiplicity of language-games in the following examples, and in others:
> Giving orders, and obeying them—
> Describing the appearance of an object, or giving its measurements—
> Constructing an object from a description (a drawing)—
> Reporting an event—
> Speculating about an event—
> Forming and testing a hypothesis—
> Presenting the results of an experiment in tables and diagrams—
> Making up a story; and reading it—
> Play-acting—
> Singing catches—
> Guessing riddles—

Making a joke; telling it—
Solving a problem in practical arithmetic—
Translating from one language into another—
Asking, thanking, cursing, greeting, praying.

    It is interesting to compare the multiplicity of the tools in language and of the ways they are used, the multiplicity of kinds of word and sentence, with what logicians have said about the structure of language. (Including the author of the *Tractatus Logico-Philosophicus*.)

This list is as much transformative of the philosophical study of language as it is descriptive of various everyday practices of language. It envisions language in the *Investigations* as inclusive of far more than what is typically assumed. While describing the appearance of an object may seem a fairly typical use of language, the related practices of giving its measurements and constructing an object from a description (a drawing) are not. The list, amassed so early in the text, emphasizes that from the onset these philosophical investigations incorporate the aesthetic and the architectural, the spoken and the shown. The inclusiveness of the list allows that rather than dividing the territory of language, as in the *Tractatus*, Wittgenstein is investigating the shared territory of language as showing, saying, performing, and so on.

Furthering his point, Wittgenstein details in the list possible language-games, beginning with the builders giving and obeying orders and including explicit extensions of that language into architectural practices: "Giving orders and obeying them—describing the appearance of an object, or giving its measurements—Constructing an object from a description (a drawing)" are processes involved in the constructing of a building from a set of architectural drawings. While most items on the list are readily considered types of language use, such things as constructing an object from a description or drawing (the third element on the list) or presenting the results of an experiment in tables and diagrams are not. Such items instead conform to what can only be thought of as the builders' extended activities.

Wittgenstein also invokes architectural drawings as explanatory, particularly of ongoing practices. This occurs further on in the *Investigations* when Wittgenstein again associates "pictures" with scale drawings, like those adhered to in the practice of architecture. In both cases architectural drawings function within language in much the way architecture functions within the *Investigations*: as a language-game that provides a model of the functioning of language:

291. What we call "descriptions" are instruments for particular uses. Think of a machine-drawing, a cross-section, an elevation with measurements, which an engineer has before him. Thinking of a description as a word-picture of the facts has something misleading about it: one tends to think only of such pictures as hang on our walls: which seem simply to portray how a thing looks, what it is like. (These pictures are as it were idle.)

The distinction between functioning and being "idle" is a crucial one that Wittgenstein instills in the *Investigations* to further differentiate his view of language from the one he presents in the *Tractatus*. What begins in the *Investigations* by considering the desire for a "complete" language leads to an examination of the multiple practices that constitute language. The multiplicity of language-games involved in the construction process, as either a previous or a future stage, result from a continually changing language, one that while never completed, was never incomplete. Language as such is depicted not as lagging behind building but as interwoven in its construction.

In section 18 of the *Investigations*, Wittgenstein employs the builders specifically to address the demand that language be complete. Again the builders' language emerges as an issue, as it consists solely of orders, and the response is to compare it to a more developed image of building:

18. Do not be troubled by the fact that languages (2) and (8) consist only of orders. If you want to say that this shews them to be incomplete, ask yourself whether our language is complete;—whether it was so before the symbolism of chemistry and the notation of the infinitesimal calculus were incorporated in it; for these are, so to speak, suburbs of our language. (And how many houses or streets does it take before a town begins to be a town?) Our language can be seen as an ancient city: a maze of little streets and squares, of old and new houses, and of houses with additions from various periods; and this surrounded by a multitude of new boroughs with straight regular streets and uniform houses.

The description of language as an ancient city is a spatial-historical description of how a city such as Vienna grew from a medieval mazelike series of streets outward around that inner core to twentieth-century suburbs. By beginning with the language of the builders and again making specific references to the ways a city develops architecturally and urbanistically, Wittgenstein reinforces the association between the builders and the practice of architecture, in effect placing the builders in the conjoined context of the practices of architecture and language.

Architectural references throughout the *Investigations* repeatedly emerge as ways of visualizing the repeated demands for completion, finality, and foundation. In these sections, architecture is pondered as a possible criterion of finality; architecture fails in that endeavor, however, as does the "language" it is brought in to support. Wittgenstein's frequent appeals to architecture are thus not in the hopes of providing a final answer but for potential justification. In his discussion of the justification for following a rule in a particular way, Wittgenstein reaches a problem similar to that of what constitutes a final definition or explanation, that of the feeling that every justification itself seems in need of additional ones. Architecture, again summoned as the final form of justification, is revealed to be incapable of providing a foundation and when employed to such ends, produces only a superfluous formal gesture. "Solid" foundations are themselves shown to be a barrier to the continual search for (further) justification rather than a provider of ultimate justifications:

217. "How am I to obey a rule?"—if this is not a question about causes, then it is about the justification for my following the rule in the way I do.
If I have exhausted the justifications I have reached bedrock and my spade is turned. Then I am inclined to say: "This is simply what I do."

The act of reaching bedrock provides the end point of moving forward in a particular direction, after which the spade is turned, capable only of continuing on in some other direction or manner. With this, Wittgenstein is left not with complete legitimation but rather with the realization that there is no ultimate justification apart from the functioning of language in our lives. That is, architecture does not offer a foundation but is as much involved in the process as are other practices. This can be seen as the search for justification in the use of language increasingly gives way to investigation of the practice(s) of language itself. "This is simply what I do" can then be taken not as the justification for action *but as the site— doing—in which to study language* and to consider what it is we do in the everyday functioning of language. This forces a shift in direction or framework of how language is investigated. The spade is turned in the direction of an examination of practice, following which architecture reenters the discussion as another possible criterion: "(Remember that we sometimes demand definitions for the sake not of their content, but of their form.

Our requirement is an architectural one; the definition a kind of ornamental coping that supports nothing.).»[13]

Architecture in this instance is shown to be incapable of contributing more than the image of a foundation or justification. Again it is compared to language that had already failed to provide an absolute, external justification. What the architectural "definition" has provided (if, however, as ornamental coping it supports nothing) is to suggest that it has failed no more than other elements, that what seems to be foundational is revealed as another element in the process.

CHAPTER 3

The Stonborough-Wittgenstein House

The Stonborough-Wittgenstein House did not enter into the discourse of modern architecture until some forty years after it was built. Following the model set forth by Bernhard Leitner's 1970 article in *Artforum* and three years later by his more complete documentation of the work in his *Architecture of Ludwig Wittgenstein,* the house has not been discussed without at least acknowledging the question of the relation it bears to Wittgenstein's philosophy.[1]

The existing literature on the house treats this question in a variety of ways. A main purpose of Bernhard Leitner's inaugural book on the house was to document and publicize the house prior to its threatened sale and destruction. The documentation includes a short history of the house, a reprint from Hermine Wittgenstein's family recollections about her brother,[2] a few formal analytical remarks by Leitner, and a limited quotation from Georg Henrik von Wright, a philosopher and former student of Wittgenstein's. This last inclusion, while only minimally defining a relationship between Wittgenstein's architecture and philosophy, has had a surprisingly strong and enduring influence.

Two sentences from von Wright's statement are of particular interest. Von Wright declares the beauty of the architecture of the Kundmanngasse[3] to be "of the same simple and static kind that belongs to a sentence of the *Tractatus.*" At the same time, von Wright finds a "striking contrast between the restlessness, the continual searching and changing in Wittgenstein's life and personality, and the perfection and elegance of his finished work."[4] To this, Leitner himself added that the "hall on the main floor and the spaces surrounding it are highly characteristic of this balanced and static quality."⁵ In von Wright's first statement, the house is ostensibly presented in aesthetic or formal relation to the *Tractatus*, sharing with it a type of beauty. The second statement, however, contrasts the house to the shifts, phases, and continual searching definitive of Wittgenstein's "life and personality." Taken together, these comments set Wittgenstein's life against his work, conceiving the work to be static and perfected and the life to be fragmented and in continual flux.

Von Wright's comments have done much to set both the tone and the parameters for the philosophical study of the house, although, problematically and interestingly enough, they are unable to locate it as either part of Wittgenstein's life or part of his work. In setting tone and parameters, the remarks replicate the philosophical inability to reconcile the indeterminate status of aesthetics and aesthetic objects with a simultaneous desire to found that study. Importantly, the difference in the reception of Wittgenstein's early and late work reappears in discussions of the house, so that the acceptance and use of the early work (for example, interest by members of the Vienna Circle) resurfaces around consideration of the house, while the difficulties and uniqueness of the late work elude grasp within the discussion of the architecture.

Despite its apparent similarity with the perfected elegance of the *Tractatus* and its implied separation from the "restlessness" of Wittgenstein's life and personality, the house cannot help but be associated with (if not actually definitive of) that restlessness. A notable aspect of Wittgenstein's continual searching is the drama of the ten-year period during which he abandoned philosophy; Wittgenstein's two-and-a-half-year practice of architecture strongly contributed to the understanding of that period of his life as one of restlessness. Comparably, far from separating his life and work, the break with philosophy, with its dramatic shifts and returns, contributes to the inseparability of the two. Beyond the importance of the specific intervening events, the movement in and out of philosophy and other disciplines acts as more than a disruption of or break in Wittgenstein's philosophical output. Instead, it contributes to the advancement of his late philosophy, which itself exhibits related shifts not just of topic but of scope and view, moving from without to within and developing from stasis to transgression to inhabitation. On this thinking, and given von Wright's comments, the house exhibits aspects of both stasis and movement, leaving it caught between the two and leaving indecipherable the question as to whether it is part of Wittgenstein's life or of his work.

While von Wright associates the house's formal simplicity and static qualities with the *Tractatus* and contrasts it to both the restlessness and the series of phases and shifts in Wittgenstein's life and personality, von Wright also clearly dissociates the architecture from the philosophy; he is not suggesting that the architecture is like the philosophy of the *Tractatus*, but only like the form of the *Tractatus*—possessing similar qualities to a "sentence of the *Tractatus*." This statement simultaneously distances not only architecture from philosophy but form from content, all the while paradoxically emphasizing the *Tractatus*'s unique form. Focusing on the form of the *Tractatus* apart from its thinking, however, cannot bring the architecture and philosophy into comparison, as it shifts the line of division to within the philosophy, leaving the architecture and philosophy distinctly separate.

Von Wright's association of the image of the house and the image of the *Tractatus* thus limits the architecture-philosophy association to the *Tractatus* in more ways than one. While this approach may initially seem obvious because for a long period the *Tractatus* was synonymous with Wittgenstein's philosophy, by ignoring the late philosophy of the *Investigations*, von Wright also ignored a philosophy that is neither simple nor static. The *Investigations* is a philosophy that both appears and functions differently from much of traditional philosophy. Because of the positioning of the house in Wittgenstein's life and work, any philosophical frame for viewing the house cannot be solely the early philosophy of the *Tractatus* but must literally be the formation of the early-late distinction around the period that includes the house.

Two effects ensue from reducing the philosophy–architecture–philosophy order of Wittgenstein's productions to philosophy–architecture by limiting the architecture association solely to the *Tractatus*. First, this intimates that the architecture be seen in the receptive and reflective mode, which disallows the positioning of the architecture as constructive of the late philosophy and leaves architecture, no longer the central term, to appear solely as the product of the earlier philosophy. And second, it limits possible associations between philosophy and architecture by restricting the terms in which the house is considered. This is not simply a problem of excluding the architecture from consideration regarding the philosophy but is an epistemological concern in that it is important to the apprehension of the architecture not only to recognize what ideas, practices, and so on may have contributed to it but also to examine what ideas, practices, and methods it produced.

Approaching the house from the standpoint of the early philosophy allows that any understanding of it lies in relation to the *Tractatus* in more ways than one. Beyond the (often rejected) possibility of the house revealing, reflecting, exploring, or otherwise instituting concepts from the *Tractatus*, the *Tractatus* is reinscribed in the house in a more fundamental manner; discussions of the house (and thus how we come to know it) employ ideas and distinctions based in the *Tractatus* or a *Tractatus*-like way of thinking in which sense is determinate and showing is sharply distinguished from saying. That is, von Wright's thinking, along with that of others, views the house as if through the conceptual lens of the *Tractatus*, with all the baggage and long-standing influences that accompany this view. Of course, it is just such a restricted view that Wittgenstein explicitly and repeatedly summons, only to reject, in the *Investigations*.

The *Tractatus*–Stonborough-Wittgenstein House association, typically presented, reinforces the line of thinking that demands architecture be understood as structured, concrete, and absolute. Turned back on the *Tractatus*, this substantiates the (erroneous) view that the *Tractatus* is itself architectural with its exacting "static" ordering and its demand that all its elements, thoughts, and meanings be contained in and defined by that order, as manifested by its numbering system. Equally, von Wright's split thinking reiterates the *Tractatus-Investigations* break that places the late philosophy only in direct relation to the early work, thereby eliminating everything in between as inconsequential, the house and the practice of architecture included. In mimicking the *Tractatus*'s exclusion of life, subjecthood, and practice from its pages and its philosophy, von Wright forces the distinction between product and method, omitting practice along the way. The result further separates the house from Wittgenstein's work by excluding the *Investigations*'s practice-based philosophy from discussions of the house. The life/work separation does more, however, to define the *Tractatus-Investigations* split than it does to locate the practice of architecture. Whereas locating the house in relation to these texts—relocating it, really—reveals much about these texts as well. Locating and relocating, which were central to Wittgenstein's life, can also be understood as central to his work and central to understanding and engaging with that work.

Leitner did confirm in his book the need to define a relationship between Wittgenstein's architecture, life, and philosophy by reprinting an excerpt from a family recollection written in the 1940s by Wittgenstein's younger sister, Hermine Wittgenstein[6] Leitner's own conclusions seem greatly influenced by this. The recollection offers an image of Wittgenstein's involvement with architecture and other aesthetic practices.[7]

Several of Hermine's statements have been quoted repeatedly, and her recollections, as with von Wright's comments, have greatly contributed to both our knowledge and the mythology of Wittgenstein's practice of architecture. The reprinted section focuses on her brother's development from childhood through the period in which he worked on the house and serves to broach the question, by attempting to provide a foundation for it, of how a philosopher untrained in architecture came to practice the discipline.

Hermine recalls Wittgenstein's history of involvement with architecture and technical and aesthetic activities, with the technical and aesthetic offered as components of the architectural. She begins by explaining that in "his youth Ludwig showed great interest in technical things." The example she includes is of a ten-year-old Wittgenstein constructing from sticks and wire a model sewing machine that was capable of sewing a few stitches. Hermine describes what she refers to as Wittgenstein's "other interests" from the period of the house's design and construction, all of which involved the arts, including Wittgenstein's relationship with the sculptor Michael Drobil. During the house design and construction period, Wittgenstein

> became very much interested in the sculptural projects which the artist had embarked upon, and even influenced him in a way.... He even began to sculpt, since he was tempted to make his own version of a head which he had disliked in one of Drobil's sculptures. He actually managed to produce something very graceful, and the plaster cast of the head was set up by Gretl in her house.[8]

In another example, Hermine Wittgenstein describes a series of primary school lectures Wittgenstein gave while a teacher at a boys' occupational school prior to his involvement with the house. In these lectures, Wittgenstein had the students invent a steam engine, draw a sketch construction of a tower on the blackboard, and depict moving human figures.

Hermine summarizes her recollections of Wittgenstein's architecture with an interpretation of the house derived from the *Tractatus*. With it, she describes Wittgenstein as a logician who transfers that thinking to architecture. This often quoted remark, again similarly to von Wright's, emphasizes the tie between the house and the *Tractatus*:

> For instance even though I admired the house very much, I always knew that I neither wanted to, nor could live in it myself. It seemed indeed to

be much more a dwelling for the gods than for a small mortal like me, and at first I even had to overcome a faint inner opposition to this "house turned logic" as I called it, to this perfection and monument size.[9]

Wittgenstein's lifelong interest in "technical matters" and issues of construction, coupled with the idea that it would be a sort of therapy for his mental state following the end of the war, are often suggested as the reasons that Wittgenstein's sister Margarethe proposed he work on the house. Wittgenstein's interest in the spatial, the technical, and the constructional—all considered as outside the bounds of philosophy—have, in the recollections and elsewhere, been segregated from discussions of his philosophical production. They are introduced instead as a series of discrete episodes on their own, with only limited and largely unidirectional connections made to his philosophical work. Understanding the house and ultimately the philosophy, however, requires that Wittgenstein, although rightly taken first as a philosopher, be recognized as a philosopher for whom the visual and spatial are themselves central or integral to philosophical thought.

Hermine's recollections outline Wittgenstein's education, beginning with the Technische Hochschule in Berlin from 1906 to 1908, during which "he occupied himself extensively with questions concerning aerodynamics and experiments." Her recollections emphasize how it was precisely at the time when he "was suddenly seized so strongly and so completely against his will by philosophy, i.e., by reflections about philosophical problems, that he suffered severely under this double and conflicting calling, and felt inwardly divided." As described, this period is the reverse of Wittgenstein suddenly abandoning philosophy following the completion of the *Tractatus*. In Hermine's example, Wittgenstein forsakes a previous course of study for philosophy. This shift furnishes an additional correlate against which Wittgenstein's life and work may be seen—that of the technical.

Although Hermine offers Wittgenstein's intense interest in philosophical questions as a sudden personal crisis causing Wittgenstein to choose between courses of study, his actions also suggest that for Wittgenstein philosophical concerns arose from within an immersion in the technical and the mechanical. If you take the emphasis of the recollections—not simply to outline Wittgenstein's engagements with the arts and "technical matters" but to show within Wittgenstein a long and continual interest in such matters—then two possibilities emerge that are useful here. First, Wittgenstein might not, as Hermine suggests, have been seized so much by something external to what he was studying but *by something he knew to be deeply connected with it*. And given that, second, these technical and aesthetic interests not only intermingle with or even pervade his philosophy but may *play an active and formative role within that philosophy*.

It is this understanding of Wittgenstein's not merely dual but deeply interrelated thinking that I want to develop here and see as indicative of the philosophy-architecture association in his work. It is my belief that the practice of architecture played such an influential role in his philosophical development not because it was unrelated to his previous work or presupposed an entirely separate set of issues but rather, in proffering and demanding a new but associated way of thinking, it forced the reconceptualization of his philosophical practice because he was already concerned with related and shared issues.

In the confrontation with architecture and necessarily having to work with new practices and processes, not only did Wittgenstein's thinking change but ideas arising from the architecture can be seen to emerge and enter into the late philosophy. The resulting intersection of ideas, constructs, and themes is not simply the result of Wittgenstein's having been a philosopher who then worked on a house but whose philosophy and methods themselves already contained related ideas, one whose philosophy already perceived the bounds of philosophy as not only potentially contingent and permeable but also necessarily requiring transgression in its construction. Through the work on the house, through the literalization, manifestation, and materialization of the architectural process, the thinking of the *Tractatus* reemerges transformed in the late philosophy, as evidenced by the opening construct of "the builders" and the renewed focus on issues of spatiality, visuality, limits, rule-following, boundaries, and inhabitation; that is by various manifestations, references, and constructs from Wittgenstein's involvement with the Stonborough-Wittgenstein House.

The Stonborough-Wittgenstein House appears from the exterior as an unadorned, white, asymmetric, cubic building with a main central section and a largely regular grid of vertical windows (fig. 3). Because of these basic characteristics, the exterior has repeatedly been compared to the modernist designs of the Viennese architect Adolf Loos. The interior, on the other hand, is what Leitner calls unique and Paul Wijdeveld states: "appears to be at first an unattributable example of early modern architecture." Looked at more closely, he says:

the design and the many peculiar details of its construction are so unique within the context of early twentieth century architecture that one is led to suspect that it must be the result of the deliberate application of "the" principles of "Wittgensteinian aesthetics" under the direct supervision of the philosopher himself.[10]

Definitive building plans of the Stonborough-Wittgenstein House date from the official purchase of the site on October 22, 1926.[11] The building plans were approved a few weeks later, on November 13. The Kundmanngasse site where the house was built was, however, not the original choice of site. The original site was similarly parklike but located instead in a more aristocratic residential district of Vienna near Wittgenstein's parental home on the Alleegasse. The new site was selected and purchased by Margarethe when the architectural designs were nearly complete, but as the proposed design had placed the building in an orientation and scale that worked equally well for either site, the design, despite the change in site, remained unaltered.

Margarethe's choice of the Kundmanngasse property was very unconventional for the type and scale of house Margarethe planned to build. The 32,000-square-foot site occupied the larger section of a city block in the third municipal district of Vienna. It had formerly been a horticultural nursery and had only recently been rezoned for residential use. The unbuilt-upon section of the site recalled the site's previous use, remaining densely covered with trees forming a garden or park. The site originally sloped downward continuously along the street, leaving the northern section, where the house was to be situated, at the lowest point. The decision was made to erect a retaining wall that permitted the northern end to be raised above the street, making it level with the highest section of the site and situating the house a full story above street level. The raising of the site, which created an enclosed plinth upon which the house was built, along with the grove of trees at the southern end effectively isolated the house from the city beyond.

The entrance to the site was originally along the Kundmanngasse. There, the entry drive began at the rear of the house and curved behind the house through the park to the main entrance at the opposite Parkgasse side. The entrance was thus an inversion of typical orientations, beginning at the rear of the house rather than the front. This reversal, while a response to the elevation of the northern end, furthers the sense that the house is more a part of its site than of the street. In 1971 that changed. The house and property were sold by Margarethe's son and heir, Thomas

Stonborough, to a real estate developer who wanted to construct an office tower on the site. In opposition to the house's immanent destruction Bernhard Leitner organized a protest that included architects, art historians, and philosophers from around the world. Just prior to its scheduled destruction, the protesters succeeded in having the house declared a protected monument.[12] Although the house was saved, the remaining section of the site was allowed to be sold to the developer, forcing the demolition of the drive and the relocation of the site's main entrance to the Parkgasse side.

In its grand scale, the Stonborough-Wittgenstein House functioned as a typical aristocratic residence. On the ground floor, the house contained a salon, a library or informal living room, a dining room, a breakfast room, Margarethe Stonborough's private rooms, and the central hall around which many of the rooms are situated (fig. 5). The upper floors contained Margarethe's husband's rooms, the children's rooms, guest rooms, rooms for a governess, secretary, and dressmaker, servants' rooms, and bathrooms. In the basement was the kitchen, an additional servant's room, and another bathroom. Hence in size and program the house was to be traditionally aristocratic, although the architecture of the house was always meant to be "modern" in accordance with Margarethe's thinking.

The house was conceived of in November 1925. At that time Margarethe Stonborough-Wittgenstein initially mentioned the idea of building a large city house in Vienna, for which she engaged the architect Paul Engelmann (1891–1965), a family friend and a student of the Viennese modernist architect Adolf Loos, who had previously acted as the architect for the interiors of their brother Paul's apartment in Berlin. Engelmann, who ultimately became a friend of both Wittgenstein and his family, had been introduced to Wittgenstein through Loos ten years earlier. Their meeting occurred during the war, when Wittgenstein was sent for officer training to Olmutz, Engelmann's family home.

Work on the Stonborough-Wittgenstein House began in April 1926, when Engelmann, in what Hermine describes as "close cooperation" with Margarethe, drew a series of sketches of possible designs for the house.[13] The sketches focused on the overall form or massing of the building as well as the layout of the rooms on the ground floor. It is unclear what the extent of Wittgenstein's influence was in the early phases of the design, but, as Hermine's recollections suggest, he would have at least commented on the various phases of the sketches during that period,[14] forming the origins of his growing involvement in the project. Whatever the contribution during that early phase, it is clear that despite her much stronger

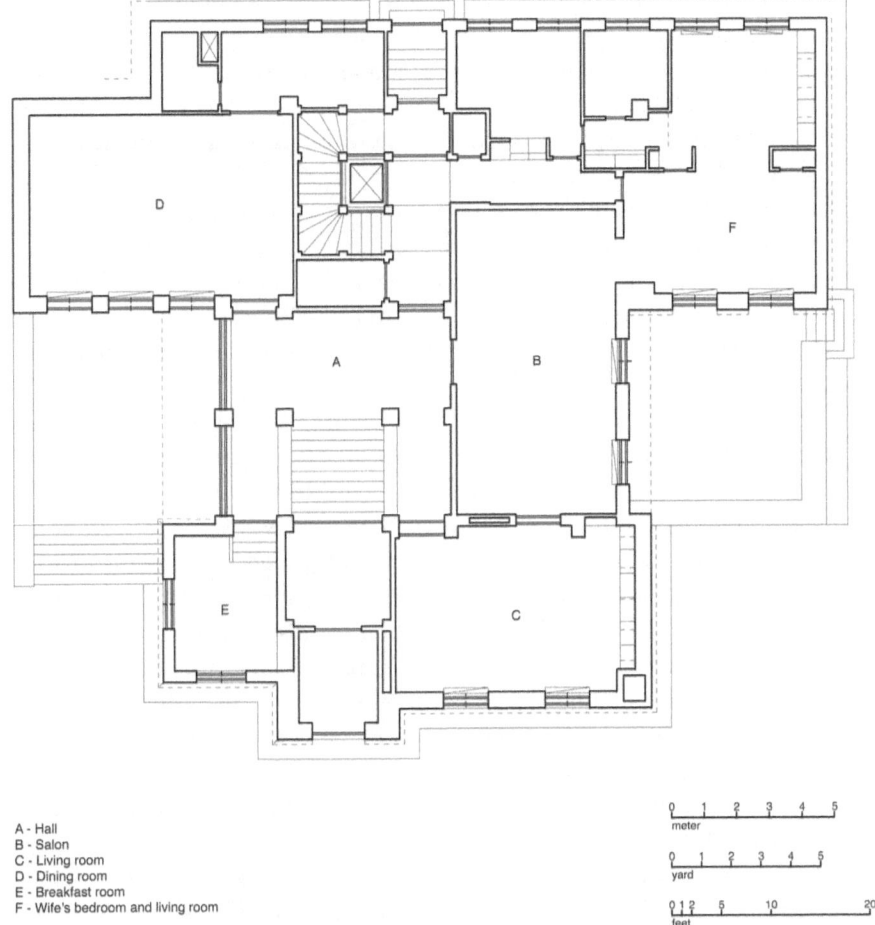

A - Hall
B - Salon
C - Living room
D - Dining room
E - Breakfast room
F - Wife's bedroom and living room

Figure 5. Stonborough-Wittgenstein House: ground-floor plan. Illustrator: North Keeragool.

role in the design with Engelmann, Margarethe granted her brother, once he became involved, "a free hand in all matters concerning the house":

> At this point Ludwig joined them, showed in his usual intense way great interest in the plans and models, began to alter them, and became more and more absorbed in the matter until he finally took it over completely. Engelmann had to give way to the much stronger personality, and the house was then built, down to these smallest detail, according to Ludwig's plans and under his supervision.[15]

Engelmann's final sketches, dated May 18, 1926, form the starting point of Wittgenstein's revisions. Wittgenstein, however, waited until the fall of 1926 to leave his job as gardener and devote himself to the full-time role of architect, officially becoming co-architect in September 1926, as evidenced by the inclusion of his name along with Engelmann's on the drawings. Engelmann's name would later disappear from the completed plans. As usual, Wittgenstein's life and work were inseparable; once part of the project, he became completely absorbed in it, going so far as to move onto the construction site and live in the small house that served as the architecture office for the project. As Wittgenstein entered into and took over the design process, the collaboration with Engelmann completely fell apart.

During that period, according to Engelmann, Wittgenstein pushed his own plans through in such an "uncompromising manner" that Engelmann felt he no longer played a role in the design. In February 1928, Engelmann went to his hometown of Olomouc and did not return until after the house was completed. During that period the interior of the house was designed and built, a task wholly appropriated by Wittgenstein. Later on Engelmann would write regarding the dissolution of the collaboration: "This solution proved to be a very happy one, for him [Wittgenstein] as well as for the building. From that moment he was the actual architect, not I, and though the plans were ready when he joined the undertaking, I regard the result as his achievement, not mine."[16]

As both Engelmann and Wittgenstein were involved in the design of the Stonborough-Wittgenstein House, the question of attribution invariably arises. Wijdeveld takes this question to heart by analyzing the sketchbook Engelmann presented to Margarethe in December 1926.[17] Wijdeveld notes that what he describes as Wittgenstein's "architectural gesture" began with Paul Engelmann's preliminary designs; he portrays Wittgenstein as acting to purify and clarify Engelmann's "classicizing" design by removing all ornament, taking volumetric clarity to its limit, and accentuating the asymmetry of the design.[18]

What is clear in Wijdeveld's discussion is that Wittgenstein altered Engelmann's final plans in four main ways. First, he augmented the floor plan of the basement and ground floors of the house by adding a continuous horizontal block with an angled skylight roof running along the entire rear of the building (fig. 6). The angled roof, continuous skylight, and window organization mark this section of the building as noticeably different from the remainder of the house. The addition had a very specific purpose, allowing Wittgenstein to situate all of Margarethe's private rooms

Figure 6. Stonborough-Wittgenstein House: northwest façade, original state, 1968. Photographer: Franz Hubmann. Copyright: Wittgenstein Archive, Cambridge.

on the ground floor, as she desired; Engelmann's plans had not been able to accommodate her. Wittgenstein's extension included Margarethe's salon, dressing room, bathroom, and a servant's room with a private connecting corridor. Additionally, the extension provided a secondary corridor linking these rooms as a separate apartment removed from the main path through the house.

The segregating of Margarethe's private rooms facilitated Wittgenstein's larger reorganization of the ground floor, whereby he interchanged the library and Margarethe's private living room, allowing him to place the library at the front of the house and Margarethe's rooms to the side and rear. This move achieved two things; first, it allowed for the grouping of all of Margarethe's private rooms together on the ground floor, and second, it collected and separated the more private from the more public spaces, with Margarethe's private living room serving as the connecting element between her rooms and the main salon.

The second main way in which Wittgenstein altered Engelmann's plans was to remove various aspects of the building, primarily a mock attic story, the exterior balustrades that were used to delineate roof lines, and various types of ornament. Third, Wittgenstein reproportioned or relocated elements from Engelmann's designs. He revised the proportions of both the entire building and individual rooms; he elevated the breakfast room on the ground floor to provide the height necessary for a cloakroom below; and he omitted, reproportioned, and redesigned window and interior openings throughout the building. These changes tended to elaborate the asymmetry of Engelmann's design by, for example, adding an off-center entrance portal projecting slightly from the front elevation of the house to accentuate the main entrance. Wittgenstein also extended the steps leading to the southwest terrace along the terrace's entire width (fig. 7) in contrast to the small perpendicularly situated flight of stairs descending from the northeast terrace.

Finally, and perhaps most important, Wittgenstein designed or redesigned all elements in the interior, including all windows and doors, choosing all materials and finishes, details, and the mechanical, plumbing, and electrical systems. He also designed elements such as the stair/elevator combination in the back section of the house. The design combines a concrete frame, a glass elevator cage, and a glass enclosure for the elevator mechanism that allows the mechanism to be visible even as the stair wraps around it.

Engelmann himself commented on how the plan of the house had changed from what he had envisioned. In a letter in response to photographs of the house that Hermine sent to him after the house's completion, Engelmann wrote:

> The pictures of the rooms in the Kundmanngasse pleased me extraordinarily and I thank you very much for that. As pictures they are truly exceptionally beautiful. That is your achievement. In addition, one can also see

Figure 7. Stonborough-Wittgenstein House: south aspect, view of the southwest terrace, spring 1929. Photographer: Moritz Nähr. Copyright: Wittgenstein Archive, Cambridge.

the achievement of your sister and your brother. So, even though I have no share at all in these pictures, I am satisfied with the thought that I had something to do with the origin of such beautiful things, regrettably more in a negative than in a positive way: at that time I wanted something different, something of myself. Now that the work of your brother can be seen in them in its final form, it is clear how much this something of myself would have paled in comparison to this accomplishment, which is better, and which at that time I barely understood. Unfortunately one only becomes wise after the event and therefore I then acted rather as a hindrance than a help. Anyway, I was there, if that can be said to be an achievement.[19]

The question of attribution, though, continues well beyond designating which aspects of the house Wittgenstein contributed and which ones Engelmann did. Rather, the question of attribution designates the site of the underlying issue of how to correlate Wittgenstein's philosophy to his architecture. To enter into that question it seems necessary carefully to distinguish Engelmann's contribution from Wittgenstein's and thus indicate to what extent and in what elements the philosophy may be located. This authorial designation defines the extent of Engelmann's contribution in order to insure the authenticity of the object in question: the house. Declaring the house, or aspects of the house, to be solely or largely Wittgenstein's is what allows for the possibility that the house may be rightly associated with the philosopher and the philosophy.

The question of the point at which Engelmann's contribution stopped and Wittgenstein's began becomes of interest, then, not because of the possible answers but because of the question itself. While the clarity of the separation between Engelmann's and Wittgenstein's respective contributions might be important for certain readings of the architecture-philosophy relation, Wittgenstein's architectural practice cannot simply be equated with the house. Instead, it is possible to theorize Wittgenstein's architecture-philosophy relation as not solely revolving about the object in question. My contention is that Wittgenstein's architecture needs to be situated not simply within the object produced (the house) but within the *practice* of architecture—a place where the exact limits of Wittgenstein's contribution or the espoused architectural value of the house (another question requiring legitimation of the object as worthy of study) is neither central nor foundational.

Approaching the house as a series of concepts and problems situated within a practice requires considering Wittgenstein's engagement or confrontation with the practice of architecture also to be a way of looking at "the house." Furthermore the shift to practice—or from product—allows the Stonborough-Wittgenstein House to be viewed not solely as Wittgenstein's (the philosopher's) contribution to architecture but rather as representative of (the practice of) architecture's contribution to (the practice of) philosophy. *Wittgenstein's architecture is thus not merely coincident with the house he designed but must be understood within his engagement with the practice of architecture,* as it is through architecture that Wittgenstein found a way to overcome the idealized solipsism of the *Tractatus* and to reintegrate both the subject and the practice of philosophy with the wider culture.

Treating architecture not as object but as practice—a key concept in Wittgenstein's late philosophy—allows the practice of architecture to act as far more than a confrontation with the everyday or a repository of aesthetic thinking, as has been suggested. The house instead makes manifest what was implied in but absent from the early philosophy. The *Tractatus*'s discussion of boundaries, its flattened and restricted visual space, its defining of the limits of the ethical and aesthetic from without, and its emphasis on saying over showing all exhibit and describe a severely restricted and idealized implementation and recognition of space. Yet equally, the *Tractatus* is deeply engaged in producing a philosophy in accordance with that restricted space. Exactly because of that, the practice of architecture was in a position to transform fundamentally the manner in which architecture inhabits Wittgenstein's philosophical work. It did this by invigorating and inhabiting the definition, viewpoint, and functioning of space in the text itself, from the prehouse *Tractatus* to the posthouse *Investigations*. Wittgenstein's practice of architecture forms a site where the spatial and visual limits, borders, structures, and so on produced in architectural practice can intimately confront their philosophical accomplices. That confrontation forces Wittgenstein in the late work to reevaluate the spatial constructs inherent to his philosophy, including the limits of language, the functioning of boundaries, and the requirements of exacting correspondence.

Approaching the Stonborough-Wittgenstein House from the point of view of practice resituates the house in relation to the philosophy so that it is no longer conceived of solely as a product of the *Tractatus*. Instead, it fosters the possibility that the *Investigations* is in part a product of Wittgenstein's practice of architecture, a practice that is not limited to a series of operations to produce an object but rather is productive and informative in its specifics, both architectural and philosophical. As with Wittgenstein's jettisoning of the search for the essence of language and the general form of propositions by considering the multiplicity of practices that are involved in language, understanding the Stonborough-Wittgenstein House as the compilation and interpenetration of a series of practices allows architecture not to be synonymous with its object, the house. As such, the Stonborough-Wittgenstein House is no longer an object in comparison to philosophy, but a process that as with the philosophy of the *Tractatus* and the *Investigations*, is concerned with a series of topics, including boundaries, limits, visuality, spatiality, inner-outer relationships, rule-following, meaning, representation, and so on. This view does not force Wittgenstein's work to be viewed as a continuum or as a series of shifts and phases, but permits both continuity and disjunctions. Not uncoincidentally, this shift in method and practice is also a way of understanding the move from the *Tractatus* to the *Investigations*, from the applied method of logical analysis in the *Tractatus* to the investigation and description of the multitude of practices that comprise language in the *Investigations*.

The Practice of Architecture

The Stonborough-Wittgenstein House is perhaps most associated with its austere exterior image, an image taken to reflect the seemingly similar image of austerity and precision of the writing of the *Tractatus* (fig. 3). Both of these images define the view from without. I want to contrast that image with one from the interior, with the view from within, the scene of inhabitation. There, beginning with entry into the central hall of the house, the visitor is presented with a scene of quiet conflict where the idealized pictorial view dreamed of by the *Tractatus* fully encounters the spatial practices of architecture subsequently developed in the *Investigations*.

To enter the Stonborough-Wittgenstein House, the visitor passes through the front glass doors into a small vestibule with light walls and dark floor, through another set of glass doors, up the dark stone stairs, and into the brightly lit space of the central hall. The dark stairs recessed into the center of this space are framed at their end by two white columns. To the left, a glass wall and doors admit light into the hall and passage out to a terrace. To the right, a solid wall harbors a set of paired metal doors (fig. 8).

The central hall is luminous, defined by a series of eight paired glass-and-steel doors on six different surfaces, set into both solid wall and glass plane and leading into the house from the main entry, out to the southwest terrace, and to the dining room, breakfast room, library, and the staircase and upper floors beyond (fig. 9). To the right, the metal doors lead to the

Figure 8. Stonborough-Wittgenstein House: the hall with a view of the sculpture "Discobolus" at the top of the stairs and the double-door leading to the salon, spring 1929. Photographer: Moritz Nähr. Copyright: Wittgenstein Archive, Cambridge.

Figure 9. Stonborough-Wittgenstein House: the hall looking toward the southwest terrace, spring 1929. The original silk-covered lamps can be seen between the columns. Photographer: Moritz Nähr. Copyright: Wittgenstein Archive, Cambridge.

main salon. Straight ahead is a wall with two pairs of translucent glass doors set off to either side, with those on the left leading to the dining room and those on the right to a hallway, a staircase, and a suite of private rooms. Turning around 180 degrees to face the entry, the visitor encounters four sets of the glass doors (fig. 4). In the center, two telescoped pairs of entry doors lead successively from the exterior to the entry vestibule and from the vestibule to the central hall. On the left, one pair leads to the library, and to the right, raised up two steps, are those to the breakfast room (fig. 10).

Figure 10. Stonborough-Wittgenstein House: the hall, looking toward the southwest terrace, original state, 1975. Photographer: Rudi Vrooman. Copyright: Wittgenstein Archive, Cambridge.

The central hall sits poised between the simplicity and austerity of its exterior and the almost mazelike series of reflections produced by these paired glass doors erupting all around to define the movement through the hall as that between the practices of vision and of space. At the moment of arrival into the house, the austerity, monumentality, and isolation of the house that confronts the visitor from without yields to these like-designed paired glass-and-steel doors, each reflecting and reiterating the others. It is the repetition of this image that forms the focus of the house, both within and from without. Repetition is not, however, the sole activity here. More precisely, the image does not repeat exactly but is subtly transformed each time it is relocated and reinvented as if to presage Wittgenstein's note that the grammar of "language" is related to that of "invent."

The doors of the central hall appear simple yet are of an intricate construction that readily allow for these continuous mutations. The doors are tall and structured by thin metal frames. Typically each glass panel has one vertical division and no horizontal ones. The exception to this lies in the pair of doors connecting vestibule and hall, in which the glass is not subdivided but allows for an unobstructed view of the entry doors beyond. The plain metal bipaneled doors opening to the salon appear as if in counterpoint to the glass. By employing the doors to create seemingly simple

THE PRACTICE OF ARCHITECTURE   97

yet actually complex boundaries between spaces, Wittgenstein builds on the doors' dual nature in a similar way to how he offers and expands the builders' language in the *Investigations*.

Owing to the climate, double exterior windows were a necessary and common practice in Austria. Wittgenstein, however, extended this double construction to the interior, throughout the central hall and in the salon. With the exception of the doors to the breakfast room and those connecting vestibule and hall, all of the glass-and-steel doors in the interior are bipaneled double doors that open out into both of the rooms they connect. On the exterior, both sides of the double glass-and-steel doors contain the same transparent glass, but on the interior doors, that is not the case. While the mediation between interior and exterior is equalized so as to present the same image of complete transparency on either side, the complexity of spatial relations on the interior disrupts any singularity of approach. Instead, rather than simply reiterating one another, the series of glass doors in the central hall defines a range of possibilities. The doors connecting the living room and hall repeat the exterior condition of clear glass on both sides, while those between dining room and central hall and staircase and central hall are differentiated one side from the other. Each of these paired doors are clear glass on the hall side and translucent glass on the other. The total effect furnishes varying degrees of separation and privacy provided by both the visual coding and restriction of vision, depending on which panels are open and which closed.

In each of the instances in the hall where two different materials or degrees of transparency are brought together, the less transparent material is placed on the more private side of the doors and the more transparent on the more public side. This would seem to form a rather straightforward approach, even constituting a rule. But what seems to be a simple declarative principle confronts in spatial practices a complex series of relationships to yield curious reversals of association. Examples of this occur in both the dining room and the salon. In the dining room the doors to the hall are on a wall with three similar sets of paired glass-and-steel doors that lead directly outside to the southwest terrace (figs. 11, 12). This sets up a sequence of four such pairs along the same wall. The situation creates a dilemma as to whether the dining-room-to-hall doors should exactly match the other three sets along the same wall, as they do in size and detail, or whether they should also mark their difference—that they lead not to the exterior but to another interior space.

While passage between the interior and exterior terrace through the three sets of doors in the dining room is alike from either approach, the

Figure 11. Stonborough-Wittgenstein House: the dining room, state in 1992. Photographer: Margherita Spiluttini. Copyright: Wittgenstein Archive, Cambridge.

interior connection between dining room and central hall is more complex. Wittgenstein's decision to place translucent glass on the dining room side and clear glass on the hall side distinguishes the two spaces even as it connects them. This decision highlights the complex nature of the boundary as connector, divider, and sign by emphasizing its materiality and location in space and allowing it to present disparate faces as it is approached from opposite sides. This last aspect literally constructs Wittgenstein's fundamental understanding of language in the *Investigations* as presenting distinct images when viewed from divergent points: "Language is a labyrinth of paths. You approach from *one* side and know your way about; you approach the same place from another side and no longer know your way about."[1]

A similar situation to that of the dining room doors appears in the paired doors leading from the salon to Margarethe's private living room. This connection further illustrates the complexity of the boundary conditions Wittgenstein constructed as a central part of the functioning of the

Figure 12. Stonborough-Wittgenstein House: the dining room, view of the southwest terrace through the open glass doors, state in 1989. Photographer: Margherita Spiluttini. Copyright: Wittgenstein Archive, Cambridge.

design of the house. In this instance, as all of the interior doors leading to the salon are metal, when paired with those to Margarethe's private living room, they no longer combine two types of glass to create the transparent/translucent pairing but glass and metal to form a transparent/opaque combination. As with the dining room–hall connection, the doors in question are placed along a plane that also contains a series of exterior doors opening onto a terrace (fig. 13). While the sets of paired doors leading out to the terrace are, as with the dining room, clear glass on both sides, the interior doors connecting hall and salon and salon and library are metal doors. Additionally, while the exterior glass doors are doubled, opening both out and in, the metal doors connecting salon and hall are unidirectional, opening only out from the salon.

The choice of material becomes even more significant in the salon as it is the only room in the house to possess metal doors. These doors exist in sharp contrast both in material and resulting opacity to the glass doors of

Figure 13. Stonborough-Wittgenstein House: view from the library/living room into the salon to the right and the hall on the left, state in 1992; the opening between library and salon is not the original. Photographer: Margherita Spiluttini. Copyright: Wittgenstein Archive, Cambridge.

the central hall and throughout the public rooms and areas comprising the ground floor. Owing to this, metal comes to be identified solely with the salon. The connection between salon and private living room thus has to navigate a series of three potentially conflicting rules: 1) the continuation of the glass doors along the exterior wall; 2) the placing of the more opaque material on the more private side; and 3) the rule that all interior doors to the salon and only to the salon are metal. These could not all be satisfied at once.

Ultimately, Wittgenstein opted to place metal on the salon side and clear glass on Margarethe's private living room side. This allowed the metal doors to remain associated solely with the salon but it disrupted the succession of glass doors along the same wall and left the private living space designated by the more transparent material. Furthermore, the decision also raises the question as to why Wittgenstein saw the need at this juncture to utilize double doors, as the remaining interior entries to the salon employ only one pair of metal doors. Doubling the doors to Margarethe's private living room from the salon thus proves to be another anomaly. The glass doors remain unseen from the salon when the metal doors are closed, and provide an unoccluded view into the more private space when those same doors are open. Their function then becomes more of a sign of the complexity of that juncture. This boundary is also of interest as it is a connection to the section of the house that Wittgenstein appended to the footprint of Engelmann's initial designs, a section added to allow Margarethe's rooms to be fully accommodated on the ground floor.

The differences in materiality from one side to the other of the paired doors compound these relations. While the transparent glass allows full vision, the translucent glass limits that vision, and the metal denies it. Hence transparency furthers familiarity—you can see where the space leads—while the other materials limit that view. This resolves in some way the mystery of the glass doors leading to Margarethe's private living room. While making her rooms more visually accessible, these doors also allow her greater visual control. The varying materiality of the glass of the doors itself contributes an additional level of significance to Wittgenstein's parable of the glasses in section 103 of the *Investigations*. In the passage, Wittgenstein describes being trapped in an unrecognized narrow conception of language that he compares to the limitations of viewing language through "a pair of glasses on our nose through which we see whatever we look at." What was only imaginable as clear glass now recalls Wittgenstein's experimentation and implementation of different types of glass throughout the ground floor of the house.

The question of difference raises related questions as to the functioning and purpose of the doors. Again the focus away from object (door) and onto practice is operative in making connections to philosophical practice. So what appears to be a focus on the details of the doors—their proportions, the degree of transparency of their materials, and the divisions of the glass into panes—can now be understood in terms of the complex relations, meanings, functions, and concepts they enter into as active agents in the construction of space, movement, and association. While doors are typically seen as openings, in a wider sense they establish the particulars of a given boundary condition.

The importance of these operations becomes multiplied in the Stonborough-Wittgenstein House through the multiplication of the doors and in their doubling to form compound boundaries. To which room and which wall do the doors belong? What boundaries do they define? How do these boundaries function and for what purposes? The doors thus reiterate many of the concerns of the *Tractatus* as to the limits of language emerging along the boundary that divides sense from nonsense, showing from saying. But they encapsulate many of the complex boundary questions posed by the *Investigations* that place greater stress on how boundaries function within a particular game or practice rather than as an absolute limit to that practice that the boundary between saying and showing implied.

This discussion of this series of boundary rules and conditions and their accompanying and almost endless list of exceptions began with the apparent singular and repeated image of double glass doors but yielded a multitude of possibilities arising from the specifics of site and the complex demands of use. These developments accumulate throughout the house as if to enact de Certeau's description of Wittgenstein's own transformation of ideas and disciplines; through

> his experience as a superior technician, then as a mathematician, Wittgenstein had, like Musil's Ulrich, the man without qualities, a "second try" and a third try. . . . He, too, possessed "fragments of a new way of thinking and feeling" and saw "the spectacle of novelty, at first so intense," dissolve "into the multiplication of details."[2]

The continual differentiation and specification of the doors through their relocation and repetition initially suggests the attempt on Wittgenstein's part to construct exacting and determinate conditions of place and boundary akin to the *Tractatus*'s understanding of the functioning of meaningful language. In that view, the continual redesign of the doors seems to aspire to establish a one-to-one correspondence between door (as sign) and space beyond that reiterates the attempt at a one-to-one-to-one correspondence of sign, meaning, and place first appearing in the *Tractatus*'s numbering system. The anomalies that arise in the application of that system in the *Tractatus* are here played out in architectural space, rendering its paradoxical reversals and its immanent possibilities more readily apparent.

What commenced, then, as an attempt (in each case) for absolute clarity and differentiation ultimately yielded in the house a series of complex situations whose ambiguities contribute as much to the defining of the nature of these boundaries as does their attempted clarity. It is that lesson or cycle that finds its way into the *Investigations*, where it repeatedly reenacts the replacement of the limited view of the *Tractatus* by the at times conflictual view that develops through visual and spatial practices.

Arising in the reiteration or redefinition of the paired doors of the Stonborough-Wittgenstein House is Wittgenstein's continuing concern with what it means to follow a rule. Concerns about rules and rule-following play a substantial role in the *Investigations*. Furthermore, these discussions are repeatedly played out around questions of visuality and spatiality, so that the text grapples with many of the same concerns as arose with the house, including questions of what constitutes a rule and what it means to follow a rule. What particularly recalls the complexity of decision-making in the work on the house is the manner in which Wittgenstein describes rule-following in his late philosophy. In one particularly well-known series of passages, Wittgenstein first describes rule-following in terms of the visual extended into three dimensions to become fully spatial. He then continues on to reject that possibility as being definitive of rule-following, replacing it with the notion that rule-following is a blind practice, one that created conflict in his experiences in the spatial practice of architecture. Wittgenstein's spatial confrontation with rule-following appears in these passages from the *Investigations*:

> 218. Whence comes the idea that the beginning of a series is a visible section of rails invisibly laid to infinity? Well, we might imagine rails instead of a rule. And infinitely long rails correspond to the unlimited application of a rule.

> 219. "All the steps are really already taken" means: I no longer have any choice. The rule, once stamped with a particular meaning, traces the lines

along which it is to be followed through the whole of space.—But if something of this sort really were the case, how would it help?

No; my description only made sense if it was to be understood symbolically.—I should have said: *This is how it strikes me.*

When I obey a rule, I do not choose.

I obey the rule *blindly*.

Together these differing views show the opposing pulls Wittgenstein felt in initiating a rule as seen in the design and implementation of the doors and then attempting to enact it in the space of the central hall, a space that brought with it more possibilities than a series of singular or linear rules could accommodate. In this instance, rather than mitigating a proposed rule, resultant spatial conflicts reveal the existence of potential rules, their determinants, and possible iterations.

What the analysis of the doors on the main floor points to, then, is that the central hall, when considered outside of the *Tractatus*'s restrictive frame, does not simply reiterate the stasis often attributed to it. Instead, the complexity of the hall multiplies effects and situations, and in so doing, defines and plays out philosophical issues related to visual and spatial concepts, including ones such as boundary, limits, correspondences, rule-following, and clarity that from within philosophy are not often recognized as spatial propositions. As they multiply and mutate in the space of the hall, the doors' clarity and transparency are destroyed both literally and metaphorically as the rules/meanings themselves become commingled, even occluded. The compiling of transparent and translucent glass serves to form the core of a discussion of transparency and correspondence, central philosophical concerns in the *Tractatus*'s philosophy of language. The doors and windows of the house both encode what lies on either side of them—an act tied to a specific location—and, in their repetition, act out variations on a theme played out in multiple situations.

Similarly, in the move from the *Tractatus* to the *Investigations*, the singularity of view is destroyed, leaving not *one* clear view, or *over*view, but a series of competing and conflicting ones. This creates the situation that later plays a constitutive role in the *Investigations*, where the understanding of language takes on a decidedly spatial slant so that the approach from one direction is quite different from the approach from another; this is the disorienting labyrinth of paths by which Wittgenstein described language in the *Investigations*. It is the repetition of an element or relationship in varying contexts that works to shift the focus from specific views to the connections and relations between the views and within them.

Repetition and connections take on a central role in the house as Wittgenstein's architecture comes into being as connections—visual, material, spatial, and epistemological. The doors visible from the entry hall, in their varying locations and degrees of illumination, are a prime example of this. Despite their overall similarities, the doors, which differ in detail, also differ in size, with even those in close proximity exhibiting subtle differences. For example, the flanking sets of doors on either side of the entry stairs, leading to the library on one side and the breakfast room on the other, are at different elevations and of different heights. The base of the doors to the breakfast room is raised up two steps. Their upper edge moderates this difference, with the breakfast room doors just inches closer to the ceiling than those of the library, illustrating how the height of the doors becomes determined by locations. Additionally, the door handles are at varying heights according to door type: glass door handles are at five feet, three inches, marking the intersection of their diagonals, and placing them near eye level. The handles of the metal doors of the salon door are a little lower at four feet, eight and a half inches, even though the doors themselves are taller. And finally, the handles on the glass entrance doors are still lower at four feet, one inch. There are also size distinctions between the door handles on the ground floor and those on the upper ones.

The continual transformation or mutation, in all respects, in the design of the glass doors produces what will emerge as a major theme of the *Investigations*: the repeated locating and relocating of an element, such as a language-game or word, as a way of grasping and elucidating its role in various language-games. This is important because it indicates the process by which a dynamic spatial practice emerged out of the attempt to produce a one-to-one-to-one correspondence of place, meaning, and object that generated the complex door boundary conditions. That is, the doors began in a manner akin to the *Tractatus*'s attempt literally to construct unambiguous meaning and in that attempt precisely to correlate meaning and place through the specifics of the doors, to produce a practice of location and relocation that enables—requires, even—elements and contexts to be continually rethought.

By placing the doors in a multitude of positions and in a variety of places and configurations, Wittgenstein instigates the activities the *Investigations* subsequently associates with the construction of a perspicuous representation, the acts of "seeing connections" and the "finding and inventing of intermediate cases." The central hall of the Stonborough-Wittgenstein House—*as a distributor of both space and spatial concepts*—acts to allow Wittgenstein to create a series of intermediary connections and cases later averred in the *Investigations* as the necessary activity by which philosophy may achieve clarity. Those intermediary connections are a result of the endeavor to make sense, to see clearly from within language, something not necessary in the view from above that appeared capable of rendering unimpaired vision.

In section 122 of the *Investigations,* Wittgenstein directly confronts this impediment to clarity posed by the view from within. This challenge arises as the *Investigations* dismantles the *Tractatus*'s all-encompassing view from without and above and with it the *Tractatus*'s construction of clarity. The *Investigations* brings with it the possibility of a previously unimaginable form of clarity, one no longer based on a total view but on the continually unfolding processes of viewing:

> 122. A main source of our failure to understand is that we do not *command a clear view* of the use of our words.—Our grammar is lacking in this sort of perspicuity. A perspicuous representation produces just that understanding which consists in "seeing connexions." Hence the importance of finding and inventing *intermediate cases.*
>
> The concept of a perspicuous representation is of fundamental significance for us. It earmarks the form of account we give the way we look at things. (Is this a "*Weltanschauung*"?)

In introducing the inventing and finding of cases, the paired doors in the central hall function to break down the absolute correlation of place, element, and meaning that forms the fundamental relation of correspondence constructed by the *Tractatus.* The doors repeatedly pose the question of the functioning of boundary markers and determinants in diverse situations, or language-games, as Wittgenstein calls such examples in the *Investigations.* Accordingly, the continual altering of the design of the doors disallows the simple association of doors with a single use or site. For example, the image of the doors also presents the question of their association with windows that bear the same glass-and-steel image but do not function to allow passage and so do not develop the complex boundary conditions enacted by the doors.

In addition to their structuring and transforming, the conflicting reflections by each pair of doors in its other creates a visual-spatial collapse. When looked at directly, the two layers composing a pair of the double doors coincide so that the front metal frame completely obscures the frame beyond. Moving off to one side disrupts the singular image to reveal a double image emerging as a spatial dislocation. The marked distance between the layers of glass accentuates this. The importance of this and of related circumstances that rely on the visual alignment of architectural elements in space is their ability to reveal their dependence on a fixed observer. Movement through space destroys that single, fixed image and reveals it as an idealized condition that gives way to the vicissitudes of movement and space. This is an important product of the design of the central hall; in the *Investigations*, Wittgenstein distinctly associates movement through space with everyday language, in contrast to a fixity resulting from the *Tractatus*'s collapse of language and logic that restricts language and our ability to navigate within it. That is, it restricts movement between language-games and hence limits use. This concept is realized most succinctly in the *Investigations* through its contrast between the immobility of being stuck on the seemingly ideal ice and the desire to walk:

> 107. The more narrowly we examine actual language, the sharper becomes the conflict between it and our requirement. (For the crystalline purity of logic was, of course, not a *result of investigation*: it was a requirement.) The conflict becomes intolerable; the requirement is now in danger of becoming empty.—We have got on to slippery ice where there is no friction and so in a certain sense the conditions are ideal, but also, just because of that, we are unable to walk. We want to walk: so we need *friction*. Back to the rough ground!

Spatial issues similar to those arising with the doors occur throughout the Stonborough-Wittgenstein House, such as the location and alignment of the floor joints, the location of window and door openings, inside and out, problems of localized symmetries within the overall asymmetric floor plan, and issues of proportions, lighting, materials, the various mechanical systems, and so on. These issues raise the questions of the specificity of site and how that affects and informs the design of architectural elements—in other words, the issue of the relation of place and meaning. Unlike what Wittgenstein said about philosophical problems in the *Tractatus*, these problems do not dissolve through analysis but arise from it. This shift is a primary example of the practice of architecture's ability to provide a new, enhanced forum for the construction and discussion of spatiolinguistic concepts and constructs.

PRECISION

Both inspection of the Stonborough-Wittgenstein House and endless stories about it reveal an emphasis on the precision of the design and construction of elements in the house such as radiators, metal curtains, and mechanical systems along with the construction and functioning mechanisms of the doors and windows. These elements draw much of the visual focus of the house, as demonstrated by any photograph or experience, particularly of the entry hall and rooms on the ground floor. These elements are repeatedly referred to as having been designed as if they were precision instruments. For example, the glass doors were equipped with metal curtains that rose from their unseen storage in a slot in the floor just below the inner pair of doors. This added to the notoriously difficult manufacture of the glass doors themselves, which required substantial communication between Wittgenstein and the fabricators. The main difficulty in fabricating the doors lay in preventing breakage of the tall, narrow glass panes, the largest of which measured only ten and seven-eighths inches wide yet was nine feet, ten inches tall. As Hermine records in her family recollections:

> Ludwig designed every window, door, window-bar and radiator in the noblest proportions and with such exactitude that they might have been precision instruments. Then he forged ahead with his uncompromising energy, so that everything was exactly manufactured with the same exactness. I can still hear the locksmith, who asked him with regard to a keyhole, "Tell me, Herr Ingenieur, is a millimetre here really that important for you?" and even before he had finished the sentence, the loud, energetic "Ja," that almost startled him.[3]

The interrelated concepts of exactness, precision, and measurement that Wittgenstein discusses in the *Investigations* recall his own battle with the exactness of dimension and precision of fabrication and installation that he encountered in the design and construction of his sister's house. As much as the idea of precision might be readily associated with the exacting demands of logic put forth in the *Tractatus,* it plays quite another role in the *Investigations,* which launches a critique of the early philosophy's overexacting demands for precision. The *Investigations* repeatedly questions the *Tractatus*'s extreme requirements of exactitude by offering examples of physical and spatial practices of measurement such as Wittgenstein encountered in his work on the Stonborough-Wittgenstein House. This suggests that his concern with precision in the practice of architecture was in a position to alter his views by providing an alternative practice (akin to another language-game) within which to engage the enacting of precision. In the *Investigations* Wittgenstein points to the limits of meaningful precision, asking: "Am I inexact when I do not give our distance from the sun to the nearest foot, or tell a joiner the width of a table to the nearest thousandth of an inch?"[4] Similarly, Wittgenstein's comments on proportion in his 1938 lecture on aesthetics proffer the example of finding the right dimension for doors and windows as a means to discuss aesthetic concerns.

Design and construction issues concerning precision and relational proportions arose for Wittgenstein in the navigation from a two-dimensional set of drawings to the three-dimensional house. These appear both in the construction process and in the philosophy of the *Investigations*. The issue of how two-dimensional images, when projected into space, may produce different three-dimensional objects works its way into the *Investigations* as examples of the functioning of language:

> 140. Then what sort of mistake did I make; was it what we should like to express by saying: I should have thought the picture forced a particular use on me? How could I think that? What *did* I think? Is there such a thing as a picture, or something like a picture, that forces a particular application on us: so that my mistake lay in confusing one picture with another?—For we might also be inclined to express ourselves like this: we are at most under a psychological, not a logical, compulsion. And now it looks quite as if we knew of two kinds of case.
>
> What was the effect of my argument? It called our attention to (reminded us of) the fact that there are other processes, besides the one we originally thought of, which we should sometimes be prepared to call "applying the picture of a cube." So our "belief that the picture forced a particular application upon us" consisted in the fact that only the one case and no other occurred to us. "There is another solution as well" means: there is something else that I am also prepared to call a "solution"; to which I am prepared to apply such-and-such a picture, such-and-such an analogy, and so on.
>
> What is essential is to see that the same thing can come before our minds when we hear the word and the application still be different. Has it the *same* meaning both times? I think we shall say not.

This same concern arose in Wittgenstein's work on the Stonborough-Wittgenstein House, where the translation from a two-dimensional set of drawings to the three-dimensional house did not always go smoothly for him, as various anecdotes reveal. After the initial construction, Wittgenstein remained dissatisfied with several aspects of the design, which he then proceeded to amend as long as his sister would allow. These changes most infamously include his raising of the ceiling of the salon by about three inches. As typically recounted, this story speaks as much to the myth of Wittgenstein's work on the house as it does to an unusual concern with precision. The raising of the ceiling initially sounds more unusual, exacting, and trivial than may be seen. While three inches may represent an insignificant shift in relation to the entire height of the wall, it is substantially more critical in relation to the datum line created by the top of the doors displaced around the room that defines an approximately two-foot space below the ceiling. Within that band, the three-inch shift is both noticeable and nontrivial. It is also not an unusual architectural concern but is one frequently encountered in the practice of architecture.

The exception in this case lies in Wittgenstein's close relation to the client, his sister, allowing him greater freedom to carry out such changes. But even her largess toward her brother had its limits. At the end of the construction process, when he was finally forced to complete the work, Wittgenstein still remained dissatisfied with three windows on the rear facade along the staircase. This situation resulted in the one time that the philosopher bemoaned having relinquished his share in the family wealth that would have allowed him to pay for the cost of further reconstruction; Wittgenstein later confessed to having purchased a lottery ticket with the hope of winning the money to cover the costs of further alterations.

INTERIOR/EXTERIOR

The complex mediation between interior and exterior, while clearly one of the main themes of the Stonborough-Wittgenstein House and of architecture in general, is also central to Wittgenstein's late philosophy. As Stanley Cavell put forth in *The Claim of Reason*, it is one of the main themes of the *Investigations*: "I would have been glad to have suggested that the correct relation between inner and outer, between the soul and its society, is the theme of the *Investigations* as a whole."[5] Although Cavell's comments may refer to another sense of inner and outer than the architectural, it is important to reiterate that the spatial conception of inner/outer still comes into play directly in Cavell's comments, as the philosophical and spatial concerns remain interdependent. This is borne out in Wittgenstein's model of family resemblance, while in many cases that interdependence suggests that the architectural—including but not limited to the literal, physical understanding and production of space—underpins the philosophical and linguistic sense. Yet the house also contains elements that relate directly to the subjective sense of inner and outer.

There are three main aspects of the Stonborough-Wittgenstein House that actively mediate interior and exterior relations. The first emanates from the split Wittgenstein develops and encodes between the public and the private areas of the house. The second concerns the emphasis in the house and the design of the house on the making of connections—philosophical, spatial, and visual ones. The third entails the complex spatial relations between the interior and the exterior of the building.

The house's design, both in its encoding of surfaces and its zoning of the various functions of the house into sections, initiates a public/private discussion throughout the house. Functional groupings of rooms and spaces in the house define three zones stemming from divisions on the ground floor. Located along the southwest side, the first sectioning delineates the line of breakfast room–dining room–pantry and kitchen below. The central zone of the house defines passage. It contains the entry, the vestibule, the central hall, the stair/elevator combination to the rear of the house, and the connecting hallway (fig. 14). The third section, which runs along the northeast side of the house, comprises the living areas, including the library, the salon, and Margarethe's private rooms. Additionally, the plan distinguishes between the public rooms, such as the library and salon, and the private ones by situating the public spaces along the front of the house, where they are directly accessible from the central hall. The private rooms are placed in the rear of the house and are accessed not directly from the central hall but only through the salon or interconnecting hallway.

The doors become of importance once more in distinguishing between public and private areas. Acting as almost literal signs of Enter, Don't Enter, Open, Closed, they define an array of possible options or actions to be taken. Oscillating between the defining of physical and visual space, the doors serve to organize movement through the central hall. With their layering of clear and translucent glass, the doors in the public rooms blur the strict dichotomy between open and closed. Although glass doors generally make such distinctions ambiguous, those in the Stonborough-Wittgenstein House define a complete range from open to closed all within the space of the central hall. By contrast, the salon delivers only the extremes: either plain metal or clear glass. The hall thus emphasizes the varying (visual) degrees between open and closed, between visually accessible and separated, between the continuation of space and the disruption of it. These variations produce movement both implied and actual. The salon, in comparison, suggests the extremes of transgression and inhabitation.

Figure 14. Stonborough-Wittgenstein House: view of the stairs with the elevator shaft on the ground floor, 1983–1984, state after the renovation of 1976–1977. Photographer: Margherita Spiluttini. Copyright: Wittgenstein Archive, Cambridge.

As evidenced here, materials act throughout the house as fundamental transmitters of meaning, place, and difference. The simplicity of the architecture and contrasts of materials emphasize the surfaces. The interior walls and ceilings are off-white plaster which plays sharply against the gray-black artificial-stone flooring that runs throughout the public spaces of the main floor. Against these extremes, the glass-and-steel doors define the central hall, and the metal doors the salon. Together these set up other dichotomous pairs—not solely of light and dark, as with the walls and floor, but also of transparent and opaque, inside and out.

In contrast to the ground floor, the upper floors are of quite another character, diverging in both materiality and spatial disposition. The upper floors are comprised of closed or isolated spaces with limited connections between them. Except for the circulation area of the stair and elevator, only the front room on the first upper floor is cited as being of aesthetic note. In what seems to be a design problem of filling a largely predetermined volume, large storage areas line the hallway on both sides, creating a sort of buffer zone of uninhabited, inactivated space between the hall and the private rooms. The hallway floor, although of the same artificial-stone flooring as the ground floor, is here oddly undifferentiated, with no joints to mark alignments, make connections, or suggest direction. This blankness seems to acknowledge the lack of spatial, visual, or social connections in this section of the house.

The floor material of the rooms themselves on the upper floors is wood, which, along with the wooden doors of these rooms, defines a different language from that of the more public rooms below. As such, the floors signify an alternate system, entailing other types of boundary conditions. In that view, the storage closets as buffer zone can be seen as an expanded boundary condition in comparison to the doors of the central hall below. Rather than presenting potentials, ambiguities, and complexity between spaces, though, that boundary condition along the linear hall offers an enforced border that disallows discourse except at the discrete moments of the opening of the wooden doors themselves. The blankness and singularity of not just the doors but the entirety of the hall as well suggests that without the "public" or social component, there seems to be no intricate mediating between interior and exterior, and thus limited associated discourse.

This lack of discourse has a potential philosophical counterpart in Wittgenstein's late philosophy. In the *Investigations*, Wittgenstein presents the possibility of a so-called "private language" as a central component of his discussion of the relation between the interior of the individual and the public externality of language. Against the thrust of the *Investigations*'s presentation of language as a public practice, the private-language argument considers the possibility of a private language, one that is theoretically impossible to teach or convey to another person. While Wittgenstein posits the question, he rejects, if not the possibility of the existence of such a language, the means by which to discuss it. Here, the *Investigations*'s spatiality, its view from within, does not end in transgression of language but ponders and encircles it. The transgression of language it suggests is more difficult to imagine, no less to achieve, from within language. Yet the question, once asked, persists. In effect, this concern posits a new unsayable, a new realm of silence, although one unlike that of the *Tractatus* in that it is no longer definitive of the showable and therefore cannot even be pointed to from within language—even as a transgression of sense. Instead the *Investigations* remains enfixed not in position but within the inner workings of language that define and come about through intersubjective practice, marking the inner/outer connection fundamental to the apprehending and envisioning of language.

Comparably, interior workings and connections pervade the Stonborough-Wittgenstein House to redefine or relocate the interior/exterior association as a complex network of interior/interior associations. The interior/exterior connection emerges, then, as akin to this series of interior connections rather than as fundamentally different from them. The boundaries forming the inner/outer relations raise a series of concerns that emerge in the practice of architecture. In the architectural design process, the inner/outer relation frequently exhibits a surprising lack of coincidence that makes visible previously nonapparent dissociations. The effect exposes the inner/outer relation to be less transparent than it initially seems. Engaging in the practice of architecture ultimately dismantles an assured idea of a one-to-one correlation of interior and exterior. This finding is not unlike the relation between a word and meaning that Wittgenstein develops in the *Investigations*, where the association is less of direct correspondence and more of an intricate and internal hook that extends beyond the limitations of an isolated word.

In a deceptively simple building such as the Stonborough-Wittgenstein House, the relation across a wall from interior to exterior or between interior spaces appears to form direct correspondences. Alignment would seemingly result from the sheer act of coincidence. But that is not always the case, as with, for example, the attempt to construct a symmetric, centered window in the breakfast room on both interior and exterior elevations. Here problems arise due to the thickness of the wall and the location of exterior perpendicular walls that disrupt the symmetry of adjoining spaces. In this instance, in order to maintain symmetry on the interior, Wittgenstein had to project a section of the window wall into the interior to account for the perpendicular wall on the exterior that determines the outside frame of reference and centerline of the window. Inside, the projection along the wall creates an equal length of wall on either side of the window. This move allows both interior and exterior placement of the window to be in the center of the section of the wall each defines. As this complex and compromising situation repeats in various ways throughout the Stonborough-Wittgenstein House, it needs to be recognized as common to the practice of architecture rather than a unique situation.

In its formation and inhabitation, the Stonborough-Wittgenstein House necessitates a continual series of shifts from the asymmetry of the overall plan to the localized symmetry of many of the spaces, rooms, and surfaces. The overall massing or form of the house initiates this condition. Viewed from the front, the house is composed of a main central section flanked by two not quite symmetric wings extending to terraces on either side. Although replicating comparable formal aspects of one another, the terraces further extend the house's overall asymmetry because one terrace is oriented forward toward the front of the house and the other one is rotated outward toward its side.

Movement through the house continually shifts from localized symmetries to overall asymmetry. Commencing about the point of entry, the oscillation between these two spatial principles takes form as a series of asymmetrical moves and reciprocal acts instituted to create or restore local symmetries. This occurs with the elevations (both interior and exterior) and in the plans. The series of shifts and moves begins from the outside with the creation of a projecting entry that disrupts the symmetry of the front elevation, displacing the door and entry section from alignment with the window grid above. This slippage disrupts the symmetry and regularity of the left bay as well as the entire front facade. Upon entering the house, the entry's underlying centrality is manifest. While from the exterior the center of the doors occupies the left bay, on the interior the entry aligns with the center of the U-shaped main hall that envelops it. The projecting entry thus creates a situation of asymmetry from the outside, while the front doors centered within it restore local symmetry to the entry and the interior. The restored centrality of the entrance resonates through the house, setting up the interior central axis. Repositioning the entrance block while accentuating the asymmetry of the exterior simultaneously aligns the front doors with the center of the interior and removes them from the regularity of the facade's grid of windows. The result of this one move is therefore to disengage or dislocate about the point of entry the exterior centerline of the building from that of the interior. This accumulation of moves defies an overall principle, producing in its place a series of specific locations.

The conflict between the overall asymmetry of the house and desired localized symmetries within it required that Wittgenstein devise a series of adjustments comparable to the thinking he employed in centering the breakfast-room window on both interior and exterior elevations. For example, Wittgenstein introduced a structurally unnecessary column in the library along the same wall as a structural one in order to ensure a symmetric elevation on the north wall of the room. Another example occurs with the markings and orientation of the flooring grid. The flooring material found throughout the ground floor is a poured artificial stone that allows for subdivisions in any manner desired. The joints in the flooring at times suggest a ground plane that spreads out beyond the dividing walls while at other times they clearly demarcate individual rooms (fig. 15). When the grid is not coincident with or contained by the walls, as in the library, it implies a continual ground plane extending beyond the specific room. That suggestion, however, is deceptive. The floor grids, in fact, are always room- or area-specific, employed to produce, extend, or emphasize spatial relations. The grids change in alignment, pattern size, and shape from room to room in order to mark local centers of doors or align with windows and other openings. At one extreme of the variations produced, the central hall presents the most unique and complex grid pattern, marking, among other things, some of the only visible structure in the house. By comparison, at the other extreme is the floor of the hallway above, which, although of the same material, is entirely undelineated, as if there were no associations to mark whatsoever, not even forward progression along its path.

While the central hall is in many ways the focus of the house, it is not the house's only center. Instead, the plans suggest the construction of multiple centers that further the oscillation from symmetry to asymmetry, both formally and conceptually. Both the central hall and the salon occupy complex positions as simultaneous programmatic, conceptual, and spatial centers within the house. The salon parallels the importance and functioning of the central hall. From the central hall, the salon's importance is clear, as it is distinguished by the metal doors connecting the two spaces. Located between the entry hall, the library, the southwestern terrace, and Margarethe Stonborough-Wittgenstein's private rooms, the salon acts as an even more internal, competing center, distributor of space, and datum

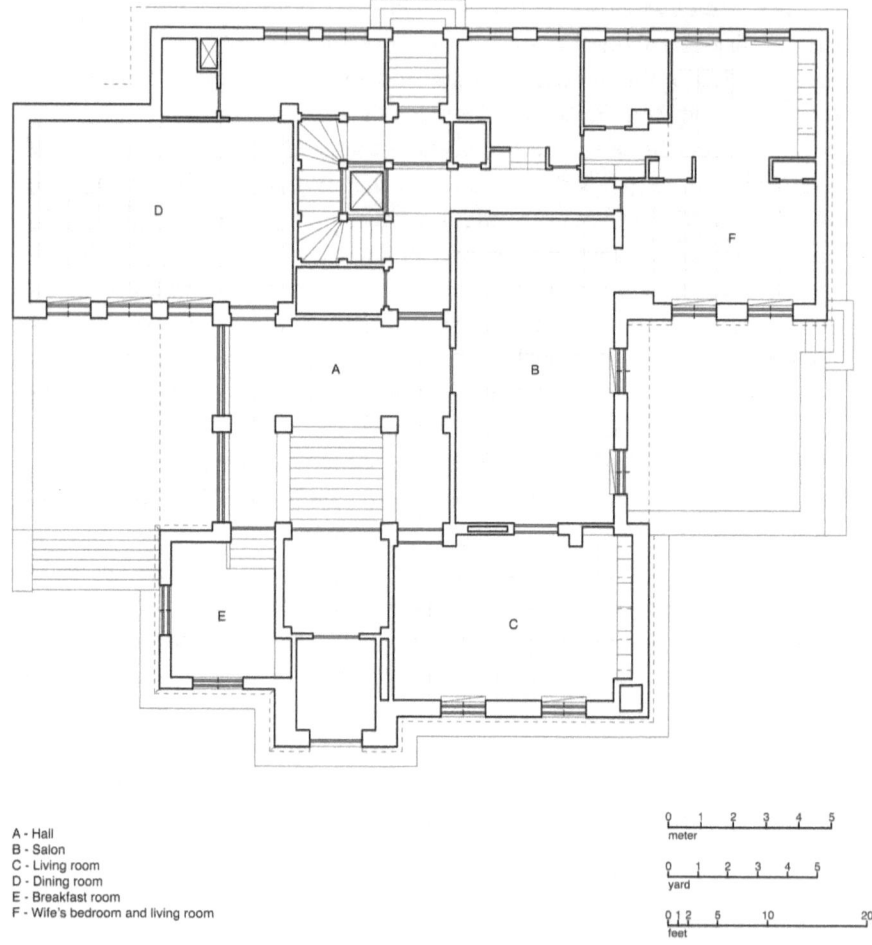

A - Hall
B - Salon
C - Living room
D - Dining room
E - Breakfast room
F - Wife's bedroom and living room

Figure 15. Stonborough-Wittgenstein House: plan of the ground floor showing the pattern of the joints on the floor. Illustrator: North Keeragool.

of meaning. And this is perhaps why it needs to be separated so definitively by the metal doors from the central hall. As much as variations of glass and light define the hall and movement through it, the datum material of the salon is metal, which contrasts sharply with the glass to form an interior/exterior distinction even at the crucial juncture of the public/private relation with the entry doors to Margarethe's private rooms. All the metal doors in the salon mark interior connections—to the central hall, to the library, and to Margarethe's private rooms—while glass doors are used to lead from the salon to the southwestern terrace in the same manner in which they are used throughout the ground floor.

Other spaces in the house exhibit to a lesser extent some of these "connective" properties, with Margarethe's private living room also acting as a connection between her private rooms, their internal corridor, the salon, and the terrace. Her private living room is already once removed from the centrality or publicness of the hall or the salon, although this all changes on the upper floors, with any central space or sense of connection severely limited to the hallway running down the literal center of the building and leading to the stair-elevator at one end, the main room at the other, and a series of private rooms and storage spaces along both sides.

Similar decisions intended to establish and reestablish local symmetries and alignments occur throughout the design of the house, with the rearranging of rooms on the ground floor and the reproportioning of those rooms, windows, and exterior elevations. Importantly, such localized associations and relations are experienced differently from a totally symmetric plan (or the use of a map to find one's way). Rather, in being localized, symmetry is encountered in specific locations from *within* the rooms or spaces. An entirely symmetric plan instead would not be as readily experienced to its full extent but would exist largely in plan or in conceptual reconstructions that act as if the entire house is seen from beyond and above. As if to make this clear, the central hall, while largely symmetric about its long axis in plan, is asymmetric when comparing its two long elevations, with one wall composed of glass and leading visually and spatially outdoors and the other a solid wall containing metal doors leading to an unseen room.

Beyond the specific aspects and resolutions of these conditions, these issues point to the design problems Wittgenstein would have faced as an architect. This situation emerges in some of the discussions of Wittgenstein's architectural work, which are curiously written as if the writers were themselves confronting architectural problems for the first time. As a result they find Wittgenstein's concerns with such issues as the aligning of the joints in the floor with the center lines of doors and windows to be particularly striking or unusual. It is not, however, that these concepts—alignment, boundary, proportion, materials, and so on—are such profound or unusual activities or issues arising from the design and construction processes, *but exactly that they are typical of the architectural design process.* It is this set of problems, occurring and recurring at various levels from floor plans to construction details, that repeatedly confront

Wittgenstein in the practice of architecture; *in spatializing his understanding of limits, boundaries, relations, practice, and correspondence, these problems literally define a place from which Wittgenstein could reconsider the limits and functioning of language and philosophy.* The movement through space and the disposition of use that fostered the reconsideration of the relation of the visual and the spatial, complex associations and identities, and so on, reveals again and again how *spatial concepts cannot be discarded to leave philosophical problems intact.* It is this understanding that underlies the creation of a practice-based philosophy by showing that spatial problems share territory with traditional philosophical problems in logic and epistemology as well as aesthetics. It is out of the reworking of that shared territory that Wittgenstein came to reconceive language and philosophy.

In providing examples of the functioning of language in the *Investigations,* spatial issues and problems are consequently offered as an inseparable part of the language itself in exactly the same way that all meanings of a word or examples of a practice contribute to our understanding of a word, concept, or spatial construct. As Wittgenstein tells us when he offers these examples, often without further explanation, he does not offer less than he knows himself. Rather, offering the spatial examples as one of the ways in which he knows language to function, Wittgenstein is revealing not just what he himself knows but the ways in which he came to apprehend these concepts. This includes the understanding that the linguistic and the spatial are inseparable, although, importantly, not identical.

PART TWO

IMAGES OF ENTANGLEMENT

This entanglement in our rules is what we want to understand (i.e. get a clear view of).—*Philosophical Investigations*, sec. 125

Images of Entanglement

There are several terms readily associated with the *Philosophical Investigations*: ordinary language, family resemblance, language-games, practice, the private language argument, and rule-following. There is also a series of images associated with the *Investigations*, although they are not often mentioned as such. A number of these images—the overlapping fibers that form the thread of family resemblance, the depiction of an immobilized Wittgenstein stuck out on an extended plane of frozen ice, the delicate spiderweb that the philosopher's crude fingers are incapable of repairing, the crystalline purity of logical structure, and the endlessly crisscrossing paths used to describe both language and our engagement with it—form what I call "images of entanglement."

Images of entanglement can be understood as a specific series of what Wittgenstein designates in the preface as landscape sketches. These are sites in which the enmeshment of associations that Wittgenstein brings together in the *Investigations* coalesces into a specific image. They are spatial configurations made manifest through the processes of philosophical investigation. Wittgenstein employs images of entanglement to define the reconceived spaces, practices, methods, structures, and contents of the text. Beginning with their protoformation in Wittgenstein's 1929 lecture on ethics[1] and developed extensively in the *Investigations*, these constructs are repeatedly posited by Wittgenstein to describe, structure, initiate, and investigate the functioning and image of language.

Entanglement emerges in the *Investigations* most succinctly in two interrelated passages: the assertion in section 125[2] that: "This entanglement in our rules is what we want to understand (i.e. get a clear view of)" and the statement a page earlier, in section 122, wherein Wittgenstein outlines the conditions for such a clear view: "A main source of our failure to understand is that we do not command a clear view of the use of our words.— Our grammar is lacking in this sort of perspicuity. A perspicuous representation produces just that understanding which consists in 'seeing connexions.'" Together these two passages call for the construction of clear images of entanglement or, rather more precisely, clear constructions or views of the entanglement with our own rules that pertain not solely to philosophy but to the whole of the workings of language. The unexpected union of clarity and entanglement developed in these passages is definitive of the work of the *Investigations* in its aim to describe the phenomena of language through a depiction of its complex surface. No concept is more definitive and emblematic of this involvement than Wittgenstein's concept of family resemblance.

Family Resemblance

The first suggestion of an image of entanglement occurs in the untitled 1929 lecture on ethics that Wittgenstein delivered to a popular Cambridge society known as the Heretics.[3] The lecture was issued shortly after Wittgenstein's return to philosophy following the completion of the Stonborough-Wittgenstein House. In it, Wittgenstein presents an early (proto) version of his as-yet-unnamed concept of family resemblance. To enable his description of ethics, Wittgenstein refers in the lecture to Sir Francis Galton's experiments in composite photography, combining multiple images onto a single photographic plate. Wittgenstein introduces the composite images as a model for the reexamination of G. E. Moore's description of ethics. Subsequently, in the *Investigations*, Wittgenstein develops this image into a model not just of ethics but of the functioning of meaningful language. The image of entanglement introduced here serves another purpose as well: it stitches together Wittgenstein's philosophical and architectural developments, beginning with his early philosophy, via the words of G. E. Moore on ethics and continuing through the introduction of spatial imagery. This process allows Wittgenstein to transform Moore's approach by introducing an aesthetic and spatial principle to produce the underlying determinant of his late philosophy of language.

The use of Moore as a stand-in for his Wittgenstein's own earlier thinking sets another practice in motion because it presages Wittgenstein's later use of Augustine's words to begin the *Investigations*. In both cases Wittgenstein implements the narrow views of others (which he proceeds to broaden) as a form of distancing or estranging from his own earlier thinking—a view of his own philosophy from a new position. The lecture on ethics introduces this process as its starting point:

> I will now begin. My subject, as you know is Ethics and I will adopt the explanation of that term which Professor Moore has given in his book *Principia Ethica*. He says: "Ethics is the general enquiry into what is good." Now I am going to use the term Ethics in a slightly wider sense, in a sense in fact which includes what I believe to be the most essential part of what is generally called Aesthetics. And to make you see as clearly as possible what I take to be the subject matter of Ethics I will put before you a number of more or less synonymous expressions each of which could be substituted for the above definition, and by enumerating them I want to produce the same sort of effect which Galton produced when he took a number of photos of different faces on the same photographic plate in order to get the picture of the typical features they all had in common. And as by showing to you such a collective photo I could make you see what is the typical—say—Chinese face; so if you look through the row of synonyms which I will put before you, you will, I hope, be able to see the characteristic features of Ethics. Now instead of saying "Ethics is the enquiry into what is good" I could have said Ethics is the enquiry into what is valuable, or into what is really important, or I could have said Ethics is the enquiry into the meaning of life, or into what makes life worth living, or into the right way of living. I believe if you look at all these phrases you will get a rough idea as to what it is that Ethics is concerned with.[4]

With these opening remarks, the lecture transposes Galton's method of composite photography to philosophy in order to provide a model for the reexamination of Moore's definitive statement concerning ethics. The importation of Galton's process is central to this endeavor. Its introduction likens the ability of a single collective photograph combining, in this instance, Chinese people's faces to stand as an example of a "typical" Chinese face with the ability of a single expression to account for the range of what is called "ethics." The comparison to Galton's photographic experiments widens the characterization of ethics by envisioning it through the lens or workings of an aesthetic practice. Wittgenstein's inclusion of Galton's photographs achieves more, however, than an expansion of Moore's explanation of "ethics." Rather, the example opens up entirely new possibilities for both ethics and language by absorbing this transformative practice into philosophy.

Francis Galton was a British statistician and inventor of the term "eugenics" whose composite photographs were first published in 1877. While Galton's work was widely propagated and received great honors for more than three decades, it was discredited following World War II because of Hitler's use of eugenic theories. Galton's aim in developing this form of photography had been to construct a series of composite photographs of given "types" of people in order to produce archives of essentialist physiognomies of race, class, religion, disease, and criminality (fig. 16). His method involved placing successive exposures of the individuals in the sample group onto a single photographic plate. Each exposure time was the inverse of the total number of exposures so that if there were nine total images combined on one plate, for example, each exposure would receive one-ninth of the total exposure time. Galton employed this process in an attempt to identify the essential physiological characteristics associated with each group. The process was designed to emphasize the features common to the sample group, since such features would receive greater combined exposure time, and simultaneously to deemphasize or even

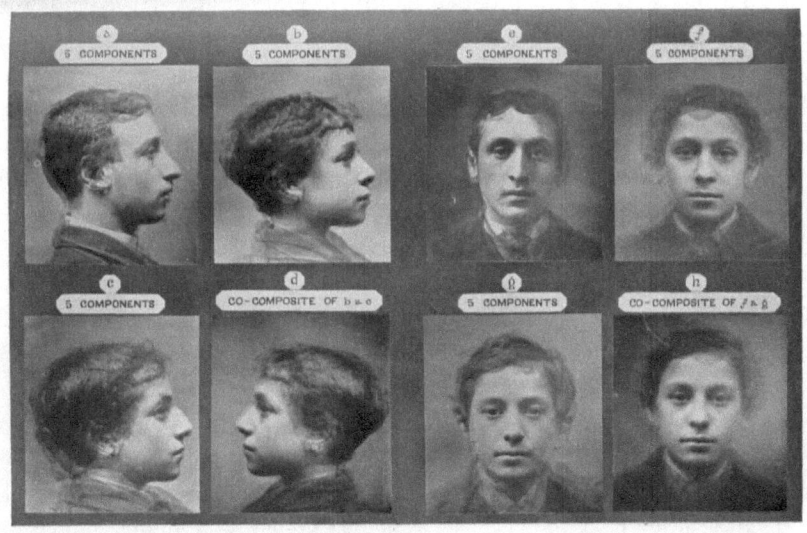

Figure 16. "The Jewish Type." Photographer: Sir Francis Galton, from Karl Pearson, *Researches of Middle Life*, vol. 2 of *The Life, Letters and Labours of Francis Galton* (London: Cambridge University Press, 1924), plate 35.

drop out more unusual or idiosyncratic characteristics that would receive insufficient exposure time to be clearly visible. Wittgenstein's use of Galton's method as an example, however, functions differently. As Galton's search was for that which was essential or biologically determined in a given group of people, his goal was to identify physiologically apparent characteristics. However, the superimposition of photographic images yielded not a typical face with clearly defined "essential" features but a somewhat blurred one. So while there are clearly emphasized features, those features themselves are not clearly defined.

Galton's method differed from Wittgenstein's employment of it in a crucial way. Whereas Galton began with multiple samples and concluded with a single, essential one, Wittgenstein reversed that process by commencing with Moore's definitive expression of ethics and expanding it into a multitude of related expressions. The model Galton offers Wittgenstein is therefore not strictly one of method or goal but of image. That is, Wittgenstein was not repeating Galton's essentialist practice but reconceiving it. Wittgenstein tells us in the lecture on ethics that he wanted to achieve the same sort of *effect* as Galton's photographs by substituting multiple expressions for Moore's sole one. As Galton's process ultimately blurs, at least to some extent, the sharpest of features, Wittgenstein's aim in following this model is not to produce definitive essence, or at least not the exacting quality of essence associated with the *Tractatus*. This is part of what Wittgenstein claims in the lecture regarding ethics, explaining that despite their appearance of producing definitive statements or facts that define the world of the *Tractatus,* statements of ethics, in producing and expressing values that appear as facts (as does Moore's definition), remain indeterminate. They are blurred compared to the precise nature of facts. It is that characteristic or aspect which places statements of ethics beyond the realm of the sayable in the *Tractatus*. The blur then becomes of interest in its suggestion not of essence but of the nonabsolute realm of values and practice. Importantly, however, Galton's blur emerges not out of a lack of clarity of characteristics but out of the attempt to yield one essential or definitive set of features. Wittgenstein's use of these photographs as a model, conjoined with the series of ethical statement substitutions he offers, implies the ability to enact in words exactly what he states in the *Tractatus* cannot be done: to say what he had previously thought could only be shown, the realm of values and practice. And Wittgenstein's conjoining visual images with the series of statements makes this clear in his uniting aesthetics, ethics, and philosophical propositions.

The broadening of an absolute statement on ethics signals a significant movement beyond the proscribed thinking of the *Tractatus* that had barred such an extended discussion on the topic of ethics. As is the case in the *Tractatus*, despite some of what Wittgenstein himself says, his interest in presenting a lecture on ethics to a popular audience immediately succeeding his return to philosophy—and directly following his practice of architecture—says what he could find no way to speak about directly in the *Tractatus*. The lecture thus initiates the remaking of the boundaries of the *Tractatus* to open up a new realm of philosophical enquiry for Wittgenstein through the introduction of the proto-image of entanglement implicit in Galton's composite photography. That new philosophical realm resides within the meaningful functioning of entanglement, developed fully in the *Investigations* as the constitutive linguistic concept of family resemblance. By framing the discussion with the constructs of vision, spatiality, and language, family resemblance as it originates in Wittgenstein's use of the Galton example moves beyond permitting the discussion of ethics. Galton's example, after all, is not a simple visual one but, in its bringing multiple and ambiguous images together, literally forms a spatial, visual, and temporal collapse.

Wittgenstein's reliance on Galton's composite photographs as a model or method by which to reimage Moore's statement on ethics and later in his development of family resemblance inscribes both aesthetics and ethics into the core of his philosophy of language. Rather than exiling statements on ethics, as he had in the *Tractatus*, the lecture on ethics begins by positioning statements comprising "ethics" within language and within philosophy. Underlying and instigating this shift is Wittgenstein's insertion of a visual practice—Galton's visual search for biological essence—as the formative principle for redefining a philosophical-linguistic undertaking. This approach is in many ways the flip side of the *Tractatus*'s attempt to define the scope of sensible language by setting limits "to what cannot be thought by working outwards through what can be thought." What this suggests is that the *Tractatus* is in effect as much about ethics and the realm of the unsayable as it is about its more explicit topical discussions. Given this, it is important to note that Wittgenstein associates ethics and aesthetics in the *Tractatus* not because they share subject matter but by virtue of the method through which they are constituted in language or, more precisely, by their being beyond sensible language in their producing models in contrast to the functioning of facts:

6.421 It is clear that ethics cannot be put into words.
Ethics is transcendental.
(Ethics and aesthetics are one and the same.)

Although Wittgenstein's lecture on ethics initially appears to be mired in the same concerns of language, boundaries, facts, nonsense, and ethics that Wittgenstein presented in the *Tractatus*, there are several important distinctions between the *Tractatus* and the 1929 lecture.

Consider, for example, the conclusion to the lecture:

I see now that these nonsensical expressions were not nonsensical because I had not yet found the correct expressions, but that their nonsensicality was their very essence. For all I wanted to do with them was just *to go beyond* the world and that is to say beyond significant language. My whole tendency and I believe the tendency of all men who ever tried to write or talk Ethics or Religion was to run against the boundaries of language. This running against the walls of our cage is perfectly, absolutely hopeless. Ethics so far as it springs from the desire to say something about the ultimate meaning of life, the absolute good, the absolute valuable, can be no science. What it says does not add to our knowledge in any sense. But it is a document of a tendency in the human mind which I personally cannot help respecting deeply and I would not for my life ridicule it.

In referring to the boundaries of language, philosophy, sense, ethics, and so on, the lecture's closing remarks suggest a crucial aspect enabling the transformation of the role and understanding of ethics in philosophy. It is at this moment that Wittgenstein inserts the key element by which ethics/aesthetics can become a model for the functioning of language in the *Investigations*: the spatial concept of boundary. While the *Tractatus*'s rigid structure disallows such an undertaking, remaking the concept of boundary along with the boundaries of language themselves permits for the derivation of a perspicuous entanglement within language in the *Investigations*.

It is concerning this reformation of boundaries that Galton's composite images have their greatest influence. In the "Lecture on Ethics," Galton's photographs combine with ethics and its multiple and unplaceable meanings both to challenge the concept of boundary in the *Tractatus* and to dislodge entrenched boundaries themselves. As a result, Galton's images emerge at the root of Wittgenstein's late philosophy of language. In redefining and resituating that which had been marginalized, even evicted from the sphere of sensible language in the *Tractatus,* the "Lecture on Ethics" resurrects those arenas as the (as yet unacknowledged) core of linguistic expansion in the *Investigations.* The *Investigations*'s extension of the use and importance of the ideas of association in Galton's photographs thereby takes what is initially presented as a model for depicting "ethics" to become the model for the overlapping of not just expressions, but practices and meaning. Wittgenstein gives the name "family resemblance" to this, recalling and reassociating genetic traits but, importantly, without continuing Galton's goal of producing essence.

Family resemblance coalesces in the *Investigations* to characterize the relationship between the various meanings and uses of a word or the various kinds of words that comprise language. The idea of family resemblance is introduced and summarized in sections 66 and 67 of the text. The description begins—as does Wittgenstein's introduction of the Galton model—with the visual, in this instance by literally looking at a wide range of the practices designated "games" and demanding that the reader do the same. In this endeavor, Wittgenstein cautions the reader not to proceed with a preexistent idea of how language functions. "Don't say: 'There *must* be something common, or they would not all be called "games"'—but *look and see* whether there is anything common to all." In enacting this examination, Wittgenstein leads the reader through a heterogeneous set of everyday practices comprising games. His concern here is that we not overlook seemingly dissimilar uses of a word by requiring in advance that they all exhibit a common essence or element. This approach underlies Wittgenstein's shift from a focus on linguistic terms to an examination of the practices in which we encounter and employ those terms. His opening description of that which we call "game" as "proceedings" is testament to the emphasis on practice, as is his choice of the word "game." As such, Wittgenstein presents "game" as a visual survey of the everyday sites where the word is encountered:

> 66. Consider for example the proceedings that we call "games." I mean board-games, card-games, ball-games, Olympic games, and so on. What is common to them all?—Don't say: "There *must* be something common, or they would not all be called 'games'—but *look and see* whether there is anything common to all.—For if you look at them you will not see something that is common to all, but similarities, relationships, and a whole series of them at that. To repeat: don't think, but look!—Look for example at board-games, with their multifarious relationships. Now pass to card-games; here you find many correspondences with the first group, but

many common features drop out, and others appear. When we pass next to ball games, much that is common is retained, but much is lost.—Are they all "amusing"? Compare chess with noughts and crosses. Or is there always winning and losing or competition between players? Think of patience. In ball games there is winning and losing; but when a child throws his ball at the wall and catches it again, this feature has disappeared. Look at the parts played by skill and luck; and at the difference between skill in chess and skill in tennis. Think now of games like ring-a-ring-a-roses; here is the element of amusement, but how many other characteristic features have disappeared! And we can go through the many, many other groups of games in the same way; can see how similarities crop up and disappear.

And the result of this examination is: we see a complicated network of similarities overlapping and criss-crossing: sometimes overall similarities, sometimes similarities of detail.

67. I can think of no better expression to characterize these similarities than "family resemblances"; for the various resemblances between members of a family, build, features, color of eyes, gait, temperament, etc. etc. overlap and criss-cross in the same way.—And I shall say: "games" form a family.

And for instance, the kinds of number form a family in the same way. Why do we call something a "number"? Well, perhaps because it has a—direct—relationship with several things that have hitherto been called number; and this can be said to give it an indirect relationship to other things we call the same name. And we extend our concept of number as in spinning a thread we twist fibre on fibre. And the strength of the thread does not reside in the fact that some one fibre runs through its whole length, but in the overlapping of many fibres.

But if someone wished to say: "There is something common to all these constructions—namely the disjunction of all their common properties"—I should reply: Now you are only playing with words. One might as well say: "Something runs through the whole thread—namely the continuous overlapping of those fibres."

Wittgenstein's illustration of game is telling, both in its obviously being a practice and in its association with the other paradigmatic appearance of "game" in the *Investigations*—the concept of language-game first introduced into the text through the builders' language. In the opening pages of the book, Wittgenstein tells us that he uses these language-games to serve as models or examples of how we use language. The presentation of language-games to our view is the cardinal philosophical method Wittgenstein advances in the *Investigations,* describing it as the fundamental way in which we apprehend and explain the operations of words and concepts. Importantly, in the introduction of the concept of family resemblance through the example of games, Wittgenstein inscribes a socially and conventionally constructed practice rather than some naturally determined notion of essence such as that upon which Galton based his (failed) research. This supposition reappears in Wittgenstein's correlated examples of language and language-games that similarly reject essence in favor of socially constructed, publicly (and visually) accessible meaning.

The concept of family resemblance enters Wittgenstein's philosophy not simply to explain the multiplicity of meanings and operations associated with a given word or expression but also to describe how the "whole" of language can be deemed meaningful without dependence on a single common aspect. That is, family resemblance offers a model of an intelligible language that is not dependent upon any essential aspect or form. This can be directly contrasted to the example of the ladder in the *Tractatus.* Whereas the ladder's two upright posts run throughout the entirety of the ladder literally to enframe and structure it, the fibers forming the twine do not. The fibers describe and form the structure of the twine but do not envelop it. Consequently the search for the general form of propositions that preoccupied Wittgenstein in the *Tractatus* is literally misguided, because it probes for something not there to be found:

> 65. Here we come up against the great question that lies behind all these considerations.—For someone might object against me: "You take the easy way out! You talk about all sorts of language-games, but have nowhere said what the essence of a language-game, and hence of language, is: what is common to all these activities, and what makes them into language or parts of language. So you let yourself off the very part of the investigation that once gave you yourself most headache, the part about the general form of propositions and of language."
>
> And this is true.—Instead of producing something common to all that we call language, I am saying that these phenomena have no one thing in common which makes us use the same word for all,—but that they are *related* to one another in many different ways. And it is because of this relationship, or these relationships, that we call them all "language."

As the overarching image of language, family resemblance becomes the primary image of entanglement driving Wittgenstein's late philosophy.

Through the entwining of meaning with practice, as in the multiple and inseparable uses of a word and in the image of the fibers of the thread itself, family resemblance produces an image in sharp contrast to the *Tractatus*'s hierarchical and discrete depiction of language and philosophical thought as a ladder. The *Tractatus*'s language, in being separate from the world it depicts, leaves the early philosophy in search of a hook to connect language to the world, and the hook it developed was an ineffable logic—a logic at odds with the visible surface of language explored in the *Investigations*. The connectivity attributed to and required of logic in the *Tractatus* becomes transformed in the *Investigations* as the entangled spatiovisual practice of family resemblance. Throughout the *Investigations*, family resemblance emerges in discussions of the practices of reading, calculating, rule-following, agreement, boundaries, and the image of entanglement itself. In a particularly telling example, the concept of family resemblance is employed to unite the meaning of one word with another, as in the interwoven practices of "agreement" and "rule" that rather than directly correspond, are described by Wittgenstein in familial terms as "cousins":

> 224. The word "agreement" and the word "rule" are *related* to one another, they are cousins. If I teach anyone the use of the one word, he learns the use of the other with it.

> 225. The use of the word "rule" and the use of the word "same" are interwoven. (As are the use of "proposition" and the use of "true.")

Beginning with the example of "games" and quickly becoming an example for all of language, the construct of family resemblance spreads throughout the text to produce a wide-ranging series of examples. As such, the example of family resemblance remains the most precisely defined yet far-reaching of the images of entanglement Wittgenstein produces. Whereas other images of entanglement arise within specific discussions, family resemblance quickly becomes the guiding principle for the reexamination and reimaging of language itself.

Family resemblance proves more than descriptive; it is generative as well. Examples of images of entanglement emanating from family resemblance proliferate throughout the text as if to act out in various ways family resemblance's practices of associating, interweaving, overlapping, appearing, disappearing, and reappearing that are first presented in the observing of games. The resulting spatiovisual constructs bring forth the specifics of these interactions, the delicacy of connections, and the attempt to capture these potentially fleeting images. Additionally, Wittgenstein offers a number of possibilities for producing such images: the landscape sketches, the frames for viewing them, the labyrinth of paths, the mechanisms for collecting and assembling reminders, and the construction of an album in which to record these events and provide a basis for further observation. The final challenge presented for images of entanglement is to navigate the newly constructed notion of boundary and boundary practices they help to introduce, and with that, the shared territory in which they reside—that is, sites in which to survey and incorporate their own spatial territory.

The Landscape of Language

The *Tractatus*'s closing image of the ladder is replaced at the onset of the *Investigations* by the image of the landscape and its associated landscape sketches introduced in the preface. That transformation from the vertical, hierarchical, and iterative rungs of the ladder to the horizontal, expanded, and unbounded landscape is indicative of the development from the *Tractatus* to the *Investigations*.

Wittgenstein uses the image of the landscape to describe the *Investigations*'s endeavors. In the preface to the *Investigations*, Wittgenstein posits two analogies as a means of explaining the text that follows. The first analogy obtains between the investigations of language and a series of "long and involved journeyings," "criss-cross in every direction." The second navigates the territory between the "philosophical remarks" that form the book and "a number of sketches of landscapes" made during those journeys. Together these analogies equate philosophical, specifically Wittgensteinian investigations to the sketches and language to the landscape the sketches traverse.

Rather than seeing the text as a final version of a single sketch, Wittgenstein describes the text of the *Investigations* as a collection and "arrangement" of these landscape sketches that together offer a "picture of the landscape." This recognition of the fragmentary nature of the enterprise leads Wittgenstein to the conclusion that the book "is really only an album." The sketches themselves are presented in much the same manner in which the structuring of the remarks that comprise the text is, with a comparable concern for how each is formed into an interrelated whole.

Introducing the question of how and when the sketches are produced, the criteria by which they are judged, the practices by which they are combined, the rejections, repetitions, editings, croppings, arrangement, and rearrangement they require provides the tools for examining how the landscape sketches describe the surface of language. As with the example of the builders who inseparably intertwine the learning and the use of language, Wittgenstein here emphasizes the inseparability of the processes of philosophy from what they produce. Accordingly, discussing the processes by which the sketches come into being proves essential to perceiving how they constitute a philosophical study of language and philosophy. This self-reflective description of the philosophy of the *Investigations* thereby posits a literal image of the text: its formal order of a series of short paragraphs or remarks. Notably these short paragraphs do not build upon one another directly in a predetermined manner, as do the rungs up the ladder, but provide another spatial model:

> The thoughts which I publish in what follows are the precipitate of philosophical investigations which have occupied me for the last sixteen years. They concern many subjects: the concepts of meaning, of understanding, of a proposition, of logic, the foundations of mathematics, states of consciousness, and other things. I have written down all of these thoughts as *remarks*, short paragraphs, of which there is sometimes a fairly long chain about the same subject, while I sometimes make a sudden change, jumping from one topic to another.—It was my intention at first to bring all this together in a book whose form I pictured differently at different times. But the essential thing was that the thoughts should proceed from one subject to another in a natural order and without breaks.
>
> After several attempts to weld my results together into such a whole, I realized that I should never succeed. The best that I could write would never be more than philosophical remarks; my thoughts were soon crippled if I tried to force them on in any single direction against their natural inclination.—And this was, of course, connected with the very nature of the investigation. For this compels us to travel over a wide field of thought criss-cross in every direction.—The philosophical remarks in this book are, as it were, a number of sketches of landscapes which were made in the course of these long and involved journeyings.
>
> The same or almost the same points were always being approached afresh from different directions, and new sketches made. Very many of these were badly drawn or uncharacteristic, marked by all the defects of a weak draughtsman. And when they were rejected a number of tolerable

ones were left, which now had to be arranged and sometimes cut down, so that if you looked at them you could get a picture of the landscape. Thus this book is only an album.[5]

Through the intimate association intertwined between landscape sketches and viewer (or draftsperson), Wittgenstein from the start inculcates spatial thinking to define and later to achieve his philosophical objectives. The importance of apprehending language as a landscape is twofold: first, it builds upon the landscape's implied inclusivity so as to define the investigation of language from within. And second, the avowed need to traverse the landscape, criss-crossed in every direction, in order to see and experience it insists that both language and the *Investigations* cannot simply be "understood" but must be reenacted by the reader in order to be known. The landscape sketches delineate a practice and can only be understood as such. In practice the metaphor of the landscape and the journeying through it to produce the sketches inherently requires the entry of a subject into language and philosophy that had been barred from the *Tractatus*.

The image of the landscape set up by the preface engages the study of language at definitive junctures within the body of the text, most succinctly in Wittgenstein's directly equating the landscape with language:

> 203. Language is a labyrinth of paths: you approach from *one* side and know your way about; you approach the same place from another side and no longer know your way about.

Landscape sketches and the depicted landscape itself, as metaphors for the relation between viewer and language or between language user and terrain, each combine spatial, visual, and verbal components. The spatial organizations they suggest, however, are of essentially opposing kinds, because the implied subject is positioned in relation to each in dissimilar ways. While a sketch is something we view from the outside, a pictorial image with defined boundaries, the landscape itself is not contained. Sketches, as a particular type of image, also suggest a rough rather than finished drawing or description, potentially preliminary or preparatory to future work. Wittgenstein's discussion of the sketches' dependence on a "draughtsman" reinforces the association between the viewer and practice in the construction of language, unifying the two through the act of making sense rather than finding it. The landscape, on the other hand, is three-dimensional; it is something we are or can be in. It surrounds the viewer with no defined boundaries—or perhaps no boundaries at all. Presenting the landscape as a two-dimensional image by depicting it, as in the landscape sketches, necessarily creates boundaries that limit the view of the landscape. Altering the viewer's position in relation to the landscape by moving through it—here by continually producing new sketches or multiple ones of the same place—overcomes some of those limitations. Integrally binding together acts of viewing, subjects, the processes of depiction, and the landscape of language in the construction of the text and the continuous construction of new images defines the work of Wittgenstein's *Investigations*.

As much as Wittgenstein's remarks in the preface to the *Investigations* are directed at the writing of the text, they function equally as remarks about how to read the *Investigations*. These quasi-instructions focus on the written components and their structuring into a whole in relation to the subjects of study. This can be seen in the preface's not opening with the image of a landscape but by describing the (seemingly) literal organization of the *Investigations*, stating that the book is composed of "remarks" or "short paragraphs, of which there is at times a fairly long chain about the same subject" with sporadic jumps from one topic to another. This description itself is interrupted by what Wittgenstein refers to as his "previous" intention of "welding" the results of these investigations into a unity in which his thoughts would "proceed from one subject to another in a natural order and without breaks." In acknowledging his failure to achieve this goal, Wittgenstein finds instead that his "thoughts were soon crippled" if he tried to force them in any "single direction against their natural inclination." This admission leads to the conclusion that this result "was of course, connected with the very nature of the investigation." It is at this crucial point—where the "very nature of the investigation" comes into contact with the method of investigation—that Wittgenstein's writing turns to analogy and metaphor, and he begins to speak of landscapes and sketches.

In addition to providing a useful metaphor for understanding the text, the analogies of the landscape that Wittgenstein employs also spatialize the process of philosophical investigation. This spatialization engenders what began with an attempted linear ordering of subject matter more akin to the *Tractatus* and concern for potential disruptions in the unity of thought to culminate with the construction of an extended horizontal network of investigation. In so doing, the analogies to the landscape restructure the text in their ability to provide a newly made model for meaning as well as site for study. Through this spatial framework, Wittgenstein replaces the linear, vertical, fixed, and hierarchical *Tractatus* with a complex and interwoven network of thought, language, meaning, images, and practices.

Wittgenstein's declaration of the need to move through the landscape in a crisscross manner marks an ultimate break with the rigidly defined structure of the *Tractatus*. As a direct consequence, the philosophical remarks that comprise the text cannot remain the compilation of more or less traditional philosophical subjects, the concepts of meaning, understanding, and so on, that Wittgenstein lists at the onset. Instead, they are constituted by the ways in which they define the extended surface of language and via which they will be repeatedly studied. The surface or landscape of language thus serves as both the content and the ground for the "long and involved journeys" as it simultaneously provides the necessary means for self-examination along with the topics of study themselves. As Wittgenstein reiterates throughout the text, *language as landscape is both the object and means of study*.

The sketches necessarily and equally become their own source of study by occasioning the surface that they study rather than simply observing it from a distance. This allows the investigation of language in the book to undertake a series of observations manifested in rather than simply recorded by the sketches of the landscape. Whereas the *Tractatus*'s thinking proceeds along a series of predetermined and more or less discrete topics, the nonlinear construction and understanding according to the logic of surface disallows the *Tractatus*'s hierarchical structure, implementing in its place a redefined nature and method of approach. The emphasis on language as surface alters the study of the philosophy of language. As surface sites, topics in the *Investigations* are accessible through their operations of spatial locating and visual depicting. This working method of traversing and surveying of the landscape destroys the clarity and singularity of the map or view from above produced by the *Tractatus*. Incapable of offering the clarity and completeness of a well-defined and ordered language, the *Investigations* instead must undertake a search for connections between the many sketches that the collection is meant to facilitate. The result is the production of an album, with its inherent concerns of categorizing, grouping, and ordering.

In direct opposition to the preset and confined frames of the *Tractatus*, the multiplicity of views in the *Investigations* that begin with the preface's initial possibility of movement insert the question of choice. Because the *Tractatus* is able to develop only in accordance with its one strictly correct method, leading to a predetermined result, it effectively offers not method but correctness. Wittgenstein's explicit concern in the *Investigations* is instead with making method visible. This becomes emphasized through its suggestion of multiple possible methods that arise from the diverse journeys and means of constructing and arranging the sketched recordings of these journeys.

In the movements from remarks to sketches and back, the preface readily develops from what seem to be purely linguistic or verbal issues of grasping language to the understanding that language has visual and spatial components that also require study. Investigating language for Wittgenstein thus becomes realized as the complex process of coordinating our movements through space with our visual observations and depictions of those processes. The resultant philosophical remarks of this travel are the landscape sketches that fuel and record the journey. Necessarily approaching the same places from new directions redefines and redepict the landscape into a series of sketches that together can be collected to produce an album. The goals of the *Investigations*' journey—to produce pictures of the landscape—lie in opposition to the construction of a map or its employment in navigating that same landscape. The album's method of investigation rejects the reliance on preexisting maps that function akin to Wittgenstein's implementation of a fixed structure to guide us through the *Tractatus*.

Wittgenstein's interest in the landscape does not stop with the preface's remarks, however, but continues throughout the body of the text. A paradigmatic example of the use of the landscape metaphor surfaces in Wittgenstein's discussion of the experience of being guided in diverse cases. The example intimately associates family resemblance—the cardinal image of entanglement—with another image of entanglement: the landscape of language. The wide-ranging situations described in these sections seemingly act out the variants of the crisscrossing of the landscape, as if in accord with family resemblance, to emphasize how no one aspect is common to all manners of traversing it:

> 172. Let us consider the experience of being guided, and ask ourselves: what does this experience consist in when for instance our *course* is guided?—Imagine the following cases:
>
> You are in a playing field with your eyes bandaged, and someone leads you by the hand, sometimes left, sometimes right; you have constantly to be ready for the tug of his hand, and must also take care not to stumble when he gives an unexpected tug.

> Or again: someone leads you by the hand where you are unwilling to go, by force.
>
> Or: you are guided by a partner in a dance; you make yourself as receptive as possible, in order to guess his intention and obey the slightest pressure.
>
> Or: someone takes you for a walk; you are having a conversation; you go wherever he does.
>
> Or: you walk along a field-track, simply following it.
>
> All these situations are similar to one another; but what is common to all the experiences?

Wittgenstein's metaphor of the sketches consequently serves two main philosophical objectives: it shows that we go awry when we try to construct a map or other overview of the geography, and it emphasizes that we equally err when as philosophers we separate the reading of philosophy from its construction by offering such a map to others as a way of practicing philosophy. Consequently, the *Investigations* rejects any method of philosophy that does not rely on and make visible or otherwise theorize its own practice. Following this, Wittgenstein constructs the *Investigations* as a series of sketches or an album of reminders and images that act as sites to encounter or recall issues of language, meaning, understanding, and so on—without losing track of the fact that process and product are as inseparable in language and philosophy as they are in other practices.

Nets and Webs

There are two fundamental types of images of entanglement that emerge in the *Investigations*. Each designates a specific relation between philosophy and language. The first form of entanglement arises in relation to the *Investigations*'s examination of the view from without constructed by the *Tractatus*. It emerges in the form of repetitive problems and situations manifest as images of nets, spiderwebs, and immobility, each of which leaves the subject fixed in place. The second form of entanglement is produced in conjunction with the *Investigations*'s construction of the view from within. In opposition to the fixity of the first form, these images of entanglement develop in the movement through space to chart acts of spatial location and dislocation. This entanglement is depicted as images of mazes, paths, and roads. Although only fully developed as such in the *Investigations*, the first type of entanglement is reiterative of the thinking of the *Tractatus* or, more correctly, of the *Investigations*'s reexamination of that thinking. The second type of entanglement—mazes, paths, and roads—makes its initial appearance in the preface to the *Investigations*, where the text's crisscross movement over the surface of language emerges as definitive of the text's structure. This movement instigates the spatial production of images of entanglement that had been disallowed by the neatly defined and hierarchically distributed levels of language in the *Tractatus*.

Section 106 of the *Investigations* portrays a primary example of the first type of entanglement, that associated with fixity and the view from without. The example renders the search for absolute clarity of expression in the *Tractatus* as the confrontation with a spiderweb, in the face of which the subject is removed and helpless:

> 106. Here it is difficult as it were to keep our heads up,—to see that we must stick to the subjects of our every-day thinking, and not go astray and imagine that we have to describe extreme subtleties, which in turn we are after all quite unable to describe with the means at our disposal. We feel as if we had to repair a torn spider's web with our fingers.

The spiderweb, although it appears in the *Investigations*, is an image constructed by the view from without. Confronted with the torn web, the attempt or compulsion is to engender to repair it. That compulsion, however, draws the reader into the web: "it is difficult as it were to keep our heads up." The web threatens to entangle the reader by seemingly demanding that the reader intervene at its level of intricacy and scale but without supplying the tools necessary to make such an intervention feasible. The threat produced by our attempted engagement with the web, though, proves to be, as it were, a spatial illusion, a trick of scale. The problem as presented is that we are too large, our fingers too crude in their functioning, to engage with the web, not that it can engulf us. Yet that threat remains. It is a spatial fear that disallows any room for movement or any space in which to succeed, because the reader is at once too large to enter the web and, as the fear of being pulled in suggests, too small to withstand its attraction. It is as if the exactness demanded by the criterion of logic, the need "to describe extreme subtleties," leaves no space in which the reader may act. Given this dilemma, the view from without developed in the *Tractatus* can now be understood as *an attempt to evade the image of entanglement presented by the surface of language,* in response to which the *Tractatus* pulls back in order to view that surface from above rather than to engage with or be drawn into its misleading and conflicting *appearance.*

In a later section of the *Investigations*, in order to examine the *Tractatus*'s insistence on the one-to-one correlation of word and meaning, Wittgenstein again relies on the association of an image of entanglement with the view from without. In this instance Wittgenstein sets up a similar problem to that of the spiderweb, but it is not the surface of everyday language but our own capacity to think that takes on a sense of estrangement:

> 428. "This queer thing, thought"—but it does not strike us as queer when we are thinking. Thought does not strike us as mysterious while we are

thinking, but only when we say, as it were retrospectively: "How was thought possible?" How was it possible for thought to deal with the very object *itself*? We feel as if by means of it we had caught reality in a net.

The image of thought attempting to capture reality in a net refers to the *Tractatus*'s exacting correlation of thought and reality, here presented as if the two are disconnected, having lost the determinate a priori connection provided by logic. This sense leaves language continually searching for a way to hook onto or ensnare the world to which it refers. The net becomes the means by which language connects to some otherwise amorphous and elusive world, as if it were catching butterflies in the air or fish in the ocean. Although the net here is in our control as opposed to the spiderweb that had threatened to engulf us, the two have more in common than not. In each passage the image arises out of a discussion that compares everyday thinking to some unattainable ideal in whose light the everyday seems clumsy and ineffectual. In section 106, the idealized and intricate structure of the spiderweb cannot be engaged with the tools we have at hand (our fingers), a situation that reveals the ineffectuality of responding to entanglement from without. This inability produces a gap or estrangement between us and the literal task in front of us: by implying first that our everyday language or thinking is too crude to be able to engage the delicacy and intricacy of the spiderweb and then, by extension, that our language is too imprecise to describe the extreme subtleties demanded by philosophy.

The image of the net constructs a similar situation to that of the web, despite the fact that the image initially seems reversed. While in section 106 we are unable to engage with the web, in section 428 Wittgenstein acts out this scenario from a different viewpoint, proffering the image in its absurdity as estrangement itself. With this image, our everyday thinking is again examined for the gap between it and some "reality beyond," as if the connection between the two were now if not missing, at least elusive. The search for a connection or correlation of language and the world provides no certainty; rather it posits in its place a missing connector in the form of a net. The net, like the web, is then inserted in place of the lost or hidden connection that an ineffable logic and a transparent language previously provide in the *Tractatus* but which is now obscured by language's ambiguous and opaque surface. The image of the net emerges from this situation as the embodiment of the persistent doubt of language's ability to function without an exact one-to-one correlation of word to meaning.

Crystalline Purity

Precipitating a turning point from entanglement from without to entanglement from within is Wittgenstein's description of being transfixed by the ice. The example, which arises immediately following the image of the web in section 106, again presents that which is perceived to be in our control ultimately controlling us. This example is pivotal, though, because with it Wittgenstein is able directly to confront the thinking of the *Tractatus* by explicitly introducing the crystalline purity of logic itself as the express image of "the entanglement with our own rules." Yet the image itself of a crystalline structure, compounded by the added requirement of purity and the association with logic, initially suggests quite the opposite from entanglement.

The *Investigations*'s discussion of the crystalline purity of logic impressed upon language in the *Tractatus* demonstrates that the attempt at a completely clarified form of expression produces what would seem to be the furthest thing from it: entanglement. In this instance, entanglement arises in the form of a fixity likened to the frozen position of the view from without:

> 107. The more narrowly we examine actual language, the sharper becomes the conflict between it and our requirement. (For the crystalline purity of logic was, of course, not a *result of investigation:* it was a requirement.) The conflict becomes intolerable; the requirement is now in danger of becoming empty.—We have got on to slippery ice where there is no friction and so in a certain sense the conditions are ideal, but also, just

because of that, we are unable to walk. We want to walk: so we need *friction*. Back to the rough ground!

The image of crystalline purity, first attributed to the requirements of logic and then transferred to the ice, creates a very similar situation to the previous section's spiderweb, with each image depicting a latticework of interwoven strands and segments. This similarity exists despite the fact that crystalline structures are typically offered as articulate and webs as confusing.

This duality of crystalline structure—as both clear and overwhelming—allows for an important development in the text from the image of fixity (web, immobility) to one of movement and spatial relocation. The *Investigations*'s persistent demands for movement across the landscape of language provide the necessary impetus to transform the image of entanglement from without to one from within. Through its depiction of an extended and idealized plane, the image of the crystalline purity of the ice becomes explicitly associated with the scope, limits, and demands of logic as they appear in the view from above in the *Tractatus*. Offered at the onset as the materialization of complete clarity, in its entrapment of Wittgenstein the ice becomes yet another image of entanglement. The immobility enforced by the ideality of the friction-free surface of the ice acts to ensnare anyone who is lured onto it. When viewed as the essence of language, the narrowness of the scope or frame of examination fostered by the crystalline structure of logic is shown to produce not the ultimate clarity once hoped for but an intolerable conflict that disallows movement, a failure akin to the philosopher's inability to repair the torn spiderweb or capture reality in a net. In a similar impasse to that which occurs at the end of the *Tractatus* which forces the transgression of its self-imposed limits, the spatial crisis of these sections requires that the subject/philosopher/reader successfully endeavor to define ways to engage entanglement rather than be immobilized by it. Transgression is again demanded here, but this time in the form of movement capable of transforming the image of entanglement into one that can truly be inhabited. Whereas the *Tractatus*'s transgression was up the ladder and beyond language to produce the removed view from without, the *Investigations*'s transformation requires the construction of inhabitation.

The transformation from fixity to movement in the development of images of entanglement occurs at the moment when the ice does not yield the expected ideal result, when its ideal friction-free surface proves to be more of an impediment to action than an aid. The shock of the resultant suspended movement reveals the ice's true nature and acts to shatter the illusion that the ice can fulfill the desire for frictionless motion or, by extension, that language can be transparent to meaning.

The desire to move ultimately wins out in this passage. This makes it necessary to disentangle oneself not from the ice but from the desire for ideality and crystalline purity—or at least from the belief that they are the prerequisites of the meaningful practice of language. This is accomplished by first recognizing that the criterion of crystalline purity imposed on language is *a form of entanglement, however ideal the structure*. Extrication from the crystalline image/structure involves redefining the aims of philosophy and specifically of the philosophical study of language. The aim of constructing a completely clarified form of expression, *once depicted*, can clearly be seen to conflict with the desire to walk, as the requirement leaves no means by which to move. Similarly, by correlating meaning and language exactly, the crystalline structure of logic equally specifies place (as does the *Tractatus*'s structure), thereby turning any possible movement into transgression. This reveals, as does the example of the spiderweb, the spatial paradox of the view from without by showing that it is a subset of the view from within language. In other words, it reveals the view from without to be in a state of limbo: outside the restricted demands of logic but inside everyday language.

Once ideality is paradoxically shown to produce fixity, the desire to move forces Wittgenstein to venture onto the rough ground of the landscape of language described in the preface, bringing the reader halfway to the second image of entanglement, that from within. Associating language and the landscape collapses the distance between the subject and language to construct a subject who inhabits everyday language, entangled, opaque, and ambiguous as it appears. That is, it constructs a subject who is able to navigate that entanglement rather than one who is fixated in its image.

Spatial Crises

The development of images of entanglement from within is initiated by Wittgenstein's movement off the ice and return to the rough ground of the landscape. That movement constitutes the culmination of a sort of spatial crisis that results in the understanding of language as spatial and temporal. The crisis is played out in successive paragraphs of the text and chronicles the development of the view from without to the view from within. The book accomplishes this through the construction of a sequence of spatial constructs.

The view from within is theorized in the space and pages of the *Investigations*, where the idealized thinking that defines and limits the frame of vision and the space of action in the *Tractatus* is confronted by the emergence of explicitly spatial practices. Beginning with the builders and reaching a sort of spatial crisis between sections 103 and 108 of the *Investigations*, this pattern of pitting an idealized conception of space against physical and social spatial practices reemerges throughout the book as if to test the limits and workings of the competing images of language and entanglement. This crisis proves transformative of the image of entanglement from that of fixity to that associated with movement.

The precipitating spatial crisis begins in the *Investigations* with the realization that the ideal view of language presented in the *Tractatus* is just that, a view:

> 103. The ideal, as we think of it, is unshakable. You can never get outside it; you must always turn back. There is no outside; outside you cannot

breathe.—Where does this idea come from? It is like a pair of glasses on our nose through which we see whatever we look at. It never occurs to us to take them off.

The explicit introduction of the view launches Wittgenstein's examination of the relation between language and vision in the *Tractatus* through the associating of "the ideal," "a pair of glasses," and "whatever we look at" around the spatial construct of inner and outer. The ideal here refers to the idealized, that is, extraordinary, understanding of language in the *Tractatus* that requires sense be determinate and showing be sharply distinguished from saying. The inclusion of the glasses points to the distinction between an imposed focus of vision defined by something external to the subject and unaided or ordinary vision. Ordinary vision is thus subjected to the glasses because the viewer is unaware, unwilling, or incapable of removing the pair from his or her nose. Typically, glasses "correct" vision, making it sharper, clearer, and with a greater range of focus. The distinction Wittgenstein sets up is thus between the ordinary or everyday unaided vision and the "improved" vision of the extraordinary ideal associated with the glasses. The exact nature of the glasses, however, initially remains unclear; they may even be plain glass, as it is impossible to determine the degree of distortion or correction until they can be taken off and the views compared. Ordinary or unaided vision in this respect is itself undetermined because it is defined in response to a set of criteria for "correct vision" that are in question. As a result, it is not immediately clear with what view the removal of the glasses leaves us.

Wittgenstein's foremost concern at this point in the text is to realize the presence of glasses defining or obscuring ordinary vision, an obscuring that is comparable to the manner in which the *Tractatus* understands ordinary language to obscure the logical form of a proposition. Wittgenstein's association of the glasses with "the ideal" is explicitly associated here with the prespecified requirements (the lens) of how we view language, while removing the glasses is integral to the attempt to investigate language as it is found in everyday practices. In other words, removing the glasses allows for the unmediated interaction with the surface and practice of language. The immanent rejection of the ideal attests that meaningful language is not a prescribed way of looking requiring a special focus to function, even for the philosopher. This leads Wittgenstein to reject the idea that philosophy should focus its efforts on unearthing a special rather than everyday view of language in its search for the general form of a proposition or the hidden logical form within language.

Section 103 inverts the *Tractatus*'s ordering of vision, space, and language to make the glasses apparent, acting as if to provide a mirror in which the subject can see her- or himself and her or his everyday practices, from which the *Tractatus* averts its gaze. Logic's relation to vision, one of the central themes and main metaphors of the *Tractatus*, is rendered unclear by this realization. Logic in the *Investigations* thus comes into question—not in its functioning within itself but in its grip on the viewing subject. The glasses, as the prescribed view described in section 103, are thus less an aid to ordinary vision than a usurping of it. To look at section 103 another way, it is not necessarily the demands of logic or vision but of philosophy that are at stake. Wittgenstein makes this explicit when he queries: "Where does this idea come from?" The "where" Wittgenstein refers to surfaces as both a disciplinary concern and a spatial one.

Examining ideal of logic as defined by the view through the glasses leads in section 103 to an immediate spatial questioning in the attempt to locate the ideal in relation to the newly acknowledged subject. The spatial questioning allows the subject to become aware for the first time of the narrowness and constricted nature of the space of the ideal. This realization brings with it a sense of confinement and with that, the simultaneous desires to escape the limits of the ideal and the fear of transgressing them. Section 103 threatens the integrity of language and meaning by revealing the tenuousness of the system understood to secure the functioning and use of language.

Tables turned, the ideal now appears imprisoning. "You can never get outside it; you must always turn back" (sec. 103). The view from outside is what defines the *Tractatus* by providing a position of safety from which to view the world and language. From that position, in its fiction, the world is contained and appears to be in perfect or perfectible order. That fiction suggests that outside of that system of logic you cannot breathe. But the fear also arises that logic's external repositioning of order may itself be unattainable or at least unsustainable. As with the *Tractatus*, the reader-viewer is forced to transgress those encroaching limits in order to see them, but here the transgression is acknowledged from the start to be part of the investigation of language. Vision—unaided everyday vision—comes into being through this act of transgression, allowing logic to appear not as language but as an imposition on language, as a narrow view and as a limitation on the practice of viewing.

Breath beyond the ideal frame of logic becomes possible, however, once it is understood that the necessity and existence of an ideal in language arises from a preconceived requirement rather than a visual inspection such as that used to examine "game's" various appearances. The idea that sensible language is confined to the system of logic can then be grasped as the fundamental misconception or misperception of the *Tractatus*. It is only from the *Investigations*, with the realization of the frame of vision defined by the glasses, that we can see the limits of the logical ideal. This spatial reconfiguration permits the *Investigations* to define itself as the view from the outside not of language but of the *Tractatus*'s concept of language. Not uncoincidentally, this is exactly the position the subject is pushed into with the climb up the ladder and the movement beyond the bounds of what the *Tractatus* declares a sensible language: inside language but outside the *Tractatus*'s limited view of language.

The following section, 104, reiterates that the discussion is about vision and representation by pointing to the initial conflation (in the *Tractatus*) of logic as a method of representation with what it is representing, a conflation that blurs what the *Tractatus*'s show/say distinction is instituted to resist. Logic's position as both divider (between sense and nonsense) and joiner (between showing and saying) is shown to be itself in conflict. "We predicate of the thing what lies in the method of representing it." The search for essence develops from this implication of universality. "Impressed by the possibility of a comparison, we think we are perceiving a state of affairs of the highest generality." That is, by following the demands of logic, we are led to such ideas as the existence of a general form of a proposition in which all language conforms to an essential structure. The clarity called for in seeing such an order within language is reliant upon the idea that the relation between language and meaning can be transparent. When logic no longer remains the essential *visual component* of sensible language, transparency is no longer guaranteed. This is the situation Wittgenstein finds in the *Investigations*, where showing and saying cannot—and do not in practice—remain distinct.

Once this new spatial construct is recognized and acknowledged, the situation changes. In showing itself as a view of rather than coincident with language, logic can no longer provide the criteria of sense in what is said. The attempt at or belief in the complete separation of showing and saying—*within language*—collapses upon itself then, when vision and subjectivity become apparent and the sharpness of that distinction cannot and need not be upheld:

> 105. When we believe that we must find that order, must find the ideal, in our actual language, we become dissatisfied with what are ordinarily called "propositions," "words," "signs."

The proposition and the word that logic deals with are supposed to be something pure and clear-cut. And we rack our brains over the nature of the *real* sign.—It is perhaps the *idea* of the sign? or the idea at the present moment?

Section 105 illustrates how the view of language aspiring to the clarity of logical expression, once instituted, makes ordinary language appear inadequate in comparison. Drawn into this way of thinking—into being overwhelmed by an unreachable ideal—the response is to "rack our brains over the nature of the *real* sign" (sec. 105). That is, Wittgenstein shows how the acceptance of the ideal of logic as the criterion of meaningful language leads philosophy into a metaphysical view of language itself, one that questions the nature of both reality and signs but without any practical understanding of what criteria would define either designation. We are led to believe we would know it when we see it (the transparency not of language but of criteria), but Wittgenstein has already questioned our vision: What can be relied upon? It is perhaps the *idea* of the sign? As it becomes clear that the logical form within language is not readily locatable, identified, or maintained ("or the idea at the present moment"; sec. 105), it becomes unclear whether even logic can continue to fulfill the ideal criteria:

106. Here it is difficult as it were to keep our heads up,—to see that we must stick to the subjects of our every-day thinking, and not go astray and imagine that we have to describe extreme subtleties, which in turn we are after all quite unable to describe with the means at our disposal. We feel as if we had to repair a torn spider's web with our fingers.

The challenge to the representative and descriptive abilities of language continues in section 106, where the inability of language to conform to an ideal (hence the failed search for the "real sign") forces language to supplant logic as the only possible form of representation, description, and thought. Wittgenstein's writing in response to this failed ideal becomes more metaphorical or literary, culminating with his conclusive image of entanglement: "we feel as if we had to repair a torn spider's web with our fingers." This expression of exasperation emphasizes the distance between our lives (and thus our language) and the demands of logic; demands that we feel compelled to fulfill despite the realization that "we must stick to the subjects of our every-day thinking, and not go astray and imagine that we have to describe extreme subtleties, which in turn we are after all quite unable to describe with the means at our disposal" (sec. 106). Those means are, of course, language, where part of the lack of descriptive ability can be attributed to "literal" language and so metaphorical language takes over to fill the gap left by logic. The (logical) requirement of clarity and transparency yields its final dissolution on the ice in section 107, initially completing the trilogy of emptiness, silence, and immobility begun by the *Tractatus*. What puts a halt to being enveloped in this is the desire of the subject to walk in section 107 and the spatial turnaround back to the rough ground that becomes fully realized in section 108.

Having reached the point in the *Investigations* where Wittgenstein acknowledges that the requirement of logic cannot be either found in everyday language nor fulfilled by it, he begins to imagine an ideal world or surface—the ice—in which it is fulfilled. The result renders visible the gap between the requirement and everyday practices of language. "The conflict becomes intolerable; the requirement is now in danger of becoming empty" (sec. 107). The dizziness of this continual loop of attempts and unfulfilled ideals creates an almost literal conflict between the desire to move and the desire for the transparency that fixes the viewer in place. "We have got on to slippery ice where there is no friction and so in a certain sense the conditions are ideal, but also, just because of that, we are unable to walk. We want to walk: so we need *friction*. Back to the rough ground!" (sec. 107). Turning back toward the rough ground, that is, to the landscape of language, defuses the emerging crisis by allowing movement.

Labyrinths and Mazes

The second form of images of entanglement, those from within, surfaces at this juncture. Unlike the first form, those from within are not produced solely by vision but through the continuous dislocation of vision constituted by movement through space. Their territory is found in the spatial field of language suggested by the landscape sketches in the preface. That crisscross movement disrupts any one-to-one correlation of image with place, thereby disavowing the image's appearance as a whole and instead requiring it be continually constructed in the subject-language association. Here, from *within* a spatial understanding of language, Wittgenstein can engage philosophical problems through methods unavailable to the *Tractatus*.

Commencing with the act of walking off the ice in the previous section, Wittgenstein adds direction in section 108: "The *preconceived idea* of crystalline purity can only be removed by turning our whole examination round. (One might say: the axis of reference of our examination must be rotated, but about the fixed point of our real need.)" Movement and space in the form of rotation are thus used by Wittgenstein to dislodge the fixed focus on a preconceived ideal image of language. Stripping away the requirement of logic becomes akin to the removal of the glasses, but, as with the glasses, it is not immediately clear with what the removal or the requirement leaves us. This rotation changes the relative positions of logic, language, and vision so that the limits of the view of language are no longer coincident with the bounds of logic. The act is one of positioning logic within philosophy as well as in relation to language and the world rather than allowing the order of logic to serve a defining role. In this new place, logic at first seems to have been altered: "For how can it lose its rigour?" leaving Wittgenstein asking: "But what becomes of logic now?" That is to ask both "How has this change come about? and "How can the investigation proceed?" (sec. 108). What is the defining method for philosophical inquiry?

The investigation about the fixed point of our real (i.e., not ideal) need is initiated by Wittgenstein's newly developed image of family resemblance that reemerges at this juncture as if to define the subsequent forms of images of entanglement. "We see that what we call 'sentence' and 'language' has not the formal unity that I imagined, but is the family of structures more or less related to one another." The evidence of this transformation becomes immediately apparent in Wittgenstein's proclaiming the spatiality and temporality of language in contradistinction to the ideality of logic: "We are talking about the spatial and temporal phenomenon of language, not about some non-spatial, non-temporal phantasm" (sec. 108). That phantom is, of course, the specter of logic.

Everyday language is acknowledged by Wittgenstein as part of the world in a spatiotemporal way that logic could not be. Ordinary language is also distinguished from logic through the publicness of its practice. Although logic was always publicly accessible in some sense, it was at the same time hidden both within language and within the discourses of philosophy and mathematics, leaving it at odds with the publicness, pervasiveness, and visibility of everyday discourse and practices.

The issue of representation returns in a new light in section 108. Throughout the *Investigations*, Wittgenstein repeatedly employs examples that emphasize the graphic nature of language. These emerge around discussions of the social and material aspects of reading and the processes of learning to read, expressing pain, recording private sensations, following a rule, and describing a geometrical projection. When the issue of representation is raised in section 104, no distinction is allowed between method of representation and the thing represented. But following the spatial rotation of section 108, Wittgenstein emphasizes the appearance of language itself, with its fundamental ambiguities of meaning and graphic appearance that describe our entanglement with language: "the philosophy of logic speaks of sentences and words in exactly the sense in which we speak of them in ordinary life when we say e.g. 'Here is a Chinese sentence,' or 'No, that only looks like writing; it is actually just an ornament' and so on" (sec. 108). By pointing to a potentially unintelligible or alien image of language, Wittgenstein's example of Chinese writing emphasizes language's graphic component, its existence as marks on a page. The second example thus takes off from the first one to allude to the inherent ambiguity and duality of language: Is it writing or is it ornament? Is it meaningful language or simply marks on a page? Once the visible, graphic, and physical aspects of language, that is, its surface appearance, are made explicit, Wittgenstein is then able to declare language to be a "spatial and temporal phenomenon."

In explicitly revealing the inseparability of the visual, verbal, and spatial, the *Investigations* undertakes philosophical problems in ways that engage all three. Hinging on such central issues as the defining of boundaries and the correspondence of word and meaning, language and the world, issues integral to philosophy, these problems include Wittgenstein's quest to define the scope, limits, and functioning of language. All of this is in sharp contrast to the *Tractatus*'s attempts to delineate clear demarcations between these aspects of language with its picture theory, show-say distinction, one correct method, and sharp categories of sense and nonsense.

Throughout the text, Wittgenstein continues to discuss language in its spatial configurations, a number of which constitute images of entanglement in the form of mazes and labyrinths or paths. These images frequently invoke the landscape sketches introduced to the reader in the preface to the text. In identical parenthetical comments at the ends of sections 525 and 534, both of which discuss the importance of context in comprehending language, Wittgenstein writes: "A multitude of familiar paths lead off from these words in every direction." And in section 426 Wittgenstein explicitly compares the view from without, the complete view, with the occluded view. The inhabiting of language in all of its ambiguities, incapable of yielding the clarity of the view from above, produces sketches of the landscape as images of entanglement:

> 426: A picture is conjured up which seems to fix the sense *unambiguously*. The actual use, compared with that suggested by the picture, seems like something muddied. Here again we get the same thing as in set theory: the form of expression we use seems to have been designed for a god, who knows what we cannot know; he sees the whole of each of those infinite series and he sees into human consciousness. For us, of course, these forms of expression are like pontificals which we may put on, but cannot do much with, since we lack the effective power that would give these vestments meaning and purpose.
>
> In the actual use of expressions we make detours, we go by side-roads. We see the straight highway before us, but of course we cannot use it, because it is permanently closed.

The multiple meanings of many concepts and contradictions or ways of viewing in the *Investigations* suggest that the work of philosophy is not solely to find philosophy's place within these sets of polarities but to reconsider the polarity of our thinking. This demands that we reconsider the limits within which we place and define our concepts. The multiplicity of methods in the *Investigations* cannot help but produce new forms of clarity that result from these redefined limits and boundaries of relations and expressions. To this end, the visual-spatial metaphor of the sketches serves a purpose other than analogy and description: in constructing and imagining new forms of clarity that provide perspicuity in a manner not previously thought possible, Wittgenstein shows that the clarity we once thought necessary may not even be possible. In its place Wittgenstein offers images of entanglement from within, descriptions of the surface of language as forms of both philosophical problems and explanation.

As such, the image of philosophical problems and of the surface of language completely collapses around an image of entanglement in the *Investigations* to produce nearly identical definitions:

123. A philosophical problem has the form: "I don't know my way about."

203. Language is a labyrinth of paths. You approach from *one* side and know your way about; you approach the same place from another side and no longer know your way about.

This image of entanglement functions as a description of simultaneously the surface of language and the philosophical problems that develop from the misreadings of that surface. Philosophical problems in the late philosophy are thus revealed not to be ultimately produced by this entanglement with our own rules (as are those of logic) *but they are that entanglement itself.* As with other images of entanglement, this image arises in passages that search for relations between language and meaning and compare the philosophical-logical solution pursued in the *Tractatus* to that found in everyday uses of language indicative of the *Investigations*. The image of language as entanglement that the idealized picture of logic is employed to repress or efface here comes to surmount the (picture of) logic in the *Tractatus*.

If philosophical problems have a certain form, what of philosophical solutions? The implication would be that the solution to not knowing one's way about is to find it. The defining relations of entanglement, however, change the *Investigations*. In section 125 Wittgenstein dispels the idea that the response to a philosophical problem should be to search for a solution to it:

> 125. It is the business of philosophy, not to resolve a contradiction by means of a mathematical or Logico-mathematical discovery, but to make it possible for us to get a clear view of the state of mathematics that trouble us: the state of affairs before the contradiction is resolved.

The *Tractatus* treats language as if it were transparent, as if you could see clearly through its surface to the meaning and logical form beneath it. As such, it posits logic as the image of language, believing it to be a faithful one. *It is this transparency and nonmateriality of language in the Tractatus that seems to require a connection to language's "objects."* The situation in the *Investigations* is quite different. Accepting the complexity and ambiguity of language leaves language no longer transparent. As a spatial and temporal phenomenon, language in the *Investigations* is always already part of the world; philosophy in the *Investigations* can no longer deny or ignore the surface of language. Instead, philosophy must now try to explain how the entanglement with language's surface is part of the functioning of language:

> The fundamental fact here is that we lay down rules, a technique for a game, and that then when we follow the rules, things do not turn out as we had assumed. That we are therefore as it were entangled in our own rules.
>
> This entanglement in our rules is what we want to understand (i.e. get a clear view of).
>
> It throws light on our concept of *meaning* something. For in those cases things turn out otherwise than we had meant, foreseen. That is just what we say when, for example, a contradiction appears: "I didn't mean it like that."

This image of entanglement at once recalls the landscape and our paths across it even as it associates that image with the construction of philosophical problems. That is, the surface of language is not covered over by philosophy, but the entanglement of language and philosophy means that each produces the other. Wittgenstein's stress on the role of the subject—"*we* lay down rules," "*we* follow the rules," "*we* are . . . entangled in *our own* rules"—in the creation of philosophical problems emphasizes the importance of considering the position of the subject in the response to these problems—"*we* want to understand," "That is just what *we* say." The role of the self is no longer denied in the *Investigations*; instead it is central to the recognition that *we* position ourselves *within* philosophical issues, which of course also means that philosophy is central to our lives. By contrast, not realizing our own role in the creation of philosophical problems has led us to think that we are outside the problem and thus, as with the web, incapable of affecting it, whereas the spatiality of language requires that we be integrally and substantially involved in our rules.

The discussion of entanglement immediately calls the criterion of clarity into question in the constructing, defining, and judging of the clarity of the views of language, philosophy, the landscape, practices, games, and so on. Clear views, however, need to be distinguished from the ability to obtain a complete view. The view from within in the *Investigations* supports no such illusion of completeness or clarity. The preface is the first site to consider this possibility in the relation it institutes between clarity and completeness by detailing how the sketches give or allow us to get "a picture of the landscape." That is, it raises the question of how a series of not necessarily complete or all-inclusive sketches can satisfactorily depict an equally undefined yet extensive landscape. The uncertainty created between what is meant by sketch and landscape, whether there are one or many, fundamentally disturbs even any initial attempt at defining a new basis for the clarity of vision. The question as to what extent the clarity of the view is contingent upon seeing the complete view becomes exacerbated by the potential for numerous views of multiple landscapes. The *Tractatus* errs both in the attempt to produce a clear view and in the belief that such a view is necessary in order to use language sensibly and to resolve philosophical problems. In response, the *Tractatus* constructs the view from without, thereby creating the illusion that a complete view is somehow accessible. But as with the example of the spiderweb, the *Investigations* denies that the view from without leaves us capable of interacting meaningfully with what is viewed. The view from without is again shown to be akin to positioning oneself on the ice. Immobility ensues. But in the *Investigations*, Wittgenstein *desires* to walk.

Albums

Presented at the conclusion of his discussion of the landscape sketches in the preface, Wittgenstein's confession that the *Investigations* "is only an album" suggests that the book is, at least metaphorically, a sketch album. And in many ways, that is the intention of the *Investigations*: to construct, edit, select, assemble, and collect depictions of the landscape of language, that is, to collect images of entanglement. Collecting and assembling are not, however, neutral activities but, as Wittgenstein acknowledges, involve work on the material collected. In addition to the method by which the collections are made, there remains the important question of what types or categories of items are being collected. In addition to the landscape sketches, the idea of an album has another association. Brought together with Wittgenstein's concept of family resemblance and its initial appearance in the example of Galton's photographs, the collection suggests a family photo album.

Galton's photographs resulted from overlaying multiple exposures to produce a composite surface constituted by a complex network of facial structures and "familial" associations. While these could be collected to form an album, each photographic image is on its own already a collection or album. The compilation and production of these complex images transforms the typical idea of an album as a serial or linear cataloguing of items, including examples and memories, into a coincident network of multiple images that focuses not on the distinct images collected but on the network of associations between images emerging within a single photograph. Each photograph acts in this way to recall the workings of family resemblance.

One way in which the *Investigations* produces an album is in its gathering of various examples, including images of entanglement. These images depict relationships between the landscape and the sketches similar to those between the specific features of individuals and those that come together to produce family resemblance. Similarly to Galton's superimposed images, the album is the aggregate construction of images of diverse linguistic practices. As an album, it is able to amass onto one extended surface diverse, even dissimilar elements comprising language, including the practices and meanings that constitute a word or expression. These are assembled alongside discussions of how language functions, the graphic appearance of language, philosophers' entanglement with language, and so on to produce an intricate network of associations organized around a series of topics that themselves form a network of relations and resemblances.

An album suggests both a book with blank pages used for making a collection and the collection itself. The proclamation that a book of philosophy is an album substantially challenges its status by suggesting that philosophy may only be a collection of found items or, worse yet, a set of blank pages waiting for some imported content. This sentiment reiterates Wittgenstein's view of philosophy as both lacking its own subject matter and incapable of supplying a foundation for other discourses. Philosophy's role, rather, becomes limited to that of collecting and assembling. The question becomes then: What is being collected? Wittgenstein answers that concern in section 127 with the provision that: *"The work of the philosopher consists in assembling reminders for a particular purpose."*

The philosopher who comes into being in the *Investigations* is thus an assembler or constructor, a role not unlike the builders of the opening sections, who, in assembling the building stones in a particular manner, are at once amassing and organizing reminders of their language: "block," "pillar," "slab," "beam." Similarly, the *Investigations* collects and arranges the everyday practices of language we encounter to produce an accumulation of reminders of the multitude of ways and places in which we encounter language, all this in contrast to the *Tractatus*'s singular picture and one strictly correct method. The succession of examples of various uses of language and the language-games of the *Investigations* are tokens of these practices. They are, however, less definitive reminders of what language is than directives for readers to recall and examine similar practices they have encountered in which a given word or expression is used. Hence in the paradigmatic example of games, Wittgenstein demands that the reader search not solely her or his memory but her or his environment as well; to look, not think.

Reinscribing the idea of a photographic album, the collection in the *Investigations* frequently are visual reminders directed at the practice of philosophy that are assembled and arrayed through spatial practices. One frequent form of (visual) reminder is Wittgenstein's admonition that it is a mistake to think that in doing philosophy, something is hidden in language that is of relevance to the work. Section 126 makes this clear because it envisions a philosophy of collecting wherein philosophy simply puts "everything before us" without explaining or deducing anything. Wittgenstein adds to this point that "one might also give the name 'philosophy' to what is possible *before* all new discoveries and inventions" (sec. 126). The series of examples that Wittgenstein puts forth and the reminders that he assembles reiterate this understanding foremost through the practice of vision. In the examples, Wittgenstein repeatedly places the burden of vision on the viewer rather than on the availability of the object to vision, thereby emphasizing the related album-constructing activities of selecting and collecting. Our position modified by the awareness that what is visible is not fixed by the object alone, it becomes clear that our practices of vision and our movements through space influence what is included in the album.

The paradigmatic symbol of the means by which Wittgenstein makes visible reminders—and reminders visible—is his spatializing, externalizing, and materializing a rule, ultimately reinventing it as a signpost in the landscape:[6]

> 85. A rule stand there like a sign-post.—Does the sign-post leave no doubt open about the way I have to go? Does it shew which direction I am to take when I have passed it; whether along the road or the footpath or cross-country? But where is it said which way I am to follow it; whether in direction of its finger or (e.g.) in the opposite one?—And if there were, not a single sign-post, but a chain of adjacent ones or of chalk marks on the ground—is there only *one* way of interpreting them?—So I can say, the sign-post does after all leave no room for doubt. Or rather: it sometimes leaves room for doubt and sometimes not. And now this is no longer a philosophical proposition, but an empirical one.

Two sections later, at the close of section 87, Wittgenstein concludes: "The sign-post is in order—if, under normal circumstances, it fulfils its purpose."

The signpost arises in Wittgenstein's discussion of the close relation between rules and explanations. Explanations are subsequently examined in these sections for their spatial and material properties in an attempt to locate them in the spatial order:

> But then how does an explanation help me to understand, if after all it is not the final one? In that case the explanation is never completed; so I still don't understand what he means, and never shall!—As though an explanation as it were hung in the air unless supported by another one. (sec. 87)

Immediately following, another reminder of practice emerges:

> If I tell someone "Stand roughly here"—may not this explanation work perfectly? And cannot every other one fail too?
> But isn't it an inexact explanation?—Yes; why shouldn't we call it "inexact"? Only let us understand what "inexact" means. For it does not mean "unusable."

The repeated appearance of the signpost in the landscape serves a threefold function in the text. It recalls the landscape sketches, it questions the role and functioning of reminders, and it dispels the view that language is comprised of self-interpreting signs. As a material manifestation of a rule, the recurring image of the signpost is emblematic of the way that topics, examples, doubts, questions, compulsions, and reminders reemerge throughout the text. Repetition itself—along with what is repeated—serves an important purpose in the *Investigations* because it reinforces Wittgenstein's view of philosophy as offering "reminders" of what we, by virtue of our being language users, already know. Philosophy, therefore, becomes the process of collecting, presenting, and revisiting everyday practices of language by forming them into an album. This view is contrasted to the common assumption that philosophy offers information, is revelatory, or oversees and comments on its own or on other discourses. Consequently, the *Investigations* constructs a method of philosophy-album that functions by reminding the reader of these practices as they occur in the everyday use of language, not as they occur in a removed and isolated philosophical practice particularly. Architecture enters here as an organizing and constitutive principle of this practice. The signpost is an image of a rule that defines spatial practices. In this view, the manifestation of the signpost confirms the supposition that philosophy is the practice of offering (spatial) reminders to find one's way across the surface of language.

The third function of the signpost—to remind us that language is not comprised of self-interpreting signs—leads to the culmination (or crisis) of one of the *Investigations*'s most important discussions of rule-following some hundred sections later, when Wittgenstein again summons the image of the signpost to try out the following of a rule in space:

> 198. "But how can a rule shew me what I have to do at *this* point? Whatever I do is, on some interpretation, in accord with the rule."—That is not what we ought to say, but rather: any interpretation still hangs in the air along with what it interprets, and cannot give it any support. Interpretations by themselves do not determine meaning.
>
> "Then can whatever I do be brought into accord with the rule?"—Let me ask this: what has the expression of a rule—say a sign-post—got to do with my actions? What sort of connexion is there here?—Well perhaps this one: I have been trained to react to this sign in a particular way, and now I do so react to it.
>
> But that is only to give a causal connexion; to tell how it has come about that we now go by the sign-post; not what this going-by-the-sign really consists in. On the contrary; I have further indicated that a person goes by a sign-post only in so far as there exists a regular use of sign-post, a custom.

The image of the signpost is succeeded by other visual reminders to be collected by the album, such as an examination of measuring in the measure of exactitude and its location in space:

> And let us consider what we call an "exact" explanation in contrast with this one. Perhaps something like drawing a chalk line round an area? Here it strikes us at once that the line has breadth. So a colour-edge would be more exact. But has this exactness still got a function here: isn't the engine idling? (sec. 88)

Section 140 contrasts this new way of seeing the various uses of a given word with the logical compulsion for a one-to-one correspondence of word and meaning in accordance with a predetermined picture of the functioning of language akin to the *Tractatus*'s picture theory. As antidote to this compulsion and to parry the fixed view of how relations between word and meaning are typically conceived, Wittgenstein substitutes spatiovisual practices, including the activity of picturing a three-dimensional geometrical object projected onto a two-dimensional plane. Harking back to the practice of architecture, the example recalls the architectural design process that develops from two-dimensional representations to the three-dimensional production. Importantly, because it is a design process, the resultant object does not precede but follows from its representation:

> 140. Then what sort of mistake did I make; was it what we should like to express by saying: I should have thought the picture forced a particular use on me? How could I think that? What *did* I think? Is there such a thing as a picture, or something like a picture, that forces a particular application on us: so that my mistake lay in confusing one picture with another?—For we might also be inclined to express ourselves like this: we are at most under a psychological, not a logical, compulsion. And now it looks quite as if we knew of two kinds of case.
>
> What was the effect of my argument? It called our attention to (reminded us of) the fact that there are other processes, besides the one we originally thought of, which we should sometimes be prepared to call "applying the picture of a cube." So our "belief that the picture forced a particular application upon us" consisted in the fact that only the one case and no other occurred to us. "There is another solution as well" means: there is something else that I am also prepared to call a "solution"; to which I am prepared to apply such-and-such a picture, such-and-such an analogy, and so on.
>
> What is essential is to see that the same thing can come before our minds when we hear the word and the application still be different. Has it the *same* meaning both times? I think we shall say not.

Wittgenstein introduces these geometrical examples as models of how reminders function within the philosophy of language. As with the signpost, Wittgenstein points to the multiplicity of usages and relations and also questions how these spatiovisual reminders operate. Do they form a particular application of the views/uses of the reminder? Grasping philosophy as a collection or assembly of reminders, visual and spatial ones included, explains in part Wittgenstein's declaration that the *Investigations* is "only an album." As with a (family) photo album, the *Investigations* is meant not to show us something unfamiliar but to remind us of that which is familiar but which we have forgotten or have occluded with preconceived ideas. It is a look at ourselves, our pasts, our practices, our language, and "forms of life" rather than an attempt to isolate the work of philosophy or to use it to consider and comment on other practices from a foundational or (literally) superior position, as in the *Tractatus*'s view from above. These images/reminders are a collection of views from within language. Yet their repeated emphasis on spatial locating and spatiovisual practices are clearly reminders of what Wittgenstein himself realized in the practice of architecture. They are his collection of reminders of how to practice philosophy in a contrasting manner to the way he had in the *Tractatus*. More specifically, they are reminders of a spatial practice that confronts the limited views of philosophy and language developed in the *Tractatus*.

Importantly, the reminders in the *Investigations*—even those arising from Wittgenstein's own experience—also differ from a family photo album in that they are based in uses of language and other public practices assembled from and accessible to the public memory. These everyday uses of language, even when not familiar in their specific form, remind the reader of kindred events and uses of language he or she may have encountered or can envision. As a guiding principle, these collected memories recall the opening sections of the *Investigations*, which brought together Augustine's memory of the acquisition of language with Wittgenstein's added practice of building in the primitive language of the builders.

The publicness of this album of reminders thereby constructs a form of history. Through the inseparability of its "theory" from its writing, history in the *Investigations* emerges as a method of inquiry. History arises in Wittgenstein's recalling his intellectual history from the *Tractatus* as well as his response to the history of philosophy in its formation of philosophical propositions and problems. By investigating not where a problem leads—to some "solution"—but how it arose from its initial misconceptions about language and misdirections in navigating the landscape of language, the *Investigations* recounts the historical development of these philosophical problems. The act of reminding thus has a double role. The reminders are not always about what we need to remember, do, or think but about where certain ways of thinking lead—say to the construction of "pseudo"-problems that leave us stuck in a repetitive pattern, mired in a narrow view of language and hence incapable of moving forward.

Surface Practices

Throughout the *Investigations,* Wittgenstein repeatedly demands that the reader maintain his or her focus on what is visible *on the surface of language.* That surface is realized as the series of landscape sketches and reminders that form the album. The processes by which the album was constructed from the sketches (including images of entanglement) divide into two primary forms: those that alter the sketches themselves by such means as cropping and editing, and those that act upon the sketches as a whole, such as rejecting, repositioning, rearranging, or regrouping. Surface practices of editing and rearrangement in the *Investigations* are offered in direct contrast to the *Tractatus*'s attempts to get beneath the surface of language to reach its hidden "essence" through the process of logical clarification. As Wittgenstein sets forth in the preface, the sketches collected in the album (the reminders) do not emerge fully formed but must be edited and rearranged in various ways.

The importance of surface for Wittgenstein cannot be overemphasized. It defines the very field of linguistic practices. Words and meaning in the many forms they take—including the spatiovisual practices Wittgenstein lists early in the text—form the surface of language. As a function of the visible surface, meaning does not merely reside in an external, public space but produces it. Nor is it the product of connecting to unseen points beneath the surface. The insistence on the surface of language thus alters the implied correspondence of word and meaning by disrupting the inner/essence–outer/surface dichotomy.

The *Investigations* plays the desire "to *understand* something that is already in plain view against the search for hidden meaning. For *this* is what we seem in some sense not to understand" (sec. 89). The following section, number 90, reiterates this pull: "We feel as if we had to penetrate phenomenon." That is, to penetrate the surface and "move beyond" what is in plain view. By contrast, the *Tractatus* requires the logical form of language to be exposed in order to resolve philosophical problems. As such, the *Tractatus* acts to unveil the logical form embedded beneath language's surface. The correlate of this method is that for logic's essential structure to be visible, language must be understood as transparent, permitting the view from *above* to be the view *through* language to meaning manifest as language's underlying logical structure, on the one hand, and its representation of the world, on the other.

The *Tractatus*'s search for essence leads to a denial of the surface of language by claiming that the real goal of investigation lies beneath that surface. The practices that emerge in the *Investigations* deny any essence that is unavailable to vision and posit instead such spatial practices as rearrangement. It becomes clear, however, that focusing on the surface of language in the *Investigations* leads to the discovery of images of entanglement that Wittgenstein tries to elude with the *Tractatus*'s methods. By placing philosophy in the privileged position of accessing language's unseen logical structure below its surface, the *Tractatus* effectively effaces the surface formed by the everyday use of language. That is, while the *Tractatus* claims to be unearthing the logical structure beneath language's confusing surface, instead it is placing the logical image of language (in the form of the view from above) over that surface, thereby obscuring everyday language. *For where else could such a logical analysis occur.* Wittgenstein's claim that this is necessary in order to clarify philosophical problems does not entirely mitigate that privilege:

> 92. This [search for a state of complete exactness in language] finds expression in questions as to the *essence* of language, of propositions, of thought.—For if we too in these investigations are trying to understand the essence of language—its function, its structure,—yet *this* is not what those questions have in view. For they see in the essence, not something that already lies open to view and that becomes surveyable by a rearrangement, but something that lies beneath the surface. Something that lies within, which we see when we look *into* the thing, and which an analysis digs out.

The *Investigations* responds to such previous eradication of everyday vision by developing a philosophical method that emphasizes the visible surface of language through the production and assembly of reminders of everyday language. This allows the *Investigations* to discuss the desire for essence as a search for a state of complete exactness that emerges around various topics, particularly the examination of the criteria for various measurement practices, as was enacted in the Stonborough-Wittgenstein House.

The concept of assembly joins here with that of reminders to define a space in which philosophy acts that does not transform language but maintains an intimate association between space and language. Philosophy as Wittgenstein tells us: "may in no way interfere with the actual use of language; it can in the end only describe it. For it cannot give it any foundation either. It leaves everything as it is" (sec. 124). No longer aspiring to uncover the purity and essence of language embedded within it, philosophy becomes forced to describe the surface of language as manifest in practice. This enjoinder effectively prohibits philosophy from redefining the core of language, as Wittgenstein attempted previously, while at the same time it collapses the spatial territory of philosophy and language. In that collapse, philosophy is redefined in relation to everyday language.

As method, the rejection or limiting of explanation, which Wittgenstein hints at from the book's opening paragraphs with his proclamation in the book's opening section that "explanations come to an end somewhere," is explicitly dealt with here through arrangement and description as the most viable practices. This declaration constitutes Wittgenstein's attempt to redefine the territory of philosophy in relation to other discourses and other uses of language—science, logic, everyday language, varying games, building, and so on—an activity that demands both transgression of the discipline and inhabitation parallel to Wittgenstein's movements in and out of philosophy. This aspect is very different from the knowledge associated with visibility of fixed places and points of view, replaced here by acts of arranging engendered by moving through space. That movement is what produces a multitude of viewpoints and depictions of the resulting views. Vision remains indispensable, but movement allows vision to be productive, turning it from a requirement into an investigation.

The embeddedness of meaning within language is reinforced by the way in which the *Tractatus* was structured, beginning with "pictures" of the relation of language to the world and then moving in, penetrating language to reach its underlying logical structure. The real need in the study of language developed in the *Investigations* does not proceed *into* a word's nature or essence but forms a surface discussion emanating from the everyday uses of language.

Surface practices, however, far from offering unmediated solutions, frequently confront the viewer or user with conflicts. In the wake of a newly defined space of language, Wittgenstein fully confronts the ambiguous image of language as specifically that of entanglement, producing images of entanglement from within and concluding in section 109 that "Philosophy is a battle against the bewitchment of our intelligence by means of language." In that passage Wittgenstein explores the deep affiliation between philosophy and language that produces "bewitchment," an image Wittgenstein no longer responds to with averted vision (as in the *Tractatus*) but with acts of arrangement. Disavowing the scientific model of facts and the natural sciences that the *Tractatus* aspires to, Wittgenstein thrusts the *Investigations* into a necessarily ongoing rearrangement of reminders of what we already know:

> 109. It was true to say that our considerations could not be scientific ones. It was not of any possible interest to us to find out empirically "that, contrary to our preconceived ideas, it is possible to think such-and such"—whatever that may mean. (The conception of thought as a gaseous medium.) And we may not advance any kind of theory. There must not be anything hypothetical in our considerations. We must do away with all *explanation*, and description alone must take its place. And this description gets its light, that is to say its purpose, from the philosophical problems. These are, of course, not empirical problems; they are solved, rather, by looking into the workings of our language, and that in such a way as to make us recognize those workings: in despite of an urge to misunderstand them. The problems are solved, not by giving new information, but by arranging what we have always known. Philosophy is a battle against the bewitchment of our intelligence by means of language.

The conclusion that "Philosophy is a battle against the bewitchment of our intelligence by means of language" immediately brings to mind the example of the Chinese sentence in section 108 and the question of whether it is writing or ornament, of whether we are seeing correctly or being bewitched by the appearance of language. The example of a visually unintelligible sentence brings with it the implied suspicion that the line between writing and ornament needs to be drawn (language needs to be bounded) for fear that the distinction could become blurred. The emphasis on battle reiterates the ongoing nature of this process that can neither be won nor simply avoided.

The battle Wittgenstein alludes to is first waged by him with the *Tractatus*. There he attempts to become unentangled from language in order to attain a completely clear view of it and of the philosophical problems it produces. Such a view is obtainable only by distancing language from world and subject alike. This disengaged view of the *Tractatus* insists that language itself reflect that clarity of the prescribed philosophical vision. Such a requirement means that language needs to be made over in an image that seems as far from entanglement and bewitchment as possible. In reconsidering the *Tractatus*'s attempt to remake language, the *Investigations* necessarily has to reconsider the image and criterion of clarity as well. In the *Investigations*, clarity arises not in opposition to but alongside, even emerging from, images of entanglement. It emerges in the production and arranging of views or sketches (depictions) of our entanglement with language from within the shared territory of language and philosophy, vision and space. Again, as in Wittgenstein's reference to Galton's composite photography in the reenvisioning of Moore's statement on ethics, Wittgenstein's method advances from a single image of clarity to multiple manifestations of it.

Amidst this dual remaking of the images of clarity and entanglement, arrangement emerges as the fundamental practice of philosophy and the study of language. This ensues from Wittgenstein's view that the philosopher always needs to work within language, the inescapability of which defines the view from within and necessitates rearrangement along language's visible surface as the fundamental working method, in lieu of effacement of or penetration through that surface:

> 120. When I talk about language (words, sentences, etc.) I must speak the language of every day. Is this language somehow too coarse and material for what we want to say? *Then how is another one to be constructed?*—And how strange that we should be able to do anything at all with the one we have!
>
> In giving explanations I already have to use language full-blown (not some sort of preparatory, provisional one); this by itself shews that I can adduce only exterior facts about language.
>
> Yes, but then how can these explanations satisfy us?—Well, your very questions were framed in this language; they had to be expressed in this language, if there was to be anything to ask!
>
> And your scruples are misunderstandings.

> Your questions refer to words; so I have to talk about words.
>
> You say: the point isn't the word, but its meaning, and you think of the meaning as a thing of the same kind as the word, though also different from the word. Here the word, there the meaning. The money, and the cow that you can buy with it. (But contrast: money, and its use.)

In this passage, Wittgenstein outlines a series of distinctions: that between the interior and exterior of words, between words and meanings, and, most curiously, less a distinction than a relation, between scruples and misunderstandings. Following this list, what initially seems to present a series of obvious distinctions becomes difficult to maintain when carefully examined. Whereas traditional philosophy has, through its search for the connection between the two, implied that words and meanings are essentially different, the connection between the two, as Wittgenstein points out, is no more nebulous than their division. "Your questions refer to words; so I have to talk about words." This is to say that meaning is neither hidden somewhere beneath the surface of language nor made of some other material. The reference to scruples thus is equally a reference to the seemingly ethical underpinning of the demand for absolute clarity that underlay the *Tractatus*.[7]

The suggestion that the "ethical principles" overriding the *Tractatus* are themselves problematic is most glaringly in evidence in the paradox between the *Tractatus*'s demands for the absolute correlation of language and logic and its simultaneous inability to make room for ethical propositions or actions themselves. By realizing that ethics in the *Investigations* is beyond the hesitation to act on some unmentioned grounds of conscience, Wittgenstein allows for practice and ethics to enter into a philosophy of language and theory of meaning; that is, the remaking of the model of meaning on the ethical/aesthetic in the *Investigations* in relation to rather than in contrast to a wider grasp of language and philosophy results from the newfound impossibility of fully separating word and meaning, inner and outer, ethics and logic, which is to say, from the production of a new spatial model.

The assembly, arrangement, cutting down, and dropping out of various sketches construct a description of what now can be understood for what it is—both an image of entanglement and one of perspicuity. The act of arranging continues on as a method for achieving clarity, but from a now recast perspective. As such, the images produced in surveying and depicting the surface of language no longer uphold the sharply defined series of boundaries and limits that defined the *Tractatus* but are images of a constitutive, productive, and inescapable entanglement.

Boundaries

Wittgenstein's discussion of boundaries in the *Investigations* arises on the heels of his introduction of the concept of family resemblance. It begins, as might be expected, with consideration of how the concept of "game" is bounded. The multitude of practices comprising games highlighted by Wittgenstein suggests that the word "game" has neither a closed nor an absolute boundary. As a result of observing the ways in which "game" or "number" function in everyday practices of language, the concept of boundary itself comes to be reconsidered:

> 68. "All right: the concept of number is defined for you as the logical sum of these individual interrelated concepts: cardinal numbers, rational numbers, real numbers, etc.; and in the same way the concept of a game as the logical sum of a corresponding set of sub-concepts."—It need not be so. For I *can* give the concept "number" rigid limits in this way, that is, use the word "number" for a rigidly limited concept, but I can also use it so that the extension of the concept is *not* closed by a frontier. And this is how we do use the word "game." For how is the concept of a game bounded? What still counts as a game and what no longer does? Can you give the boundary? No. You can *draw* one; for none has so far been drawn. (But that never troubled you before when you used the word "game.")
>
> "But then the use of the word is unregulated, the 'game' we play with it is unregulated."—It is not everywhere circumscribed by rules; but no

more are there any rules of how high one throws the ball in tennis, or how hard; yet tennis is a game for all that and has rules too.

In the passage immediately following, the discussion of the boundaries of a word, concept, or practice evolves into an explicit discussion of spatial limits and practices such as those involved in the production of architectural drawings, measurement, and building construction:

> 69. How should we explain to someone what a game is? I imagine that we should describe *games* to him, and we might add: "This *and similar things* are called 'games.'" And do we know any more about it ourselves? Is it only other people whom we cannot tell exactly what a game is?—But this is not ignorance. We do not know the boundaries because none have been drawn. To repeat, we can draw a boundary—for a special purpose. Does it take that to make the concept usable? Not at all! (Except for that special purpose.) No more than it took the definition 1 pace = 75 cm to make the measure of length "one pace" usable. And if you want to say "But still, before that it wasn't an exact measure," then I reply: very well, it was an inexact one.—Though you still owe me a definition of exactness.

Once posited, the observation that we often operate without having exactly defined or sharply delineated boundaries leads to the discussion of boundaries that are themselves not sharply defined, such as fuzzy pictures and roughly indicated places. Wittgenstein presents these in order to test how indistinct boundaries function in everyday practices:

> 71. One might say that the concept "game" is a concept with blurred edges.—"But is a blurred concept a concept at all?"—Is an indistinct photograph a picture of a person at all? Is it even always an advantage to replace an indistinct picture by a sharp one? Isn't the indistinct one often exactly what we need?
>
> Frege compares a concept to an area and says that an area with vague boundaries cannot be called an area at all. This presumably means that we cannot do anything with it.—But is it senseless to say "Stand roughly there"? Suppose that I were standing with someone in a city square and said that. As I say it I do not draw any kind of boundary, but perhaps point with my hand—as if I were indicating a particular spot. And this is just how one might explain to someone what a game is. One gives examples and intends them to be taken in a particular way.—I do not, however,

mean by this that he is supposed to see in those examples that common thing which I—for some reason—was unable to express; but that he is now to *employ* those examples in a particular way. Here giving examples is not an *indirect* means of explaining—in default of a better. For any general definition can be misunderstood too. The point is that *this* is how we play the game. (I mean the language-game with the word "game.")

The realization of unclear or even undemarcated boundaries defining games has far-reaching consequences in language. The first of these raises the question of the nature of similar boundaries that separate word from word, concept from concept. The second is the crucial question of indistinct boundaries themselves. Indistinct boundaries challenge not just the concept defined but the construct of boundary itself. As Wittgenstein draws no line between an abstracted concept of boundary and actual spatial and physical boundaries we may encounter, the shift from the functioning of boundaries in our use of language to a discussion of visual and spatial boundaries themselves is fluid. *All uses of "boundary," as of "game," participate in our understanding of the concept of boundary.* The construct of family resemblance and its concomitant images of entanglement assure us of this. Family resemblance can now be perceived in terms beyond the defining of Wittgenstein's understanding of language to reveal itself as a fully spatial practice, one that, as becomes apparent, is unthinkable without challenging the overarching concern of boundary production between showing and saying in the *Tractatus*.

The breakdown of the show-say distinction in the *Investigations* lies in the suggestion that showing this way—the pointing with the hand or the giving of or showing examples—is not indicative of an inability to express an idea in a better or more precise manner; that is, the *Investigations* makes clear that contrary to the *Tractatus*'s thinking, showing does not commence from the point at which saying fails. Nor is it an inferior method. Instead, showing implicates practice, a view disallowed by the *Tractatus*. Practice in the *Investigations* prevails, not because saying failed in its inability to define essence but because of the concrete historical failure illustrated by the construction of many philosophical theories and intractable problems, as compared with the successes of everyday forms of communication. That failure, once apparent, permits practice to move forward and furnish a method of counteracting the hierarchy of saying over showing in philosophy. Privileging saying produced mistakes based on appearance which, importantly, philosophy, by largely excluding the visual, remained untrained in and thus unable to detect. As the *Investigations* claims, the ability to distinguish amongst the appearance of words is central to philosophy. But in overlooking the visual/spatial/practical components of language, philosophy had also overlooked those components through which distinctions in appearance were revealed. The result left philosophy incapable of fully making the distinctions it demanded.

Boundaries in the *Investigations* come to exemplify not just the distance from their counterparts in the *Tractatus* but their participation in fundamentally reconfiguring philosophy. Based in and resulting from the spatial practices of design and construction Wittgenstein encountered in the practice of architecture, the specific discussions of boundaries within the *Investigations* constitute the foundation of philosophy's reconfiguration. Whereas the *Tractatus* discusses the limits of language, of philosophy, the subject, and so on, the nature and configuration of the boundaries themselves are never discussed. Rather, as the *Investigations* acknowledges, they are repeatedly reinscribed in accordance with the (nonmaterial) order of logic, in contrast to the *Investigations*'s continuously evolving construction of and challenge to those same boundaries. Not until the *Investigations* does Wittgenstein produce a philosophy capable of incorporating into its discussion the formation of its own spatial thinking or capable of theorizing its own spatial practices. Accordingly, many of the challenges to logic take form in the *Investigations* as spatial and physical measurement, where the concerns for spatial, linguistic, and philosophical boundaries are brought together in order to overcome the problems created in philosophy in its ignorance of these aspects of language.

Wittgenstein's remade boundaries of philosophy and language redefine the idea of sense and nonsense arising around diverse boundary formations. Many of these emerging types of boundaries function in ways that could not be and, more importantly, are not prescribed by the *Tractatus*. In response, questions of context and function repeatedly emerge throughout the *Investigations*. What, for example, is the purpose of the boundary in question? One purpose of the boundary is to define its own nature by specifying or producing the particular boundary function desired. As such, the nature or structure of the boundary informs how it may function and thus what purposes it may serve and by which criteria we can judge whether it has fulfilled its function:

> 499. To say "This combination of words makes no sense" excludes it from the sphere of language and thereby bounds the domain of language. But when one draws a boundary it may be for various kinds of reason. If I surround an area with a fence or a line or otherwise, the purpose may

be to prevent someone from getting in or out; but it may also be part of a game and the players be supposed, say, to jump over the boundary; or it may shew where the property of one man ends and that of another begins; and so on. So if I draw a boundary line that is not yet to say what I am drawing it for.

Boundaries arise most ardently in the *Tractatus* to define points of transgression. The *Investigations*'s acknowledging of the spatial and temporal nature of language instead alters what it means to inhabit language or transgress its bounds. From the point of view of the inhabitation of language, the transgression of the bounds of sense possible in the *Tractatus* confronts the actualized boundaries of everyday linguistic practices that disallow the hypothetical transgression of language upon which the *Tractatus* is based.

This thinking supports Wittgenstein's realization in the *Investigations* that we can no longer command an absolutely clear view in our use of words as our grammar is lacking in (that) sort of perspicuity. Clarity is dependent on a place from which one can command a "clear view," but where can that be with language? Not from seeing the whole of language, because there can be no such external position that would allow for that. Clarity and perspicuity—along with confusion and misunderstanding—must necessarily arise from within, as any attempt to define it from without is unobtainable. As with Wittgenstein's question as to what becomes of logic now, the question may be added: What becomes of clarity now? The question of clarity and the attempt to obtain a clear view reaffirm an inherent problem with the inner/outer metaphor itself: the metaphor contains the problematic implication of a possible boundary producing an external standpoint. As both imply a position beyond the limits of language, speaking of an inside is as problematic as speaking of an outside.

The concern with an inaccessible space beyond language, one linked to both the transgression and delineation of boundaries, surfaces in Wittgenstein's late work as a certain amount of spatial angst associated with these remade, inexactly defined, and potentially shifting boundaries. Passage 84 of the *Investigations* begins with the realization that as the meaning and use of a word "is not everywhere bounded by rules," the use of words themselves is not an absolutely defined practice. Uncertainty takes on a spatial dimension, becoming a sort of inverse boundary in the landscape, emerging at the juncture of landscape and building. It is this same boundary, the one separating indoors from out[8] and moving us from looking at the landscape to being in it, which also forms the operative shift between types of images of entanglement, between immobility and construction:

> 84. I said that the application of a word is not everywhere bounded by rules. But what does a game look like that is everywhere bounded by rules? whose rules never let a doubt creep in, but stop up all the cracks where *it* might?—Can't we imagine a rule determining the application of a rule, and a doubt which it removes—and so on?
>
> But that is not to say that we are in doubt because it is possible for us to imagine a doubt. I can easily imagine someone always doubting before he opened his front door whether an abyss did not yawn behind it, and making sure about it before he went through the door (and he might on some occasion prove to be right)—but that does not make me doubt in the same case.

The suggestion that there is something beyond which we cannot access emerges beside the declaration or implication of a boundary. This understanding, in denying that there can be a purely external or internal standpoint, destroys any thinking that adheres to a strict dichotomy between the inner and the outer. The desire to be outside and be able to see the complete picture no longer remains a possibility. The sketches are thus not merely preparatory for a final version. This same idea is reflected in Wittgenstein's discussion of philosophy's ability to discuss itself, where he describes philosophy as not having to move outside itself in order to "see" itself—a concept literally present in Wittgenstein's comparison of philosophy with orthography:

> 121. One might think: if philosophy speaks of the use of "philosophy" there must be a second-order philosophy. But it is not so: it is, rather, like the case of orthography, which deals with the word "orthography" among others without then being second-order.

Wittgenstein's employment of the visual and spatial along with family resemblance in his discussion of boundaries serves to reassess the emerging practice of philosophy and the association of its component parts, including the realms of aesthetics and ethics. This combination produces the only time that Wittgenstein specifically mentions aesthetics/ethics in the *Investigations*.[9] It is not coincidental that the concepts of aesthetics and ethics, the makeup of the boundaries of philosophy, and the realm of language and meaning as characterized by family resemblance should converge at this point in the *Investigations*. The juncture specifically ties together Wittgenstein's aim in the *Tractatus* to designate the scope and limits of language-philosophy with an understanding that such a goal is a spatial practice—one remade with the new awareness of space, boundaries, practice, correspondence, agreement, and so on. The working out of spatial problems in this section enters philosophy anew by referring to aesthetics/ethics and thereby fully incorporating these components into the late philosophy's reconceived limits of language and philosophy. These areas, previously labeled as functioning outside the bounds of the sayable, become in the *Investigations* the site from which the emerging understanding of boundaries and meaning explicitly emanate:

> 77. And if we carry this comparison still further it is clear that the degree to which the sharp picture *can* resemble the blurred one depends on the latter's degree of vagueness. For imagine having to sketch a sharply defined picture "corresponding" to a blurred one. In the latter there is a blurred red rectangle: for it you put down a sharply defined one. Of course—several such sharply defined rectangles can be drawn to correspond to the indefinite one.—But if the colors in the original merge without a hint of any outline won't it become a hopeless task to draw a sharp picture corresponding to the blurred one? Won't you then have to say: "Here I might just as well draw a circle or heart as a rectangle, for all the colors merge. Anything—and nothing—is right."—And this is the position you are in if you look for definitions corresponding to our concepts in aesthetics or ethics.
>
> In such a difficulty always ask yourself: How did we *learn* the meaning of this word ("good" for instance)? From what sort of examples? in what language-games? Then it will be easier for you to see that the word must have a family of meanings.

This reference to "good" completes the expansion of Moore's single and definitive statement on ethics begun by Wittgenstein in his "Lecture on Ethics" with the protoconcept of family resemblance. While the lecture remains content to expand Moore's single statement into related multiple ones, in the *Investigations* Wittgenstein inspects the propositions of aesthetics and ethics and finds the extension and definition of ethics serve an important purpose, not in simply extending the understanding of ethics but in initiating a practice. It is that practice—born of extension—in becoming visible that allows for Wittgenstein's questioning the very basis of requirements he places on language in the early philosophy. The expanded ethics, in drawing a picture, fosters the reconception of language as a practice or collection of practices, as manifest in the assembling of reminders in the form of language-games. This shift ultimately brings aesthetics and ethics into philosophy as an important model for all of language rather than a limited model for a specific region.

Shared Territory

By the end, Wittgenstein had given over two years of his time to the design and construction of the Stonborough-Wittgenstein House for his sister. In January 1929, immediately following the completion of the house, Wittgenstein returned to Cambridge and to philosophy. In a letter he wrote at that time to Moritz Schlick, the philosopher of the Vienna Circle, Wittgenstein spoke of his decision to remain in Cambridge "for a few terms and work on visual space [*Gesichtsraum*] and other things."[10] The term *visual space* is intriguing, particularly in this instance. Although it remains unclear what visual space fully includes, the idea of visual space suggests that architecture may well have furnished the site of Wittgenstein's interest in visual space as well as the starting point and final impetus for his late work. While the architecture of the central hall of the house yields some clues to the meaning of this term, with glass, for example, serving as a preeminent material for the study of visual space, Wittgenstein's incarnation of "the visual room" in the *Investigations* offers additional prospects.

Paragraphs 398 to 400 of the *Investigations* specifically discuss the concept of visual space in the form of Wittgenstein's example of the visual room:

> 398 "But when I imagine something, or even actually *see* objects, I have *got* something which my neighbour has not."—I understand you. You want to look about you and say: "At any rate only I have got THIS."—What are these words for? They serve no purpose.—Can one not add: "There is

here no question of a 'seeing'—and therefore none of a 'having'—nor of a subject, nor therefore of 'I' either"? Might I not ask: In what sense have you *got* what you are talking about and saying that only you have got it? Do you possess it? You do not even *see* it. Must you not really say that no one has got it? And this too is clear: if as a matter of logic you exclude other people's having something, it loses its sense to say that you have it.

But what is the thing you are speaking of? It is true I said that I knew within myself what you meant. But this meant that I knew how one thinks to conceive this object, to see it, to make one's looking and pointing mean it. I know how one stares ahead and looks about one in this case—and the rest. I think we can say: you are talking (if, for example, you are sitting in a room) of the "visual room." The "visual room" is the one that has no owner. I can as little own it as I can walk about it, or look at it, or point to it. Inasmuch as it cannot be any one else's it is not mine either. In other words, it does not belong to me *because* I want to use the same form of expression about it as about the material room in which I sit. The description of the latter need not mention an owner, in fact it need not have any owner. But then the visual room *cannot* have any owner. "For"—one might say—"it has no master, outside or in."

Think of a picture of a landscape, an imaginary landscape with a house in it.—Someone asks "Whose house is that?"—The answer, by the way, might be "It belongs to the farmer who is sitting on the bench in front of it." But then he cannot for example enter his house.

Wittgenstein's passages on the visual room reveal the space of architecture to be specifically a space of philosophical concern. That space defines sites of philosophical problems, and in so doing, continues the construction of a shared territory between the spatial and the linguistic that begins in the *Investigations* with the builders. Wittgenstein's raising the issue of ownership of the visual room can also be understood as questioning what disciplinary standards, concerns, and issues are in operation between architecture, space, and language. As ownership is the product of a boundary, the questions focus on the boundaries of ideas as well as those of space. These problematics, which in the *Investigations* frequently involve the move from two-dimensional space to three-dimensional space, play out time and again. One iteration appears in the examples in the *Investigations* that imagine the multiple possibilities latent in two-dimensional depiction of a three-dimensional geometric projection. In each case, ambiguities arise from the implication of more than one possible three-dimensional form capable of fulfilling the description.

Wittgenstein's curious discussion of the "visual room" constructs such an association between drawings and architecture. While invoking architectural drawings, landscapes, and houses, the discussion proves most intriguing in its association of the subject, the self, and the question of the inhabitation of language. The visual room acts out the envisioning of a visual image, either real or imagined, of a spatial "object." Although the visual room might be consolidated under Wittgenstein's discussion of the relation between the inner and outer, private mental imagery and publicly accessible language, as with his well-known discussion of pain sensations (in the so-called private-language argument), the situation here is markedly different. Rather than "language" forming the specific outward criterion, as in the earlier examples, here the visual, spatial, and architectural become the primary form of comparison. And, if only because of the example chosen, the act of envisioning a room not yet there mimics an activity Wittgenstein encountered in the practice of architecture.

The question of ownership that Wittgenstein introduces is also relevant. Ownership arises as an everyday architectural situation. When an architect designs a house, a room for someone else, whose room is it? It is the product of the designer's thinking, yet it is not "owned" by him or her. The concept also intones questions of privacy and accessibility, constructs repeatedly examined by Wittgenstein. The impossibility of entering into the *Tractatus*'s conception of solipsistic language (hence the resultant view from without) is revealed as the impossibility of entering into a nonpublic language and is contrasted here with the demand for inhabitation of the physical, not just mental, kind. As such, the exclusion of private mental space is shown, literally, to be akin to the impossibility of others entering and inhabiting that space, marking that space as inaccessible yet present.

The distinction drawn at the end of the middle paragraph between "ownership" of a physical rather than a "visual" room brings with it the question of the connection between the two—a question concerning, among other things, issues of space and inhabitation. The visual room cannot have an owner "outside or in." While this excludes inhabitation of the visual room, it does so on the basis of the ambiguous position that the "visual room" maintains between outside and in, public and private. And the visual room, as it turns out in the subsequent passage, is akin to language in that it has no outside. "One might also say: Surely the owner of the visual room would have to be the same kind of thing as it is; but he is not to be found in it, and there is no outside" (sec. 399).

Another way to approach the space between outside and in is to understand it as equally the space between the *Tractatus* and the *Investigations*.

Whereas we are not assuredly outside the *Tractatus* (and language) in the view from the ladder, the *Investigations* brings with it inhabitation and the knowledge that we are most certainly within language. The admission that we are utterly and inescapably within language (the *Investigations* disallows the possibility of being outside it) begins to dismantle the inner/outer distinctions and positioning in relation to language. The outside, as with Wittgenstein's discussion of ownership, begins to lose its meaning as we have no way of apprehending, describing, depicting, or speaking about it. As we cannot be outside language, being "inside" also loses its piquancy.

Architecture, then, becomes an even more intriguing example here for Wittgenstein. While clearly a physical room can be inhabited, owned, entered, exited, and so on, a visual room, that which arises in the attempt to comprehend a proposition (coincidentally about a room) is akin to language in its ambiguity and its relationship to ownership. With the discussion of the visual room, Wittgenstein's discussion of a private language can be understood to be examined at three different scales in relation to the subject: as on par with the subject in the discussion of a private language, pain, or sensation; on a smaller, external scale, such as in Wittgenstein's discussion of spiderwebs; and at the third scale, in the implied enclosure of the subject with the discussion of the visual room or nets. The discussion of the visual room thereby solidifies the association of the spatial and the linguistic in the inner/outer, private/public discussion.

The visual room proves its immediate usefulness in the discussion of language one paragraph later. "The 'visual room' seemed like a discovery, but what its discoverer really found was a new way of speaking, a new comparison; it might be called a new sensation" (sec. 400). The practice of architecture has thus produced a new way of speaking, accompanied by a new understanding of language. The association again of architecture and language, here particularly regarding the visual room, offers a newly realized manner of speaking in conjunction with Wittgenstein's reconception of language in the *Investigations* that binds architecture to language and the subject.

Through the incorporation of aesthetics, ethics, and practice into the philosophy of language, Wittgenstein reconceives the functioning of language. The philosophy of language, the ostensible work of the *Investigations*, is thus irreparably altered. Aesthetics, ethics, practice, epistemology, meaning, logic, and so on are all entangled in the formation of the family resemblance of philosophy. The thread of logic that runs through all parts of language and philosophy in the *Tractatus* is no longer understood as the essence of language, hidden or otherwise. Instead, it remains a fiber in the twine, but, as with all of the other fibers, it does not run throughout but is evident only at moments. Equally, its placement is not always apparent but is at times obscured, its length indeterminate. Yet it remains logic. Thus logic, along with aesthetics, ethics, and other components of philosophy, contributes to the formation of images of entanglement that emerge throughout the *Investigations*. The *Investigations* begins with this image and works to produce methods whereby it can be examined rather than replaced with a "clearer" model of the functioning of language. This is most apparent when the crystalline structure of language developed in the *Tractatus* itself becomes, once examined in the *Investigations*, another form of entanglement, not despite of but as a direct result of its goal of absolute clarity.

The proximity of Wittgenstein's introduction of family resemblance to the *Investigations*'s discussion of the breakdown of absolute boundaries and its culmination in the reference to ethics and aesthetics act to reaffirm how meaning in the *Investigations* comes to be modeled on aesthetics/ethics and not on logic. The dismantling of absolute boundaries brings along with it the destruction of the one-to-one-to-one correspondence of word, meaning, and place realized in the analysis of the function and purpose of place in the discussion of boundaries. The discussion progresses in the *Investigations* by examining the operative difference between vague and sharp boundaries and continues on to a discussion of the boundary between vague and sharp. All this occurs without separating types of boundaries, be they a wall in a house, a fence in the landscape, or a delineation between philosophical concepts. With these shifts, the *Investigations* reveals itself as the view from across the boundary the *Tractatus* attempts to draw, a boundary that operates in previously inconceivable ways so that it is able to incorporate the *Tractatus*'s views as they are relevant for a limited section of language. It is from there that Wittgenstein redraws the landscape, with aesthetics/ethics supplanting logic as the structuring order of the philosophy of language. Through the introduction of this new spatial model of boundary, borne of entanglement, what it means to structure language or philosophy is transformed.

Aesthetics and ethics reveal their importance in this process by being the original site and the first place in which definitions and depictions are seen to become not necessarily more useful when made more absolute. This, however, does not remain solely the case. Rather, as with Wittgenstein's primary examples of "game" and the concept of language itself, such functioning is far more extensive. And, as the discussion of boundaries reveals, there is no sharp distinction between vagueness and sharpness itself—this in contrast to the *Tractatus*, which draws, or attempts to draw, a sharp boundary between the sensible portion of philosophy and the unsayable propositions of ethics and aesthetics. They thus enter as a defining practice of the late philosophy, in effect becoming the model language-game or original home where such a use of language is first learned. The practice of architecture is no stranger to that home.

Wittgenstein's return to philosophy in his 1929 "Lecture on Ethics" thus initiated a process that ultimately posited a photomontaged aesthetic practice at its center. Through this image, capable of incorporating, inseparably, multiple images to create new ones, language becomes both knowable and recognizable as family resemblance. The importance of the image of entanglement providing both the inspiration and explanation for language in the *Investigations* turns out to be the effect of method in Wittgenstein's late philosophy. As the *Investigations* functions through a series of examples, models, and reminders, the image of entanglement becomes the iconic example, capable of revealing—by showing, saying, ordering, commanding, pointing, and so on—the language-game to be itself a profitable entanglement.

In having maintained the method of defining the outer by the inner, the excluded by the included, the *Tractatus* leaves the realm of aesthetics paradoxically both privileged as the outer and marginalized as silence. As the site of Wittgenstein's renewed interest in philosophy, aesthetics and ethics repeatedly resurface, initially through the practice of architecture, then in the "Lecture on Ethics," and finally in the late philosophy of the *Investigations*. Although arguably still underground in the *Investigations* when read traditionally as subject matter, aesthetics/ethics comes to the forefront when read in accordance with the *Investigations*'s emphasis on method and example. The return to the everyday as the model for philosophy is, after all, the site of the practices of aesthetics and ethics. Wittgenstein in the *Investigations* reincorporates this realm into philosophy and the everyday to serve as a corrective model for an estranging philosophy in search of a home. This does not limit aesthetics to the visual and spatial, on the one hand, or the practices of art and architecture, on the other, but *incorporates* them into philosophy to yield an alternative to the *Tractatus*'s single method, which only empties philosophy.

Guiding the methods and examples, aesthetic practices lie at the center of Wittgenstein's philosophy in the *Investigations*. This is so not simply owing to Wittgenstein's practice of architecture, his introduction of the builders, his placing a series of photographs as the first examples, or his emphasis on the visual and the spatial, nor even due to the construction of images of entanglement. Rather, it is a product of the very functioning of language as entanglement. That functioning allows for aesthetics, practice, logic, epistemology, facts, and the natural sciences all to be entwined in language, destroying the previously defensive borders drawn by the *Tractatus*. The *Investigations* thus begins from the boundaries of sense drawn by the *Tractatus* and redefines the location and nature of that boundary, redefining the relations of philosophy, sense, language, practice, showing, and saying in the process.

In placing ethics and aesthetics at the center of his late philosophy, the *Investigations* thus moves beyond the self-imposed bounds of the *Tractatus* to incorporate what previously could only be defined from without. Aesthetics and ethics thus replace, in one way, the role logic plays in the *Tractatus*. Their inclusion provides more than just the ability to dismantle traditional philosophy; rather, it creates the basis for building a philosophy—yet another role for the builders in the *Investigations*. Logic, as Wittgenstein tells us, remains intact in the *Investigations* but serves a different, more limited function, becoming a *topic* of investigation rather than maintaining its privileged role as the sole *method* of investigation. This reversal of modes of investigation shows how altering the tools, media, and approaches produces different grasps of reality, philosophy, and language. This supports a main theme of the *Investigations*, that methods, form, processes—the ways that we do philosophy—are a crucial part of the philosophy produced.

The emphasis on a multiplicity of methods in the late philosophy can be seen in Wittgenstein's work within architecture, which introduced a multitude of new practices, methods, and approaches to problems, as well as providing a field in which to experiment and examine the results of these experiments with methods of design, construction, and thought. Seemingly paradoxically, the practice of architecture, which might have been expected to shore up Wittgenstein's view of the definitive nature of boundaries in the walls of a building, instead led him to see how diverse boundaries may be. These distinctions serve clearly to differentiate operative boundaries from the absolute limits of the *Tractatus*. Boundaries instead develop from practice in the *Investigations*, where their specific qualities are determined by their materiality, location, surroundings, and required uses. In Wittgenstein's practice of architecture, boundaries emerged in a multitude of forms—as walls, windows, doors, openings, elevational changes, stairs, lines in the floor, and as opaque, transparent, translucent, and implied. In the late philosophy, this same thinking produces a use- and context-dependent structure for language and philosophy that is permeable at times, more definitive at others, allowing boundaries that were previously solely exclusionary to reemerge to produce a shared territory of philosophy and language, showing and saying, vision and space.

INTRODUCTION
SPATIAL PRACTICES FROM ARCHITECTURE TO PHILOSOPHY

1. Ludwig Wittgenstein, *Tractatus Logico-Philosophicus: The German Text of Logisch-philosophische Abhandlung*, trans. D. F. Pears and B. F. McGuinness, with an introduction by Bertrand Russell (London: Routledge & Kegan Paul; New York: Humanities Press, 1961). The *Tractatus* was first published in German in 1921, and its first English translation appeared the following year, 1922. The current translation was revised following Wittgenstein's suggestions. The *Tractatus* was the culmination of the first movement of analytic philosophy, logical atomism. Widely understood, analytic philosophy formed a systematic attempt to reconsider the assumption that language offers an accurate and truthful description of reality.

2. Ludwig Wittgenstein, *Philosophical Investigations*, trans. G. E. M. Anscombe (New York: Macmillan, 1953). The *Investigations* was published two years after Wittgenstein's death in 1951.

3. The house was built for Wittgenstein's sister Margarethe Stonborough-Wittgenstein between 1926 and 1928. It is located on the Kundmanngasse in Vienna and was declared a National Landmark following its near sale and destruction in the early 1970s. It currently houses the Bulgarian Cultural Institute.

4. See, e.g., Bernhard Leitner, *The Architecture of Ludwig Wittgenstein* (London: Academy Editions, 1995); and Paul Wijdeveld, *Ludwig Wittgenstein: Architect* (Cambridge, Mass.: MIT Press, 1994).

5. Wittgenstein, *Tractatus*, prop. 4.114.

6. Following the outbreak of World War I, Wittgenstein voluntarily returned to Austria to enlist in the army as a soldier. Once there, he insisted upon being sent to the front, where he was eventually captured and spent ten months as a prisoner of war in Italy.

7. Michael Nedo, "Introduction," in *Ludwig Wittgenstein: Wiener Ausgabe* (Vienna and New York: Springer-Verlag, 1993).

8. *Philosophical Investigations*, sec. 114.

9. Ibid., sec. 103.

10. I am referring here to the first and main part of the *Philosophical Investigations*; the second part was added by the editors after Wittgenstein's death. The editors note that part 2 contains material that Wittgenstein would have worked into the first part.

11. See *Philosophical Investigations*, secs. 2, 6, 8–10, and 17–21.

12. Henri Lefebvre's criticism of Kristeva, Derrida, and Barthes comes to mind because despite his opposing point of view, he reiterates that the debate involved is indeed a spatial one. Lefebvre, *The Production of Space*, trans. Donald Nicholson-Smith (Cambridge, Mass.: Blackwell, 1991), criticizes Kristeva, Derrida, and Barthes for "leap[ing] over an entire area, ignoring the need for any logical links" in "promoting the basic sophistry whereby the philosophico-epistemological notion of space is fetishized and the mental realm comes to envelop the social and physical ones." That they largely "spring without the slightest hesitation from mental to social" (6). Lefebvre also notes that Lévi-Strauss in all of his work "implies that from the earliest manifestations of social life mental and social were conflated by virtue of the nomenclature of the relationships of exchange" (5 n. 12).

13. Although spatial and visual metaphors are clearly evident in Wittgenstein's text, even frequently acknowledged, the implications of such insistent and repeated visual-spatial thinking within the texts has remained at a distance from the discussions of the "philosophy" of the *Investigations*. As a result, such thought has been subsumed to a philosophy understood to operate outside of or at best in association with that thinking. When discussed, visual and spatial metaphors are predominantly employed to explain "the philosophy" rather than to contemplate what, for example, the philosophy says about space or what consequences spatial thinking held for the development of Wittgenstein's philosophy. Frequently it is assumed that the importance of spatial-visual thinking is to operate as a neutral tool to discuss some other aspects of philosophy or language proper rather than to be a subject of philosophical study in its own right, Such a view reduces the importance of the specifics of the text on all levels as well as denying the specific functioning of spatial and visual thought as integral and important components of philosophical thought. To focus on the visual and the spatial within a philosophy text is to shift the focus within philosophy onto that which philosophy traditionally has repressed as merely metaphorical. For other approaches that recognize the importance of visual and spatial concepts in Wittgenstein's work but still, I believe, subsume it to the philosophy proper, see, among others, Judith Genova, *Wittgenstein: A Way of Seeing* (New York and London: Routledge, 1995); Stephen Mulhall, *On Being in the World: Wittgenstein and Heidegger on Seeing Aspects* (New York and London: Routledge, 1990); and John

Koethe, *The Continuity of Wittgenstein's Thought* (Ithaca, N.Y., and London: Cornell University Press, 1996).

14. Wijdeveld, *Wittgenstein: Architect*.

15. Book Review of *Ludwig Wittgenstein, Architect, Journal of Aesthetics and Art Criticism*, 53, 4 (1995): 451.

16. Wijdeveld, *Wittgenstein: Architect*, 194.

17. Wittgenstein himself entered this fray when in his early work he denied such a shared territory, positing in its place an indissoluble distinction between showing and saying. Yet his late philosophy opened up just such a territory by questioning the sharp line between language and other practices, suggesting, for example, that the view of animals as simply not using language can only be upheld "if we except the most primitive forms of language" and noting that: "Commanding, questioning, recounting, chatting, are as much a part of our natural history as walking, eating, drinking, playing." *Philosophical Investigations*, sec. 25.

18. Elizabeth Grosz, *Architecture from the Outside: Essays on Virtual and Real Space* (Cambridge, Mass.: MIT Press, 2001), xvi. For example, take the language Grosz uses to describe the outside. In her discussion, while underscoring fundamental differences in the modes of conceptual and other operations of the disciplines, Grosz paradoxically repeatedly interposes "term" and "space" in referring to each of the disciplines. This suggests a fundamental interconnectivity. Immanent in it is the suggestion that such language occupies both sites akin to how ordinary language permeates discourse.

19. Grosz, *Architecture from the Outside*, xv–xvi.

20. Wijdeveld, *Wittgenstein: Architect*, 194.

21. Grosz, *Architecture from the Outside*, 72–73.

22. Ibid.

23. Michel de Certeau, *The Practice of Everyday Life*, trans. Steven Rendall (Berkeley, Calif.: University of California Press, 1984).

24. *Philosophical Investigations*, sec. 116.

25. Ibid., sec. 119.

26. Ibid., sec. 120.

27. Such a purifying process was the exact intention of the *Tractatus* in its requirement that language conform to the specialty of logic. It is also how Wijdeveld comes to describe Wittgenstein's main role in the design of the Stonborough-Wittgenstein House.

28. De Certeau, *Practice of Everyday Life*, 10.

29. Ibid., 13–14. De Certeau was referring here to Wittgenstein's stating that "When we do philosophy . . . we are like savages, primitive people, who hear the expressions of civilized men, put a false interpretation on them, and then draw the queerest conclusions from it."

30. Ibid., 11.

31. Ibid., 10–11.

32. As much as de Certeau owes a debt to Wittgenstein, he does not fully see the difference between the early and late philosophy in their view of language and therefore misses the full impact of the late philosophy on spatial practices; hence he associates Wittgenstein directly with only his discussion of language rather than his wider discussion of spatial practices of the everyday.

33. De Certeau, *Practice of Everyday Life*, 10–11.

34. Slavoj Žižek, *Looking Awry: An Introduction to Jacques Lacan through Popular Culture* (Cambridge, Mass.: MIT Press, 1991), 3. For Žižek, this undertaking involves the discussion of Lacanian psychoanalytic theory as it emerges in and through various forms of popular culture.

35. The classic example of such a look awry is the use of anamorphosis in Hans Holbein's painting "The Ambassadors" (1533). For a discussion of the spatial implications, see Norman Bryson, "The Gaze in the Expanded Field," in *Vision and Visuality*, ed. Hal Foster (Seattle: Bay Press, 1988), 87–108; and Allen Weiss, "Vaux-le-Vicomte: Anamorphosis Abscondita," in *Mirrors of Infinity: The French Formal Garden and Seventeenth-Century Metaphysics* (New York: Princeton Architectural Press, 1995), 32–51.

36. *Tractatus*, props. 5.6, 5.61.

37. Ibid., prop. 5.632.

38. Ibid., prop. 6.54.

39. For a discussion of some other understandings of the numbering system in the *Tractatus*, see Verena Mayer, "The Numbering System of the *Tractatus*," *Ratio* 6 (1993): 108–19.

40. *Philosophical Investigations*, sec. 66.

41. See de Certeau, *Practice of Everyday Life*. De Certeau uses Wittgenstein's late philosophy to set up the idea of both practice and the everyday. However, he does not connect it to the view from the streets that he presents in his work.

42. Wittgenstein lists early on in the *Investigations* examples of language-games, including giving orders, singing catches, play-acting, describing an object, and "Constructing an object from a description (a drawing)" see *Philosophical Investigations*, sec. 23.

43. In the past decade there have been a number of books that—although in a very different manner and without focusing on his practice of architecture—have developed discussions of Wittgenstein's philosophy in relation to other disciplines, including psychoanalysis, literary criticism, and political thought. For examples, see Jacques Bouveresse, *Wittgenstein Reads Freud: The Myth of the Unconscious*, trans. Carol Cosman (Princeton, N.J.: Princeton University Press, 1995); Susan B. Brill, *Wittgenstein and Critical Theory: Beyond Postmodernism and toward Descriptive Investigations* (Athens, Ohio: Ohio University Press, 1995); and Alice Crary and Rupert Read, eds., *The New Wittgenstein* (New York and London: Routledge, 2000).

CHAPTER I

TRANSGRESSIONS

1. *Tractatus*, prop. 4.114.
2. Ibid., prop. 5.61.
3. Another way to understand this is to see the realm that includes aesthetics and ethics as the realm of practice. It is the realm of practice that forms the basis for the late philosophy of the *Philosophical Investigations*. While defined in the *Tractatus* as beyond the limits of the sayable, the statements of aesthetics and ethics are not outside *the structure of defining the sayable* that the *Tractatus* imposes. Rather, they remain dependent upon the *Tractatus*'s determinate delineation of spatial limits and boundaries. Wittgenstein makes this clear, writing: "[Philosophy] must set limits to what can be thought; and, in doing so, to what cannot be thought. It must set limits to what cannot be thought by working *outwards* through what can be thought" (prop. 4.114; emphasis added). As such, propositions including those from aesthetics and ethics, by virtue of occupying the realm beyond the sayable, are as if expelled from the world, jettisoned into silence, only entering the realm of the *Tractatus* by way of exclusion. Yet they can, given the method of the *Tractatus*, be understood as its subject, a subject defined from the outside. This is the case even though the text maintains that philosophy cannot talk about that realm but can only show it. This realm beyond the sayable; thus it is not unimportant or inconsequential. Instead, Wittgenstein tells us, it is of the utmost importance in our lives even though it cannot be (sensibly) formed in determinate propositions. This understanding is well argued in Allan Janik and Stephen Toulmin, *Wittgenstein's Vienna* (New York: Simon & Schuster, 1973). The authors, however, focus on the ethical rather than emphasizing the place and potential outcomes of examining the aesthetic.
4. *Tractatus*, prop. 1.1.
5. In discussing the distinction between showing and saying in the *Tractatus*, it is important to keep in mind that this is a distinction *within* language. As such, the distinction is not the distinction between the visual and the verbal per se, but *within* the verbal, even if at times it entails silence. Crucially, that such a linguistic distinction is understood to exist implies the existence of a visual component of language.
6. The preface relates that beyond ridding philosophy of pseudo-problems, logical clarification for Wittgenstein is otherwise of admittedly limited value: "the *truth* of the thoughts that are here communicated seems to me unassailable and definitive. I therefore believe myself to have found, on all essential points, the final solution of the problems. And if I am not mistaken in this belief, then the second thing in which the value of this work consists is that it shows how little is achieved when these problems are solved."
7. *Philosophical Investigations*, sec. 3.

8. Ibid., sec. 114.

9. *Tractatus*, prop. 5.632.

10. Ibid., prop. 6.54.

11. Norman Bryson, for example, discusses the development of a sense of oneself as a subject and as an object in the visual field of the other in the writings of Sartre and Lacan. See Norman Bryson, "The Gaze in the Expanded Field," in *Vision and Visuality*, ed. Hal Foster (Seattle: Bay Press, 1988), 87–108.

12. For a discussion of other understandings of the numbering system in the *Tractatus*, see Verena Mayer, "The Numbering System of the *Tractatus*," *Ratio* 6 (1993): 108–19.

13. See Brian McGuinness, *Young Ludwig 1889–1921*, vol. 1 of *Wittgenstein: A Life* (Berkeley, Calif.: University of California Press, 1988), 265.

14. Marjorie Perloff, *Wittgenstein's Ladder* (Chicago: University of Chicago Press, 1996), 42.

15. There is an interesting discussion of relations between scaffolding and the underlying structure by Mark Wigley where it becomes clear that it is the seemingly secondary or dependent nature of scaffolding that makes the structure it defines seem primary. See Mark Wigley, "The Translation of Deconstruction," in Wigley, *The Architecture of Deconstruction: Derrida's Haunt* (Cambridge, Mass.: MIT Press, 1993), 1–33.

16. This number refers to Part I, the primary sec. of the *Investigations* only. It is debated whether the second part would have been included in this text or would have formed a separate text had Wittgenstein lived to see the work published. I have chosen to focus here predominantly on Part I.

17. See *Philosophical Investigations*, sec. 103.

18. Family resemblance is discussed at length in Part Two of this book.

19. See Stanley Cavell, "The Argument of the Ordinary: Scenes of Instruction in Wittgenstein and Kripke," in *Conditions Handsome and Unhandsome* (Chicago: University of Chicago Press, 1990). Another discussion of the practice of teaching in Wittgenstein's late philosophy discusses the inequality of the teacher-student relation. See Kojin Karatani, *Architecture as Metaphor: Language, Number, Money* (Cambridge, Mass.: MIT Press, 1995).

20. Perloff, *Wittgenstein's Ladder*, xiv.

21. *Tractatus*, prop. 4.0.

CHAPTER 2

FROM WITHOUT TO WITHIN: THE BUILDING OF INHABITATION

1. Augustine, *Confessions* I.8.

2. Stanley Cavell discusses this in an unpublished manuscript, "Notes on the Opening of the *Philosophical Investigations*."

3. *Philosophical Investigations*, sec. 2.

4. Ibid., sec. 3.

5. See Michel de Certeau, *The Practice of Everyday Life*, trans. Steven Rendall (Berkeley: University of California Press, 1984); and Henri Lefebvre, *The Production of Space*, trans. Donald Nicholson-Smith (Cambridge, UK: Blackwell, 1991).

6. The possibility for "Slab!" to mean "slab" or "Bring me a slab!" a one-word or a four-word sentence, is discussed by Wittgenstein in sec. 20 of *Philosophical Investigations*.

7. The possibilities inherent in Wittgenstein's introduction of language-games are apparent in Jean-Francois Lyotard's use of language-games to reimagine language and to examine the development of postmodernist thought. See Jean-Francois Lyotard, *The Postmodern Condition: A Report on Knowledge*, trans. Geoff Bennington and Brian Massumi (Minneapolis: University of Minnesota Press, 1984).

8. *Philosophical Investigations*, sec. 17.

9. Ibid., sec. 17.

10. Ibid., sec. 23.

11. Ibid., sec. 29.

12. Ibid., sec. 18.

13. Ibid., sec. 217.

CHAPTER 3
THE STONBOROUGH-WITTGENSTEIN HOUSE

1. Bernhard Leitner, "Wittgenstein's Architecture," *Artforum*, February 1970; and Bernhard Leitner, *The Architecture of Ludwig Wittgenstein* (London: Academy Editions, 1995). The book was first published in 1973 by the Press of the Nova Scotia College of Art and Design.

2. Hermine was the younger of Wittgenstein's sisters; Margarethe, for whom the house was built, was the elder.

3. The house is referred to at times as the Kundmanngasse in accordance with the Viennese tradition of naming the house for the street in which it stands.

4. Quoted in Leitner, *Architecture*, 50.

5. Ibid.

6. See ibid., 17–23.

7. Ibid.

8. Quoted in ibid., 22. Gretl refers to Margarethe Stonborough-Wittgenstein.

9. Ibid., 23.

10. Paul Wijdeveld, *Ludwig Wittgenstein: Architect* (Cambridge, Mass.: MIT Press, 1994), 11.

11. See ibid. for a more complete discussion of the history of the house's construction.

12. From 1973 to 1975 the building, although saved from destruction, was without funds and fell into decay; in 1975 the Bulgarian Embassy purchased the building to house its cultural institute, which still occupies the building.

13. Engelmann later presented these sketches to Margarethe in the form of a book as a Christmas present in 1926. The sketchbook is currently in the reserve collections of the Getty Center for the History of Art and the Humanities in Santa Monica, California.

14. Wijdeveld suggests the possibility that Wittgenstein's ideas may be reflected by the lack or limited amount of adornment from what he defines as phase three of the sketches on, or by the verticality of the windows from his phase six on, both aspects of which were realized in the house.

15. Quoted in Leitner, *Architecture*, 20.

16. "Letter from Paul Engelmann to Hermine Wittgenstein dated January 9, 1932," in Bernhard Leitner, *The Wittgenstein House* (New York: Princeton Architectural Press, 2000), 86.

17. See Wijdeveld, *Wittgenstein: Architect*, for a full discussion. Wijdeveld divided the sketches into ten distinct phases, ranging from the beginnings as a traditional and classical version of an aristocratic house, to a series of possibilities that included a curving main facade in one phase and a forty-five-degree angle cutting through the center of the plan in another phase.

As the sketches progressed, however, Engelmann's design became more asymmetrical and simplified. Even in the later phases however, Engelmann continued to suggest ideas ultimately rejected for the final design, including planning the building based on a modular grid, which he attempted to meld with the building's massing. The last sketches began to suggest the final cubic composition of the Stonborough-Wittgenstein House, defined by a tall central block with two main wings and several smaller, asymmetrically placed volumes, with the final design phase in the sketchbook being the closest to what was eventually built.

18. See Wijdeveld, *Wittgenstein: Architect*, 159–82.

19. Leitner, *Wittgenstein House*, 86.

CHAPTER 4
THE PRACTICE OF ARCHITECTURE

1. *Philosophical Investigations*, sec. 203.

2. Michel de Certeau, *The Practice of Everyday Life*, trans. Steven Rendell (Berkeley, Calif.: University of California Press, 1984), 13.

3. Bernhard Leitner, *The Architecture of Ludwig Wittgenstein* (London: Academy Editions, 1995), 20.

4. *Philosophical Investigations*, sec. 88.

5. Stanley Cavell, *The Claim of Reason* (Oxford: Oxford University Press, 1979), 329.

PART TWO
IMAGES OF ENTANGLEMENT

1. Ludwig Wittgenstein, "(Untitled) A Lecture on Ethics," *Philosophical Review* 74 (1965): 3–12. This lecture was prepared by Wittgenstein sometime between September 1929 and December 1930. The lecture was presented to the Cambridge society the Heretics and is the only popular lecture Wittgenstein ever composed or delivered.

2. While the numbered entries forming the *Tractatus* are referred to as propositions, *Philosophical Investigations* are divided into several hundred short sections that are typically referred to interchangeably as sections or as paragraphs.

3. Wittgenstein, "(Untitled) A Lecture on Ethics."

4. Ibid.

5. Wittgenstein, *Philosophical Investigations*, preface.

6. See ibid., secs. 85, 87, and 198 for all the references made to the signpost.

7. "Scruples" is a particularly interesting choice of word as it suggests an ethical consideration or principle that inhibits on grounds of conscience. The suggestion of inhibition to act cannot help but recall Wittgenstein's image of the idling engine and his dislike associated with fixity and idleness.

8. Slavoj Žižek, *Looking Awry: An Introduction to Jacques Lacan through Popular Culture* (Cambridge, Mass.: MIT Press: 1991), offers an interesting discussion of the differences between our perceptions of space from being within to being without, such as, for example, the differences of being within and without an automobile in relation to language and the Lacanian concept of the real.

9. I refer here only to Part I of the *Philosophical Investigations*, the main part of the text.

10. Michael Nedo, "Introduction," in *Ludwig Wittgenstein: Wiener Ausgabe* (Vienna and New York: Springer Verlag, 1993), 28.

PRIMARY SOURCES

Wittgenstein, Ludwig. *The Blue and Brown Books.* New York: Harper & Row, 1965.
———. *Culture and Value.* Edited by G. H. von Wright in collaboration with Heikki Nyman, translated by Peter Winch. Chicago: University of Chicago Press, 1980.
———. "(Untitled) A Lecture on Ethics." *Philosophical Review* 74 (1965): 3–12.
———. *Lectures and Conversations on Aesthetics, Psychology and Religious Belief.* Edited by Cyril Barrett, compiled from notes taken by Yorick Smythies, Rush Rhees, and James Taylor. Berkeley and Los Angeles: University of California Press.
———. *On Certainty.* Edited by G. E. M. Anscombe and G. H. von Wright, translated by Denis Paul and G. E. M. Anscombe. New York: Harper & Row, 1972.
———. *Philosophical Investigations.* Translated by G. E. M. Anscombe. New York: Macmillan, 1953.
———. *Remarks on Colour.* Edited by G. E. M. Anscombe, translated by Linda L. McAlister and Margarete Schattle. Berkeley and Los Angeles: University of California Press, 1977.
———. *Remarks on the Foundations of Mathematics.* Edited by G. H. von Wright, R. Rhees, and G. E. M. Anscombe, translated by G. E. M. Anscombe. Cambridge, Mass., and London: MIT Press, 1991 [1956].
———. *Tractatus Logico-Philosophicus: The German Text of* Logisch-philosophische Abhandlung. Translated by D. F. Pears and B. F. McGuinness, with an introduction by Bertrand Russell. London: Routledge & Kegan Paul; New York: Humanities Press, 1961 [1922].
———. *Zettel.* Edited by G. E. M. Anscombe and G. H. von Wright, translated by G. E. M. Anscombe. Berkeley and Los Angeles: University of California Press, 1970.

SECONDARY SOURCES

Amendolagine, Francesco. "The House of Wittgenstein." 9H 4 (1982): 23–38.

Anscombe, G. E. M. *An Introduction to Wittgenstein's Tractatus*. London: Hutchinson, 1959.

Bakacsy, J., A. V. Munch, and A.-L. Sommer, eds. *Architecture, Language, Critique: Around Paul Engelmann*. Studien Zur Osterreichischen Philosophie 31. Amsterdam and Atlanta, Ga.: Rodopi, 2000.

Brill, Susan B. *Wittgenstein and Critical Theory: Beyond Postmodernism and Toward Descriptive Investigations*. Athens, Ohio: Ohio University Press, 1995.

Bryson, Norman. "The Gaze in the Expanded Field." In *Vision and Visuality*, edited by Hal Foster, 87–108. Seattle: Bay Press, 1988.

Bouveresse, Jacques. *Wittgenstein Reads Freud: The Myth of the Unconscious*. Translated by Carol Cosman. Princeton, N.J.: Princeton University Press, 1995.

Cavell, Stanley. "Aesthetic Problems of Modern Philosophy." In *Must We Mean What We Say?* New York: Charles Scribner's Sons, 1969.

———. "The Argument of the Ordinary: Scenes of Instruction in Wittgenstein and Kripke." In *Conditions Handsome and Unhandsome*. Chicago: University of Chicago Press, 1990.

———. *The Claim of Reason: Wittgenstein, Skepticism, Morality and Tragedy*. Oxford and New York: Oxford University Press, 1979.

———. "Declining Decline." In *This New Yet Unapproachable America: Lectures after Emerson after Wittgenstein*. Albuquerque, N.M.: Living Batch Press, 1989.

———. "Notes on the Opening of the *Investigations*." Unpublished manuscript.

Certeau, Michel de. *The Practice of Everyday Life*. Translated by Steven Rendell. Berkeley: University of California Press, 1984.

Crary, Alice, and Rupert Read, eds. *The New Wittgenstein*. New York: Routledge, 2000.

Derrida, Jacques. "White Mythology: Metaphor in the Text of Philosophy." In *Margins of Philosophy*, translated by Alan Bass. Chicago: University of Chicago Press, 1982 [1972].

Diamond, Cora. *The Realistic Spirit: Wittgenstein, Philosophy, and the Mind*. Cambridge, Mass.: MIT Press, 1991.

Dummett, Michael. *Origins of Analytical Philosophy*. Cambridge, Mass.: Harvard University Press, 1994.

Eagleton, Terry. *Wittgenstein: The Terry Eagleton Script, the Derek Jarman Film*. London: British Film Institute, 1993.

Engelmann, Paul, and Ludwig Wittgenstein. *Letters from Wittgenstein with a Memoir*. Translated by L. Furtmüller. Oxford: Basil Blackwell, 1967.

Genova, Judith. *Wittgenstein: A Way of Seeing*. New York and London: Routledge, 1995.

Gottlob, Frege. *The Foundations of Arithmetic.* Translated by J. L. Austin. Evanston, Ill.: Northwestern University Press, 1974.
Grosz, Elizabeth. *Architecture from the Outside: Essays on Virtual and Real Space.* Cambridge, Mass.: MIT Press, 2001.
Hacker, P. M. S. *Insight and Illusion.* Oxford: Clarendon Press, 1986.
Hollier, Dennis. *Against Architecture: The Writing of George Bataille.* Translated by Betsy Wing. Cambridge, Mass.: MIT Press, 1989.
Janik, Allan, and Stephen Toulmin. *Wittgenstein's Vienna.* New York: Simon and Schuster, 1973.
Jay, Martin. *Downcast Eyes: The Denigration of Vision in Twentieth-Century French Thought.* Berkeley and Los Angeles: University of California Press, 1993.
Karatani, Kojin. *Architecture as Metaphor: Language, Number, Money.* Cambridge, Mass.: MIT Press, 1995.
Koethe, John. *The Continuity of Wittgenstein's Thought.* Ithaca, N.Y., and London: Cornell University Press, 1996.
Kripke, Saul. *Wittgenstein on Rules and Private Language.* Cambridge, Mass.: Harvard University Press, 1982.
Lefebvre, Henri. *The Production of Space.* Cambridge, Mass.: Blackwell, 1991.
Leitner, Bernhard. *The Architecture of Ludwig Wittgenstein.* London: Academy Editions, 1995.
———. *The Wittgenstein House.* New York: Princeton Architectural Press, 2000.
———. "Wittgenstein's Architecture." *Artforum* February 1970.
Lyotard, Jean-Francois. *The Postmodern Condition: A Report on Knowledge.* Translated by Geoff Bennington and Brian Massumi. Minneapolis: University of Minnesota Press, 1984.
Mayer, Verena. "The Numbering System of the *Tractatus*" in *Ratio* 6 (1993): 108–19.
McGuinness, B. F. *Young Ludwig 1889–1921.* Vol. 1 of *Wittgenstein: A Life.* Berkeley: University of California Press, 1988.
Mulhall, Stephen. *On Being in the World: Wittgenstein and Heidegger on Seeing Aspects.* London and New York: Routledge, 1990.
Monk, Ray. *Wittgenstein: The Duty of Genius.* London: Cape, 1990.
Nedo, Michael. "Introduction." In *Ludwig Wittgenstein: Wiener Ausgabe.* Vienna and New York: Springer Verlag, 1993.
Norris, Christopher. *The Deconstructive Turn: Essays in the Rhetoric of Philosophy.* London and New York: Methuen, 1984.
Nyman, Kaj. "Wittgenstein, Meaning, and Architecture." *DATUTOP* 10 (1986): 39–66.
Pearson, Karl. *Researches of Middle Life.* Vol. 2 of *The Life, Letters and Labours of Francis Galton.* London: Cambridge University Press, 1924.
Perloff, Marjorie. *Wittgenstein's Ladder.* Chicago: University of Chicago Press, 1996.

Putnam, Hilary. *Renewing Philosophy.* Cambridge, Mass.: Harvard University Press, 1992.

Rajchman, John. *Constructions.* Cambridge, Mass.: MIT Press, 1998.

———. *The Deleuze Connections.* Cambridge, Mass.: MIT Press, 2000.

———. "Foucault's Art of Seeing." *October* 44 (1988): 88–117.

Rhees, Rush. "Wittgenstein's Builders." In *Discussions of Wittgenstein.* London and New York: Routledge, 1970.

Sluga, Hans. "Between Modernism and Postmodernity: The Case of Wittgenstein and His Architecture." Unpublished manuscript.

Staten, Henry. *Wittgenstein and Derrida.* Lincoln and London: University of Nebraska Press, 1984.

von Wright, G. H. *Wittgenstein.* Oxford: Blackwell, 1982.

Weiss, Allen. "Vaux-le-Vicomte: Anamorphosis Abscondita." In *Mirrors of Infinity: The French Formal Garden and Seventeenth-Century Metaphysics.* New York: Princeton Architectural Press, 1995.

Wigley, Mark. "Architecture after Philosophy: Le Corbusier and the Emperor's New Paint." *Journal of Philosophy and Visual Arts* 2 (1990): 84–95.

———. *The Architecture of Deconstruction: Derrida's Haunt.* Cambridge, Mass.: MIT Press, 1993.

———. "Heidegger's House: The Violence of the Domestic." *D: Columbia Documents in Architecture and Theory* 1 (1992): 93–118.

Wijdeveld, Paul. *Ludwig Wittgenstein, Architect.* Cambridge, Mass.: MIT Press, 1994.

Winch, Peter. "Wittgenstein: Picture and Representation." In *Trying to Make Sense.* Oxford: Basil Blackwell, 1987.

Žižek, Slavoj. *Looking Awry: An Introduction to Jacques Lacan through Popular Culture.* Cambridge, Mass.: MIT Press, 1991.

INDEX

aesthetics, 8, 11, 13, 59, 79, 93, 126, 175, 187. *See also* lecture on aesthetics
albums, 142, 161–67, 168, 186, 187
architectural drawings, 73, 74, 86–92, 110–11, 165–66, 183, 184
Augustine, 42, 62–65, 70, 125

boundaries, 16, 22–23, 35–36, 37, 38, 43, 59, 60, 83, 84, 93, 94, 99, 100–3, 105, 114, 130–34, 138–39, 152, 158, 165–66, 171, 173, 174–81, 186, 189
builders, builders' language, 26, 61–77, 84, 162

Cavell, Stanley, 54, 63, 67, 70, 111
Certeau, Michel de, 14–18, 26, 66, 103
clarity, 24, 26, 29–30, 36, 41, 53, 58, 105, 106–7, 117, 124, 128, 144, 148, 152–54, 157, 158, 159–60, 172, 173, 178, 186
composite photography, 125, 126–29, 161, 162
correspondence (correlation), 46–52, 57–58, 59, 105, 114, 115, 144, 145, 155, 180
crystalline purity, 108, 123, 146–48, 155

Deleuze, Giles, 13, 14
Derrida, Jacques, 13, 14
Drobil, Michael, 82

Engelmann, Paul, 3, 27, 86, 87–92
entanglement, 27, 40–42, 124, 136–37, 147, 156, 159, 161
ethics, 8, 23, 39, 59, 126, 128, 129, 173, 181, 185. *See also* lecture on ethics
ethics and aesthetics (as together), 39, 173, 180, 188, 189

family resemblance, 18, 20, 52, 123, 124, 125–35, 141, 156, 161, 176, 179, 186
Frege, Gottlob, 175

Galton, Sir Francis, 125, 126–29, 161, 162
games, 131–33, 134, 174–76
glasses, 5, 52, 149–51, 155
Grosz, Elizabeth, 12–14

images of entanglement, 28, 29–30, 123–89
images of transgression, 23, 45–60
inhabitation, 27–29, 59, 61–77, 79, 112, 148, 178

Janik, Allan, 39 (n.3)

Karatani, Kojin, 54 (n.19)

labyrinths of paths, 40, 99, 135, 138, 155–60

ladder, 23, 24, 25, 44, 46, 52–57, 133, 136, 137, 152
landscape sketches, 123, 136–40, 142, 155, 160, 161, 168, 173, 179, 187
language. *See* ordinary (everyday) language; private language
language-games, 71, 74, 75, 106, 181
lecture on aesthetics, 110
lecture on ethics, 29, 123, 125–26, 128–31, 180–81, 187
Lefebvre, Henri, 66
Leitner, Bernhard, 78, 81
limits of language, 3, 4, 16, 22–24, 25, 34, 35–36, 38–40, 42, 43, 44, 45, 65, 102–3, 129, 147, 155, 178, 180
logic, logical form, 3, 8, 9, 35–36, 38–42, 47, 50, 51, 53, 55, 57, 59, 61, 65, 82, 125, 126, 129, 140, 147, 149, 150, 151, 153, 155, 169, 170, 181–86, 188
Loos, Adolf, 84, 86
Lyotard, Jean Francois, 71 (n.7)

mazes, 40, 75, 143, 155–60
McGuinness, Brian, 46
Moore, G. E., 125, 126, 129, 180
mystical, 36, 42–45, 46

nets and webs, 40, 123, 143–45, 147, 153
numbering systems, 5, 8, 24, 46–52, 55, 56, 58, 81, 104, 156

ordinary (everyday) language, 14–19, 22, 40, 41, 46, 50, 58, 108, 148, 150, 156, 169, 170

Perloff, Marjorie, 46–47, 55
Philosophical Investigations, 2–5, 7 (fig. 2), 9–11, 15–21, 25–26, 42, 43, 49–52, 61–77, 105, 107, 108, 110, 123–89
picture theory of meaning, 24, 57–68, 170
practice, 14–18, 19, 25, 26, 28, 30, 33, 59, 61, 62, 65, 68, 69, 76, 80, 81, 92–94, 95–120, 131, 137, 138, 142, 149, 154, 162, 163, 164, 166, 172, 173, 174, 175, 177, 188, 285
precision (exactness), 11, 46, 54, 106, 109–11, 165, 169, 175

private language, 111–14, 184
pseudo-problems, 23, 41–42, 167

reminders, 142, 162, 164, 166, 167, 170, 181
Rhees, Rush, 68, 70
rules, rule following, 3, 25, 75–76, 84, 104–5, 134, 141, 146, 156, 158, 159, 163–65, 178, 179

Schlick, Moritz, 3, 79, 82
showing/saying, 3, 23, 39–40, 56, 59, 66, 81, 152, 157, 176, 189
signpost, 163–65
spatiality, 1–30, 33–45, 46–52, 59, 71, 75, 80, 81, 83, 93, 94, 104, 105, 107–8, 112, 114, 119–20, 123, 138–39, 140, 143, 144, 149–54, 155, 156–57, 168, 169, 172, 177, 178
Stonborough, Thomas, 85–86
Stonborough-Wittgenstein House, 2, 21, 25, 28–29, 78–94, 95–120; boundaries, 102–5, 120; central hall, 27–28, 94–98, 105, 116, 117, 182; interior-exterior, 96–98, 110, 111, 114, 115–19; materials, 95, 97, 99, 101–2, 109, 113–15, 117; precision, 109–11, 164, 175; repetition, 105–7; rule following, 103–6; site, 84–86; symmetry-asymmetry, 84, 115–19; and *Tractatus Logico-Philosophicus*, 79, 80, 81, 84, 93–94, 105–6; transparency, 95–103; windows and doors, 27, 84, 90, 95–102, 105–8, 113–14, 188
Stonborough-Wittgenstein, Margarethe, 27, 83, 85, 86, 88
surface (of language), 23–25, 34, 41, 55, 112, 136–40, 143, 147, 158, 159, 165, 168–73

Toulmin, Stephen, 39 (n.3)
Tractatus Logico-Philosophicus, 2–5, 6 (fig. 1), 8, 9–10, 21–25, 33–60, 61, 64, 65, 66, 72, 74, 79, 80, 81, 82, 83, 84, 93, 94, 95, 103, 104, 105,106, 128, 129, 133, 134, 139, 140, 143, 144, 145, 146, 147, 149, 150, 151, 154, 155,

167, 169, 170, 171, 172, 173, 178, 184, 186, 187, 188
transgression(s), 22, 25, 33–60, 112, 115, 147–48, 151, 178

Vienna Circle, 3, 79, 182
view from within, 20, 22–23, 25, 26, 43, 61–77, 95, 105, 148, 151, 152, 159–60, 172, 185
view from without/above, 18, 20–22, 25, 26, 34–37, 40, 41, 42–44, 53, 55, 56, 59, 95, 105, 143, 148, 151, 152, 157, 160, 167, 169, 179

viewing subject, 19–21, 22, 23, 35, 42–45, 51, 53, 55–56, 61, 70, 101–7, 108, 139, 149, 150, 151, 154, 155–56, 171
visual room, 182–85
visual space, 3, 182–85

Wijdeveld, Paul, 11 (n. 14), 13, 84, 88
Wittgenstein, Hermine, 78, 81, 82, 83, 109
Wittgenstein, Paul, 86
Wright, Georg Henrik von, 78–80, 81, 82

Žižek, Slavoj, 19–20

www.ingramcontent.com/pod-product-compliance
Lightning Source LLC
Chambersburg PA
CBHW031245290426
44109CB00012B/436